TYRONE L. GROH

PROXY WAR

The Least Bad Option

STANFORD UNIVERSITY PRESS

STANFORD, CALIFORNIA

Stanford University Press

Stanford, California

© 2019 by the Board of Trustees of the Leland Stanford Junior University. All rights reserved.

Printed in the United States of America on acid-free, archival-quality paper

Library of Congress Cataloging-in-Publication Data

Names: Groh, Tyrone L., author.
Title: Proxy war : the least bad option / Tyrone L. Groh.
Description: Stanford, California : Stanford University Press, 2019. |
    Includes bibliographical references and index.
Identifiers: LCCN 2018044084 (print) | LCCN 2018045305 (ebook) |
    ISBN 9781503608733 (e-book) | ISBN 9781503608184 (cloth; alk. paper)
Subjects: LCSH: Proxy war. | Military policy. | Proxy war—Case studies. |
    Military policy—Case studies.
Classification: LCC JZ6385 (ebook) | LCC JZ6385 .G76 2019 (print) |
    DDC 355.02—dc23
LC record available at https://lccn.loc.gov/2018044084

Typeset by Newgen in 10.75/15 Adobe Caslon

Cover photo: Kurdish fighters from the People's Protection Units (YPG) head a convoy of U.S. military vehicles in the town of Darbasiya next to the Turkish border, Syria, April 28, 2017. REUTERS/Rodi Said

Cover design: Rob Ehle

CONTENTS

ACKNOWLEDGMENTS

This book would not have been possible without the generous support I have received from so many organizations and individuals. I am especially indebted to Dan Byman and Anne Clunan for their mentorship and friendship over the past ten years while I have been working on this project. I want to thank Embry-Riddle Aeronautical University for providing financial support for a part of my research. I also want to thank the U.S. Air Force School of Advanced Air and Space Studies for giving me the opportunity to pursue such an interesting and challenging endeavor.

I am grateful to all of those I have had the pleasure of working with during this and other related projects. Although I am thankful to all of you who helped me along the way, I want to specifically recognize Pete Fesler, Brooke Shannon, Furman Daniel, Andy Bennett, Jim Forsyth, James Kiras, Michael Koplow, Chrystie Flournoy Swiney, and Alex Berg—each of you provided a critical part that helped make this possible. I would also like to thank the two anonymous reviewers for their thoughtful and helpful comments.

Lastly, this book would not have been possible without the support of my family. I would like to thank my parents, sister, and in-laws for their love and encouragement. Most importantly, I wish to thank my loving and supportive wife and my two wonderful boys, who have given me unending patience and inspiration.

CHAPTER 1

INTRODUCTION

WHEN THE decision to intervene in another state's affairs becomes a public conversation, a decision maker can be left with only deciding *how*, rather than whether, to intervene. Senator John McCain consistently pushed the White House to arm Syrian rebels as a means to bring down the Assad regime without committing America's regular forces. McCain publicly urged the president, "I want to hear him say we're going to arm the free Syrian army. We're going to dedicate ourselves to the removal of Bashar al-Assad. We're going to have the Russians pay a price for their engagement. All players here are going to have to pay a penalty and the United States of America is going to be on the side of people who fight for freedom."[1] But the threat in Syria just doesn't look threatening enough to the White House, or most American citizens, to warrant a direct intervention. Enter the idea of proxy war. If a civil war breaks out in another state and overtly threatens your own state's security, then the situation clearly warrants a direct and overt response. Such circumstances allow the decision maker to quickly move to planning for a direct intervention. If the situation influences national security, but the circumstances do not so strongly engender public support for an overt commitment, then the decision maker has a more difficult choice to make: (1) choose not to intervene and suffer the consequences of political adversaries at home and rival states abroad viewing the administration as weak on security and unwilling to stand up to threats abroad; (2) choose to intervene directly and risk failure or being labeled as aggressive and unconcerned about the ensuing loss of life; or (3) find something in between.

This book is about understanding the "something in between" policy. When "doing nothing" is not perceived as an option, yet direct intervention appears to be a step too far, decision makers and their staffs seek ways to intervene indirectly. Under such circumstances, it may seem alluring to seize an opportunity to outsource the personnel needed for a foreign military intervention. To make such a prospect even more tempting, consider keeping the policy covert and making the involvement deniable. If such a prospect appears even remotely feasible, then the question "Why fight when someone else will do it for us?" will more than likely become a dominant part of the conversation. This kind of scenario is where proxy war makes its entrance into the field of possible policy options.

The term *proxy war* carries a lot of baggage. During the Cold War, the use of proxies allowed states to be far more adventurous in their efforts to influence world events and gain an advantage over their rivals. Small states on the periphery were often viewed as pawns in a much greater game, allowing the United States and the Soviet Union to compete globally without risking nuclear war. Local actors and conflicts were hijacked to serve the interests of Washington and Moscow. This Cold War image of proxy war continues to dominate the contemporary view of indirect interventions that involve a third party to influence civil affairs abroad and helps explain its continued use (and misuse) as an instrument of foreign policy.

The usefulness of proxy war has unfortunately been overblown. Indirect intervention, and more specifically proxy war, demands more rigorous exploration and study to remedy misperceptions and misunderstanding of its use as a tool of foreign policy. To avoid adding to the confusion about different methods of indirect intervention, I find it necessary to separate the action into two distinct categories: donating assistance and proxy war (concepts I explore in detail in Chapter 2). I define donating assistance as providing resources, without intending to direct the actions of a local actor, to influence political affairs in the target state. I define proxy war as *directing the use of force by a politically motivated, local actor to indirectly influence political affairs in the target state.* Both provide a middle ground for intervention and help bypass the thresholds for direct intervention and nonintervention.

Using proxy war as a means of indirect intervention requires considering both the policy's *utility*—a short-term view that determines whether a proxy can actually provide the ability to intervene—and the *efficacy*—a long-term view that evaluates the likelihood that supporting the chosen proxy can produce a desirable outcome. Donating assistance is also a means of indirect intervention, the difference being that donating assistance cedes any control over how the local actor uses the support provided. Proxy war entails a hierarchical relationship between an intervening state and its proxy—in more formal terms, a principal-agent relationship. Proxy war requires a higher level of involvement from the intervening state. The trade-off is that proxy war offers an opportunity to help manage some of the uncertainty associated with indirect intervention. For this reason, proxy war is rarely a low-cost policy, and it is never risk free. Proxy war is also far more complex than a policy of donating assistance and therefore requires a much deeper understanding of the phenomenon if it is to be done well.

How does proxy war fit into today's context? The United States has been fighting abroad on a relatively large scale since 1991. A perception of overstretch and increasing global competition have created a growing political and fiscal impetus for conserving resources and drawing down U.S. forces and deployments. The desire, and arguably the need, for U.S. intervention, however, continues. Discussions regarding the prospects of proxy war tend to focus on the benefits of such a policy. Developing partnerships and participating vicariously through them have become an answer for shifting away from the long-held requirement of having an armed force capable of fighting two major wars at the same time.[2] Little work, however, has been done to understand the actual utility (short-term) and efficacy (long-term) of proxy war. Many studies in the realm of proxy war are made up of anecdotal compilations of superpower conflict taking place on the periphery during the Cold War. Because of that, the use of proxies continues to be portrayed as a way to reduce the costs and risks of military intervention abroad.[3]

To date, there is little consideration for the potentially negative implications of acting through a third party. For example, updates to the National Security Strategy discuss the importance of shifting costs and risks to partners due to fiscal constraints. Both the 2006 and 2010 versions of the Quadrennial Defense Review discuss the need to work with and through partners to pursue common security interests while simultaneously promoting U.S. security. There is no warning or caution about the potential for partners to use American support in ways that hinder U.S. interests, nor is there a discussion of the need to put monitoring mechanisms in place to protect against such activities. Proxies, like adversaries, are self-interested, a fact that can drive costs far beyond expectation and significantly increase uncertainty.

The world, however, is becoming increasingly competitive. Under such conditions, the United States will continue to focus on working with and through partners to pursue American interests abroad. When the United States is faced with difficult scenarios such as whether to intervene in Crimea, Syria, Egypt, or Bahrain, proxy war will likely gain popularity as a potential course of action. Before America commits to a strategy of developing partners with the intent to expand its influence via proxy, decision makers and strategists need a better understanding of the potential risks as well as the potential rewards. More importantly, policy makers and strategists need better ideas about how best to execute a proxy war under varying conditions.

Proxy war is risky, but it is not something to be avoided at all costs. This type of indirect intervention has its place; it just demands careful consideration. For the foreseeable future, proxy war will remain an integral part of any state's foreign policy options that meet the following three conditions: (1) the state's interests and identity push outside its own borders, (2) the security and well-being of the state is connected to conditions in other states, and (3) the state maintains the capacity to engage in international affairs. Naturally, the states that fit this profile best are those with significant regional or global interests and the means to pursue them, but proxy war as a tool of foreign policy does not belong exclusively to powerful states.

In today's world, a rigorous study and understanding of proxy war will only continue to grow in importance. The United States has already started on the path to proxy war in Syria and may find it extremely difficult to change course even if the context changes significantly. Caught between fiscal needs to limit military involvement and political pressures—both domestic and international—to intervene, Washington faces a potentially recurring issue in world politics: there is no good policy option. Unfortunately, intervening in world affairs will likely become more about choosing the *least bad* option. When the perceived threat to national security remains below the threshold of direct intervention and the presence of a potential partner appears workable, proxy war often quickly rises to the top of the least bad options.

OBJECTIVES OF THIS BOOK

In this book, I address interests from two different communities. For academics interested in international relations or security studies, this study delves into the ontological nature of indirect intervention. Focusing mostly on proxy war, I develop a more specific definition of the phenomenon and explore the different ways states use it to intervene militarily in conflicts abroad. In addition, I discuss how proxy war has changed since the end of World War II and provide insights about how proxy war will likely operate in the future. For practitioners involved in strategy and foreign policy, this book offers a theory of how to conduct proxy war in a way that maximizes its utility and efficacy. Further, I provide recommendations for improving how to consider and deliberate proxy war as a potential policy option.

To help balance the needs and interests of these two very different communities, this book follows Alex George's sage advice: "Scholars may not be in a good position to advise policymakers how best to deal with a specific instance of a general problem that requires urgent and timely action," but "they can often provide a useful, broader discussion of how to think about and understand that general problem."[4] Proxy war, as a phenomenon, has only been lightly explored. Three recent works have engaged on the topic of proxy war to promote a better understanding for why states choose proxy war. Michael Innes explores new lenses for analyzing proxy war to escape many of the well-established views of proxy war that have been carried over from the Cold War.[5] Geraint Hughes offers a brief but interesting exploration of proxy war seeking to shape the narrative about the viability of proxy war as a tool of statecraft.[6] Hughes also develops ideas, looking at historical cases, for why and how proxy wars have been fought in the past.[7] Andrew Mumford provides a similar effort, providing additional cases and examples that expand the scope of proxy war.[8] Although I also engage on the reasons why an intervening state might choose proxy warfare, the principal focus of this book is to understand the phenomenon better in its application. This book offers insights and explanations about proxy war to those who study foreign policy from an academic perspective, as well as those involved in the development and practice of foreign policy. The principal idea behind this book is to leave the policy making to the professionals and focus instead on providing a useful way to think about a policy of proxy war.

To deliver on these objectives, this book makes three arguments. First, I argue that the phenomenon of proxy war requires sharper boundaries. The term *proxy war* continues to be used both too broadly and too vaguely. In Chapter 2, I lay out the constitutive elements of proxy war (its ontology) and explain how it fits into the context of indirect military intervention. Proxy war involves (at least) two actors—an intervening state and its proxy—cooperating to achieve some common security objective. Cooperation, however, does not automatically indicate the existence of a proxy war policy. The practice of giving support to a third party to act on your behalf exists in very different ways. People support lobby groups with resources to forward their desired agenda. The use of a third party in this sense reflects the practice of *donated assistance*. Some organizations outsource services to a third party acting on their behalf to make the most of existing opportunities. For example, the U.S. government has a federal postal service, but it uses Federal Express (FedEx) or United Parcel Service (UPS) to ship important cargo domestically. The U.S. Postal Service could deliver the item, but the government can send it either quicker or faster (often both) using a private, third-party carrier. The relationship provides opportunities for both; the U.S. government gets a cost-effective and time-efficient means of shipping goods with an extremely high likelihood that the service will meet its expectations, and FedEx or UPS profits from the U.S. government's business.

Proxies, however, are not always so reliable. If you employ a tenant in an apartment building you own to shovel the snow off the sidewalks and walkways, the quality of the service may not be what you expect, but it does not have to be perfect either. In either case, you (as the owner) place a premium on not having to be involved on a daily basis. To manage costs, you will not pay much for the service, perhaps a small credit on the tenant's lease. The tenant is self-interested—shoveling the snow may not be a priority the same way it is for you as the owner. Under such conditions, the tenant will likely encounter a day when he or she would rather do something else and is willing to take the risk that you either do not notice or are willing to overlook the lack of service on that day. Proxies operate with the same mind-set. Having different goals and objectives complicates the relationship between an intervening state and its proxy—each wants something from the relationship and each has different priorities. Looking at a similar relationship put into another context, intervening in another state's civil war indirectly through the use of a proxy adds risk and uncertainty—the proxy may not want the same things or hold the same priorities unless made to do so by the intervening state.

Unlike direct intervention where a state's relative capability is on full display, indirect intervention affords an intervening state the ability to influence affairs in another state without such commitment. The benefit of indirect intervention comes from the avoidance of displaying those capabilities, preserving those capabilities for times of greater need, and obscuring its level of commitment and involvement to obtain a particular outcome. Direct intervention requires a win to sustain an intervening state's reputation and position in the international system. Indirect intervention broadens the spectrum of acceptable outcomes and opens the possibility that winning is not always the goal of an intervention. From this perspective, proxy war improves the state's ability to control the situation, especially when the proxy functions as intended—when it pursues the intervening state's objectives with the same commitment and vigor as if it were fighting alone. Such commitment from a proxy, however, requires an exorbitant amount of control. Without control, the proxy will likely pursue its own agenda with little regard for the costs to the intervening state. If the outcome is relatively unimportant, however, intervening indirectly through the means of donated assistance might be best. Donated assistance reflects a policy that provides an indigenous third party with the means to fight but cedes all control to the third party. Donated assistance helps reduce an intervening state's involvement in an indirect intervention but bears an equal reduction in the intervening state's ability to control the outcome.

To expand the understanding of proxy war as a means of indirect intervention, I argue that it can be divided into four distinct types: *in it to win it*, *holding action*, *meddling*, and *feed the chaos*. Each has its own purpose and utility depending on the context surrounding the intervention of an intrastate conflict. All four adhere to the idea that a state perceives that "doing nothing" is too weak and committing the state's own forces is too risky. Caught in between, an intervening state will look for opportunities to advance its vital and desirable interests.[9] Balancing the pursuit of these two types of interests contributes to how an intervening state might use the different forms of proxy war.

In it to win it should occur when a state perceives a greater need to influence the outcome of an intrastate conflict because of the intervening state's vital interests, such as its pursuit of security, or when an intervening state strongly desires a specific outcome based on its worldview and will offer more support and a higher level of commitment to enable its proxy to win. A *holding action* approach applies when localized threats to vital interests in and around the target state are low, yet the likelihood that instability could spread to other states or regions in a way that would threaten vital interests precludes nonintervention as an option. In some cases, the available proxy lacks the capability to actually win the conflict, but helping prolong the civil war may improve the outcome in terms of the intervening state's interests. A good example of this is when the available proxy has little political capacity and correspondingly engenders only minute or no support among the target state's population. In this situation, extending the conflict reduces the opposition's claim to power because it cannot control the violence within the borders and may pave the way to greater concessions that do less harm to the intervening state's interests. In any case, a holding action comes in when an intervening state wants to maintain the status quo (or at least some semblance thereof). *Meddling* finds its place when an intervening state has a desirable interest in altering the status quo, yet such a move contributes little to nothing in terms of vital interests. Further, it would enhance the state's position without risking any loss in capability or prestige. If the risk of escalation with a peer or near-peer competitor is high or there are significant constraints (internationally and/or domestically) restricting the amount of resources that can be made available to the proxy, then *meddling* offers a viable option. Lastly, *feeding the chaos* comes in when a state perceives that gains to either vital or desirable interests are unnecessary or unlikely, but supporting a proxy to alter the status quo remains possible. In cases where gains are not needed, but prolonging the violence indefinitely prevents the opposing side from adding to its own power and influence, feeding the chaos becomes attractive. This approach is similar to a *holding action*, except the intervening state wants to alter rather than uphold the status quo. Without the ability to connect support to a specific interest or threat, *feeding the chaos* is often conducted covertly to avoid international or domestic blowback.

My second argument is that how and when states use proxy war has changed since the end of World War II, but what has not changed is why states use it. In Chapter 3, I look at how the use of proxy forces has fluctuated over time. Observing different uses of proxy war since the end of the Cold War, I break them up into three separate periods that highlight the influence of different world orders: bipolarity from the end of World War II to the fall of the Soviet Union in the early 1990s, unipolarity from the early 1990s to 2006, and what I define as quasi-unipolarity from 2006 to the present. Considering systemic- and state-level influences, I explain that states choose different types of proxy wars for different reasons and that those choices have relevant effects on frequency and duration of civil wars. I acknowledge that this approach may seem a bit antiquated in light of more recent scholarship in the field of international relations. Nevertheless, I have chosen systemic-level theories to analyze changes in proxy war over time to highlight the continuing relevance of such "big" theories and for their explanative value, especially when "bridging the gap" between academics and policy makers. I also include state-level theories in my analysis because of the importance of how a state perceives the influence of world order on intervention decisions. Although some may suggest that this analysis is overly simple, I argue that the interplay between state- and systemic-level theories provides an elegant means of analyzing the changes in proxy war.

During the Cold War, the international system reflected a bipolar order. The United States and the Soviet Union stood atop the other countries in terms of capability and reach. With a few exceptions, states and relevant nonstate actors chose one side or the other. Adding to this, the presence of nuclear weapons made escalation between the United States and the Soviet Union extremely dangerous and undesirable. As a result, the two superpowers competed against one another using proxies. Smaller, regional powers engaged in proxy war on occasion to avoid drawing in one of the two superpowers. These types of external intervention prolonged intrastate conflicts and arguably contributed to initiation of many civil wars.

After the fall of the Soviet Union and the end of the Cold War, the United States became the only state capable of global reach and engagement. During this period, the duration of civil wars decreased significantly. Lacking the peer competition from the Soviet Union, the United States no longer feared uncontrollable escalation, reducing the need for indirect intervention and proxy war. Instead, proxy wars were primarily used by smaller, regional powers rather than those with global reach and interests. Without powerful intervening states backing indigenous fighters, many civil conflicts did not have the resources needed to continue the fighting. Although outside intervention occasionally helps end civil wars, "empirical studies actually suggest that interventions by other states generally tend to prolong civil wars and make conflicts more severe."[10]

The terrorist attacks on 9/11, however, saw the United States return to the use of proxy war to enable the removal of the Taliban regime in Afghanistan and aid in the capture or killing of Osama bin Laden. By the mid-2000s, intrastate conflicts and interventions once again began to increase.[11] The use of proxies increased as well. As the unipolar order slipped into a somewhat quasi-unipolar order, one where the hegemony of the United States continued to exist, but only tentatively, other states began to use proxy war more broadly.

My third argument is that proxy war can provide a useful and efficacious option, even under suboptimal conditions, so long as the intervening state sustains the coherence of the policy as conditions change and maintains near-absolute control over its proxy's actions. Coherence refers to the degree to which all aspects of the policy contribute to the intervener's desired objectives, and the policy's ability to adapt to changing conditions. Coherence demands that an intervening state tailor the policy specifically to account for local (target state), global, and domestic conditions. Ethnic and/or ideological factors found at the source of a conflict define what I call the *character* of a conflict.[12] Paying attention to the character of the conflict yields important information about the motivation of a proxy and informs an intervening state about the scope of its objectives and the potential need for additional control measures. If there are doubts or unknowns about the character of a conflict, serious consideration should be given to avoiding a proxy option no matter how enticing it may appear.

To better explain the importance of coherence in proxy war, I borrow from the work of Kichiro Fukusaku and Akira Hirata that focuses on the role of coherence on the effects of the Organisation of Economic Co-operation and Development (OECD) policies to improve development efforts.[13] Using Fukusaku and Hirata's description of the necessary elements for development efforts, I propose that a proxy intervention policy's coherence stems from five areas:

1. Internal coherence: the consistency of the intervening state's objectives with the policy, strategy, operations, and tactics used by all contributing agencies and departments when carrying out the proxy intervention.

2. Intrastate coherence: the policy and supporting actions that reflect the political and military situation on the ground in the target state.

3. International coherence: the consistency of support, or the degree of adversarial support, among states that influence those involved in the proxy intervention.

4. Domestic coherence: the consistency of support and/or opposition among parties inside the intervening state that influence the conduct of the proxy intervention.

5. Proxy coherence: the consistency of policies used by the intervening state to employ and control the proxy to achieve objectives.

Based on this model, *formulating* a coherent policy requires considerations for how to create and coordinate interactions with three different actors: its proxy, the international arena, and the domestic arena. *Sustaining* a coherent policy means that strategists must predict and manage their leaders' changing expectations, understand and work through how the uncertainty associated with proxy warfare will affect the policy over time, and deal with emerging conditions—those self-inflicted as well as those beyond control—that hinder policy coherence.

Chapter 4 also explains that regardless of the premise under which the proxy policy was selected, control can help ensure the utility (emphasizing the short-term perspective) and efficacy (emphasizing the long-term perspective) of the policy. Under ideal conditions, this is simple. If the proxy has similar political objectives, has a sophisticated understanding and a high degree of capability in the use of force, yet remains highly dependent on the intervening state for support, then the intervening state will have no issues controlling its proxy.

Intervening states can operationalize a proxy war policy more effectively if they understand the importance of the different aspects of the ideal type. Having similar political objectives minimizes the negative effects of the proxy's agency—its desire and ability to pursue its own agenda in a way that compromises the intervening state's objectives. A highly capable proxy, in terms of warfare, helps ensure that it does not have to resort to desperate tactics that rise to the level of war crimes or crimes against humanity.[14] A militarily capable proxy also minimizes the need for the intervening state to provide training or advising that risks the lives of its own forces and could potentially drag the intervening state to a higher level of involvement. Lastly, when a proxy remains highly dependent, the intervening state has more control over the proxy and can more easily bend the proxy to its will. Thus a proxy's isolation from other avenues of support has a significant impact on its resource dependence. A proxy that is highly isolated—geographically and socially—is less likely to establish and/or capitalize on outside sources of support, making the proxy easier to control. If the proxy is too isolated, the intervening state may have trouble providing the resources it needs, and it may not have the social connections needed to succeed politically. The perfect balance reflects a highly capable proxy with no option other than to subjugate its own desires and objectives to those of the intervening state, or face extinction. Unfortunately, there is no such thing as an ideal proxy. Any shortfall in any area leads to a suboptimal condition.

Once the decision has been made, an intervening state must structure its support for the proxy in a way that balances results with control. In some cases, performance-based incentives help keep a proxy focused on its performance. In others, outcome-based incentives can keep a proxy in check. The trick, however, is knowing which form of incentive is required given the conditions on the ground. Even more difficult, an intervening state must translate its intentions for incentives from the executive or highly placed government official directing the policy down to the tactical operator who is working directly with the proxy. During the execution of the proxy war, coherence demands that an intervening state continue to observe closely the opinions of domestic and international audiences and its ability to adjust the policy when warranted. Although keeping the policy covert may alleviate some of those issues in the short-run, policy analysts and strategists need to prepare for the moment when the proxy war becomes public.

In Chapter 4, I also explain how control depends largely on three conditions: *compatibility of objectives, capability of a proxy, and the dependence of a proxy on outside support.* Understanding how these three conditions affects the relationship between an intervening state and its proxy offers decision makers a reasonable means to assess the utility of a proxy war policy. First, a proxy war policy demands an in-depth study of a proxy's motivations. Policy makers should be wary of situations where an intervening state and its proxy have convergent objectives in only one particular area; this can lead to a quick decision for short-term gains and can result in long-term losses. An intervening state should weigh the overall convergence and divergence of its objectives with its proxy's, knowing that the proxy will likely withhold information that could hurt its ability to attract support. If necessary, an intervening state must be ready to limit its objectives to match its perceived ability to control the proxy.

Second, a capable proxy can lead its movement/forces and engage an adversary with relatively minimal assistance, ensuring that an intervening state can minimize its involvement. Capability, however, has two aspects: political and military. The relevance of the proxy's political capability increases as the intervening state's objectives increase in scale. For example, if an intervening state engages in a proxy war that reflects either an *in it to win it* type or a *meddling* type, meaning it wants to depose an existing regime and replace it with its proxy for the long term, then the political legitimacy and capacity of the proxy becomes an important issue in the policy's success. The intervening state must be more careful in managing how its proxy fights and how it engages the civilian population it will (hopefully) later govern. If an intervening state wants to simply perform a *holding action* or *feed the chaos* in an existing intrastate conflict, then it should limit its objectives and its support to enable the proxy to achieve tactical military victories.

With capability, however, there is a balance. As a proxy's capability increases, it challenges an intervening state's ability to control its proxy. Rapid military success can be difficult to control. The proxy may overreach and actually work against the intervening state's overall objectives. Under such conditions, a high degree of capability warrants additional monitoring to ensure control. In some cases, a proxy may be capable, but it may lack the necessary resources to enable its activities. This is how capability and dependence differ. A high-level of proxy dependence provides the means to control a proxy and counteract the negative effects of having divergent objectives or an overly capable proxy.

To put the concepts of coherence and control into practice, I recommend three maxims to help policy makers guide the formulation and sustainment of a proxy intervention policy. First, *know your enemy, but know your proxy even better.* As mentioned earlier, a state must realistically evaluate its objectives and compare those to the objectives of its proxy. If the proxy's objectives closely match those of the intervening state, then costs are likely to be low and benefits high—there is no incentive for the proxy to cheat, the intervening state does not have to offer incentives to get the proxy to do something it does not really want to do, and the intervening state saves the cost of having to implement strict measures to monitor and control its proxy. What behaviors signal a change in the proxy's stated (revealed) objectives? If a change has occurred, an intervening state must now ask what objectives are attainable with an uncooperative proxy? As objectives diverge, costs are going to increase because the policy now demands more stringent control and monitoring measures. Changes in the proxy's objectives also increase the possibility that a proxy will pursue methods or means that can harm the intervening state's interests. This becomes particularly important if the intervening state desires the ability to negotiate a settlement. If the proxy goes off the rails, its actions could damage the intervening state's ability to end the conflict when desired. *Knowing your proxy* also involves continuously monitoring the proxy's access to resources, its leadership capability (militarily and politically), and how the character of the conflict changes over time.

Second, *let the proxy lead, but only so far.* This maxim addresses issues connected to a proxy's self-interest and autonomy. By definition, war by proxy requires the creation of a hierarchical structure between an intervening state and an actor selected to serve as a proxy. Both sides will have their own desires and agendas, but the proxy's need for support and the intervening state's ability to provide that support creates a hierarchal relationship that places its desires above those of the proxy. If an intervening state doesn't get what it wants out of the relationship, it usually has the option to take its support elsewhere. An intervening state must understand the dynamics of these challenges to have the best opportunity to successfully execute a proxy war under suboptimal conditions. Autonomy must be managed carefully because of proxy self-interest; if able, the proxy will naturally tend to apply resources toward its own ends—a phenomenon that increases as autonomy increases. Having a proxy that can lead is desirable, but it requires limits. An intervening state must cultivate its proxy's ability to lead both politically and militarily, while at the same time restricting its proxy's opportunity to lead in areas that can damage or hinder the desired objectives.

Third, *cultivate proxy dependence.* A high-level of proxy dependence appears to provide sufficient control to counteract the negative effects of having divergent objectives. Cultivating dependence requires two simultaneous actions: (1) providing enough support to enable the proxy to accomplish the intervening state's objectives without the excess that can motivate or enable damaging, self-interested behavior, and (2) isolating the proxy from sources of outside support. The basic logic of agency theory (see Chapter 2) holds up in terms of incentive structure under each of the proposed conditions, except when an intervening state and its proxy have highly divergent objectives. In the absence of strong control measures or if an intervening state desires a settlement between its proxy and its adversary, an intervening state needs to assess its incentive structure and consider shifting to some form of outcome-based incentives. In addition to the use of resources to control a proxy, supporting multiple proxies and playing them off one another to deter each from pursuing their own interests offers an additional means of control. Having additional proxies does, however, add to the complexity of the policy and demands additional resources to minimize the negative effects previously mentioned regarding proxy war.

CASE STUDIES

In Chapter 3, I provide ten short case studies to explore and illustrate the different types and uses of proxy war under different world orders. I compare the choice and use of proxy war by states under conditions of bipolarity, unipolarity, and quasi-unipolarity. I have selected diverse cases in terms of regime type, relative capability, and span of interest to illustrate the influence of the world order on the phenomenon of proxy war.

Chapters 6, 7, and 8 offer three different cases that test the validity of the theory presented in Chapter 4: U.S.-Hmong in Laos, South Africa–UNITA (National Union for the Total Independence of Angola) in Angola, and India-LTTE (Liberation Tigers of Tamil Eelam) in Sri

Lanka. Each of the three cases has been selected to gain diversity needed to evaluate the different aspects of my theory. I have chosen three different states to show the difference in how policy is executed, allowing for a more generalized study of how my theory of proxy war connects to its practice in future scenarios. The cases provide variation in the types and amounts of costs and benefits each intervening state incurred and the conditions under which the proxy war occurred. Although Gary King, Robert Keohane, and Sidney Verba explicitly condemn research designs that choose cases based on dependent variables (the utility and efficacy of proxy war), Alex George and Andrew Bennett acknowledge that the practice serves a valuable role in achieving the variation necessary to conduct a useful and informative study.[15] To increase the rigor of this study across the three cases, I use the method of structured, focused comparison. For all three cases, I ask the following questions:

What were the barriers to direct intervention and nonintervention?

Why did the intervening state choose a proxy war policy?

How did the intervening state ensure coherence and what was the overall effect?

How did the intervening state use and control its proxy and to what end?

How do my proposed maxims apply to the intervening state's use of a proxy?

The U.S. support of Hmong irregulars provides a case in which an intervening state engages in the covert support of a nonstate actor (the Hmong) to conduct counterinsurgency (COIN) operations. Aside from the interesting idea of supporting a non-government-related entity to conduct COIN operations on behalf of the Lao government, the U.S.-Hmong case offers seven particularly diverse and interesting characteristics that provide the necessary variation in my three main cases to help answer the questions posed in Chapter 1 and test the validity of the propositions presented in Chapter 2. First, the United States used a politically isolated Hmong proxy as a counterinsurgency force. Second, U.S. and Hmong forces maintained a close, well-integrated relationship but could only provide the Hmong with a low degree of autonomy because of the relatively superior military capabilities of the opposing forces. Third, Washington supported the Hmong to ensure that U.S. involvement remained plausibly deniable. Fourth, the character of the war in Laos was predominantly ideological. Fifth, U.S. involvement steadily increased, causing a corresponding increase in the costs and decrease in the benefits. Sixth, the Hmong became completely dependent on the United States, in ways far beyond the actual fighting. International conditions did not support U.S. involvement at any level. The conflict has both ethnic and ideological characteristics. Finally, the case represents a situation where the intervening state gained significant benefits from the arrangement with comparatively small costs, yet the proxy incurred tremendous costs with few benefits. U.S. support of the Hmong fits the definition of a proxy war in that the United States organized, trained, equipped, directed, and supported Hmong operations against Pathet Lao and North Vietnamese Army (NVA) forces in Laos. Although the United States had forward air controllers (FACs) operating covertly inside Laos and used a substantial number of aircraft to aid indigenous forces in Laos, few U.S. personnel participated in the fighting on the ground. From a political standpoint, the Hmong were completely isolated from the Royal Lao Government (RLG) in Vientiane and had little interest in gaining a stake in the political process. Rather, the Hmong fought to avoid "any external effort to control and manage their affairs."[16]

The U.S.-Hmong case provides an example of a highly cooperative, highly dependent proxy receiving covert support, operating with a low degree of autonomy, and possessing relatively convergent objectives as the intervening state. Inside Laos, the Hmong were instrumental in forestalling communist forces from capturing Laos's capital in Vientiane, despite the fact that they were a politically isolated ethnic group with relatively weak connections to the Royal Lao Government. The United States, as the intervening state, reflects a strong democracy pursuing security interests abroad to curtail the flow of communism and the expansion of its chief rival, the Soviet Union. Soviet involvement, however, remained limited in spite of heavy U.S. involvement. Both the international community and the U.S. public were assumed by decision makers to be unsupportive, but little action was taken by either audience after news of U.S. involvement became public knowledge.

The U.S.-Hmong case is interesting because it reflects the use of a proxy engaging in a counterinsurgency *on behalf of* the sitting government. Despite its efforts, the United States failed to persuade the Royal Lao Government to commit to counterinsurgency efforts against the communist Pathet Lao. The U.S.-Hmong case is critical for four reasons. First, U.S. support to the Hmong remained highly covert for over ten years before it was publicly revealed. Even more importantly, the United States elected to continue its support to the Hmong for several years afterward; this provides an opportunity to study both the effects of keeping a proxy war secret and what happens when a covert policy is revealed. Second, this case represents one of the rare instances when an intervening state supports a proxy that is essentially unaffiliated with the sitting government. Third, the case depicts an example of an intervening state cultivating its own proxy force. Although the Hmong had already begun to band together to fight the North Vietnamese and Pathet Lao, it was not until the United States got involved that the Hmong became an influential factor in the Laotian conflict. Fourth, this case provides an opportunity to study a scenario where an intervening state received marginal benefits and incurred only moderate costs.

South Africa's use of UNITA as a proxy provides a case in which a politically isolated state got involved in the tense civil war in Angola to protect itself from communist influence and stop the South West African People's Organisation (SWAPO) insurgency from gaining ground in Namibia (South West Africa). This case is especially interesting for at least four reasons. First, it deals with somewhat divergent objectives between the intervening state and the proxy. Second, it includes the dynamics of more than one intervening state supporting a proxy. Third, the conflict in Angola had elements of both an ethnic and an ideological struggle. Fourth, South Africa's role as a regional power and pariah in the international system is unique.

South Africa's support of UNITA fits the definition of a proxy war in that South Africa provided logistics, uniforms, weapons, weapons training, and South African Defense Force (SADF) personnel serving as operational and tactical advisors. On occasion, SADF provided artillery and air support for SADF and UNITA elements engaged with Armed Forces for the Liberation of Angola (FAPLA) and Cuban regulars. UNITA's forces far outnumbered those of the SADF and did the majority of the fighting. South Africa gave UNITA a very high degree of autonomy, despite its significant support for the movement. The combination of UNITA's dependence and its closely aligned objectives enabled South Africa to maintain a relatively hands-off approach during the war in Angola.[17]

South Africa's support of UNITA during the Angolan Civil War poses two challenges to an accurate assessment of the utility and efficacy of using a proxy. First, the aims of Pretoria's policy in Angola differ significantly from conventional wisdom. Some argue that South Africa's involvement in Angola was designed to hold on to Namibia indefinitely and to uphold apartheid.[18] Pretoria sought neither to uphold apartheid nor to control Namibia indefinitely, but rather to find a means to transition to an inclusive government at home without having the country, and the region, devolve into chaotic, bitter war.[19] Ultimately, Pretoria sought an outcome that would prevent the African National Congress (ANC) from taking over South Africa by force, remove Cuban soldiers from Angola, minimize Soviet influence in the region, allow Namibia to transition peacefully into the control of SWAPO, and prevent the Popular Movement for the Liberation of Angola (MPLA) government in Luanda from destroying UNITA. Therefore, when some scholars or analysts claim that South Africa's loss of Namibia and its transition away from apartheid were costs, a better understanding reveals that the way in which these two outcomes occurred were in fact benefits.

Second, it is difficult to separate the effects of South Africa's broader regional and domestic policies from those specifically related to Angola. The issue of apartheid often overshadowed South Africa's involvement in Angola, and Pretoria's involvement in Mozambique and its affiliation with the Mozambican National Resistance (RENAMO) provided a strong source of international scrutiny. In explaining the effects of different conditions on the utility and efficacy of South Africa's proxy war in Angola, I present evidence of how conditions affected the utility and efficacy of South Africa's use of UNITA and, where identifiable, attribute effects to circumstances unrelated to the Angolan Civil War.

Like the U.S.-Hmong example, the South Africa–UNITA case demonstrates a highly cooperative, highly dependent proxy; it differs, however, in the fact that UNITA received relatively overt support, operated with a high degree of autonomy, and had highly divergent objectives. Inside Angola, support for UNITA and its rival, the MPLA, is mainly divided along ethnic lines. Internationally, this case reflected the superpower rivalry common in the Cold War, but the United States remained only a limited participant. South Africa, a regional power regarded as a pariah among most states, opposed the Soviet Union's attempt to increase its influence in southern Africa. Although the international community rhetorically opposed South Africa's involvement in Angola, the actions of the United States and Western Europe reflected a more tacit approval of Pretoria's proxy war. Domestically, South Africa's public was reluctantly supportive, but only on the condition that the costs remained low.

The South Africa–UNITA case is critical for three reasons. First, it provides an example of a high dependence and high autonomy to balance out the other two cases (U.S.-Hmong was high dependence/low autonomy and India-LTTE was low dependence/high autonomy). Understandably, I found no examples of a low-dependence, high-autonomy relationship between an intervening state and a proxy. Second, it provides an opportunity to study a scenario in which the international system should have inflicted high costs on South Africa for its proxy war policy but failed to follow through. Considering that most states had already rhetorically condemned Pretoria's government and its foreign policy in southern Africa, it is interesting that states failed to raise the international costs of South Africa's policy. Third, South Africa—unlike the other two examples—incurred very low costs yet still managed to maximize its benefits.

India's support of LTTE depicts a case in which an intervening state initially elects to covertly support one side of a civil conflict and is then later forced to intervene directly and overtly attempt to stop its proxy's operations. The India-LTTE case offers six particularly diverse and interesting characteristics. First, this case provides an example where both international and domestic pressures figured strongly into a state's interventionist policy.[20] Second, India's concern about regional and global rivals siding with Sri Lanka initially led the government in New Delhi to look for a covert way to influence Sri Lanka's foreign and domestic policy. Third, India and LTTE did not have a close working relationship; India's efforts to penetrate the organization and control it ultimately failed. Fourth, India maintained relations and provided support to several Tamil militant groups and purposely sought to keep them all relatively even to prevent one group from gaining a dominant stance among Sri Lankan Tamils. Fifth, the character of the war in Sri Lanka was predominantly ethnic. Sixth, this case provides the most obvious and devastating example of a proxy using the support it had been given against the intervening state. Unlike the previous two cases, the regional context of this case overshadowed many of the effects of the global political environment that were so influential in Angola and Laos. Although the conflict took place during the Cold War, both the superpowers remained sidelined and allowed India to exercise its role as a regional power.

India's support of LTTE fits the definition in that India provided equipment, training, and supplies to LTTE in an attempt to influence Sri Lanka's foreign and domestic policies and assert India's dominance in South Asia. None of the Tamil militant groups, including LTTE, had the resources or capability to compete with Sri Lanka's armed forces and produce an independent Tamil state.[21] Although India and LTTE had different intentions, both wanted to stop the violence and reverse Sinhalese efforts to marginalize Tamils under the auspices of Sri Lanka's constitution.

The India-LTTE case involves the support of an uncooperative proxy operating with a high degree of autonomy and possessing highly divergent objectives. For the duration of the conflict, India's support remained covert and plausibly deniable. Inside Sri Lanka, the character of the conflict was almost exclusively ethnic and involved the government in Colombo trying to prevent the emergence of an independent Tamil state. Internationally, the United States, the Soviet Union, and most other global powers, for the most part, remained sidelined. In addition, the spillover of refugees into India, the human rights violations committed by Sri Lanka's armed forces, and the covert character of India's policy all combined to help New Delhi avoid significant international costs. Domestically, India's government had to balance its foreign policy with concerns about its sympathetic Tamil population and the threat of several different secessionist movements inside its own borders.

The India-LTTE case is critical for three reasons. First, the case reflects history's most costly proxy war policy. Not only did LTTE hamper India's policy in Sri Lanka, it also led India into a disastrous military intervention aimed at reining in its own proxy's military operations and contributed to the assassination of Prime Minister Rajiv Gandhi.[22] Second, it represents a case where the desire of the intervening state's domestic public to support the proxy overwhelmed the state's ability to execute its policy. Third, it provides an example of a proxy war that remained only marginally affected by the bipolar order of the Cold War; both the United States and the Soviet Union remained relatively uninvolved throughout the conflict.

Case Study Limitations

I have chosen to focus on nonstate proxies because previous studies have mostly emphasized states serving as proxies, and the few studies that did consider nonstate proxies provided only a broad brush of the subject.[23] Further, focusing on nonstate proxies provides a more rigorous investigation of the phenomenon. As I explain in Chapter 2, a proxy war requires the presence of a principal-agent relationship. Although the proxy maintains its agency, its ability to act remains more or less constrained by the intervening state's conditional offer of support. Although a state could serve as a proxy in this capacity, it becomes more difficult to establish the principal-agent relationship. For example, Cuba has often been considered a proxy for the Soviet Union, especially in Angola and Ethiopia in the 1970s and 1980s. Cuba, however, elected to directly intervene in the affairs of both countries of its own volition.[24] The fact that states will hide the nature of their relationships with other states makes it more complicated to assume a principal-agent relationship because of international institutions and laws that grant states autonomy and the fact that the relationship could reflect a de facto alliance instead.

To narrow the scope of my research, I have chosen to focus exclusively on the period following World War II. The creation of the United

Nations and the UN Security Council has arguably altered the way states interact with one another, especially with regard to the use of force; any state that intervenes in the domestic affairs of another state without provocation or the approval of the UN Security Council violates the UN Charter.[25] This is not to say that the UN Charter has completely changed how states behave—it simply acknowledges the fact that states often seek the approval of the United Nations when using force (unless acting in self-defense).

To address the need for rigor in this study, I have chosen three cases that occurred prior to the twenty-first century. As previously argued, these cases provide suitable diversity and rich sources of information, but they may lack the ability to offer insights about how the availability of information worldwide and social media may influence the conduct, utility, and efficacy of proxy war. I do, however, offer six brief case studies from the post–Cold War era, and four from the post-9/11 era in Chapter 3. Despite increases in the availability of information and the broad reach of social media, proxy wars today question the singular effect of either factor's ability to change the phenomenon. The current proxy war in Yemen seems as quiet and unreported as did the proxy war in Angola in the 1970s. Although more recent cases may uncover some changes in the post-2000 world, the information and details available in those cases do not allow for sufficient rigor. As such information becomes available, more recent cases will offer new opportunities for further research.

SUMMARY

Proxy war is currently viewed through an overly optimistic lens, a trend that continues despite historical evidence. As a result, states can find themselves in an unpredicted and perilous situation. Proxy war may be a necessary policy choice, but it is never a risk-free, low-cost endeavor. I believe most states understand this aspect, yet often fail to take the proper measures to protect against the risks involved. The obvious first step is to understand how the policy will fit into the security interests of the state from a more holistic perspective; it pushes past indirect intervention and looks at the other factors that can affect the decision to choose a proxy, even under suboptimal conditions. Preceding that first step, however, analysts and strategists charged with analyzing and developing a policy need to understand the biases and misperceptions that will influence them and those they advise. Policy analysts, strategists, and decision makers can deliberate the policy more effectively if they understand the essence of the phenomenon. In a parallel vein, this book provides a better understanding of how proxy war might be used by a competing state. Proxy war is a policy fraught with weaknesses and challenges. Understanding the phenomenon helps a state use it as an instrument to pursue security interests abroad and helps a state counter such efforts from its rivals. Knowing how to do proxy war brings the added benefit of knowing how to undermine the utility and efficacy of a proxy war used against the state's interests.

CHAPTER 2

SHARPENING THE DEFINITIONS OF INDIRECT
INTERVENTION AND PROXY WAR

INDIRECT INTERVENTION typically occurs within the confines of an existing intrastate conflict. Indirect intervention provides a would-be intervener with an opportunity to influence the political affairs of another state in the face of perceived barriers that bar a state from directly intervening. It also provides an avenue of action for a would-be fence sitter that feels pushed to intervene reluctantly in another state's affairs. Based on a study of indirect intervention, I propose four general categories that represent the barriers that lead states to choose indirect intervention: (1) the risk of escalation increases if a state directly intervenes, (2) a lack of domestic support may risk the sustainability of the intervention, (3) a lack of international support negatively affects the cost/benefit ratio of the intervention, and (4) a lack of capacity makes direct intervention untenable. Facing these restrictions, states must decide how much control they desire over the outcome when intervening indirectly. In all four cases, a would-be intervener must consider the balance between higher degrees of control (which require a higher degree of commitment) and the ability to hide or obscure its involvement with a corresponding decrease in control. Proxy war comes to the fore because it offers a chance for balancing the desire to influence affairs in a desired way while minimizing or obscuring participation.

Proxy war is only one means of indirectly intervening in the affairs of another state. Looking more generally at indirect intervention, I suggest that it can be broken down into two general types: donated assistance and proxy war. I propose that the essential components of proxy war include an intervening state attempting to influence an intrastate conflict outside its borders, an indigenous force willing to fight or already engaged in that conflict on the intervening state's behalf, a principal-agent relationship between the intervening state and its proxy, the presence of some degree of agency afforded to the proxy, and some degree of control over the proxy afforded to the intervening state. Lastly, this chapter explains how the possibility of a proxy war fits into a state's desire to intervene in the affairs of another state.

INDIRECT INTERVENTION AND PROXY WAR

The term *proxy war* is overused and underspecified. For such a common term, *proxy war*, or more specifically *proxy intervention*, lacks a sharp explanation for what it is, as well as when and how it works. Geraint Hughes argues that nonstate actors that remain dependent on an intervening state should all be considered proxies because the degree of dependence fluctuates over time.[1] I agree that it is useful at this point to focus on nonstate actors, but only because of the difficulty associated with proving a principal-agent relationship between states. Without an acknowledgment that one of the states involved does not view itself as a sovereign independent cooperating with another more powerful state, it becomes very difficult to establish a principal-agent relationship—to know who is working for whom.

Some current works such as Michael Innes's edited volume, *Making Sense of Proxy Wars*, continue to propagate misguided images of Cold War proxies as "little more than third-party tools of statecraft without any agency, intent, or, indeed, interests visibly separate from those of a well-resourced state sponsor."[2] Innes does, however, expand previous conceptions of proxy war linked to the Cold War by suggesting that proxies exist beyond insurgents and counterinsurgents in the Third World. Innes opens the door to considering state-sponsored terrorist organizations as proxies but overexpands the concept of a proxy to things such as car bombs and multinational corporations.[3] There are two issues with these examples. Considering inanimate objects (those incapable of agency) as a possible proxy and a vehicle for indirect intervention, Innes misses an important aspect of proxy war—the fact that a proxy retains some degree of its agency, even though it enters into a principal-agent relationship. Under such a convention, it becomes possible to consider car bombs or drones a proxy, and simultaneously waters down our understanding. I also argue that using actors that lack any political motivation, such as mercenaries or private military companies, introduces a separate dynamic to proxy war. Although I agree that such actors could serve as a proxy, it is worthwhile to separate them into two different lines of inquiry.

Understanding the relationship between an intervening state and its proxy creates the distinction between two different types of indirect intervention: donated assistance and proxy war. To narrow and specify the definition of proxy, I include the idea that an intervening state has an intent to control the actions of the proxy to some degree. This does not mean that proxies are all used for the same purpose in an indirect intervention (a topic I discuss in further detail shortly). The intent to control combines with a principal-agent relationship to produce specific effects in an indirect intervention. Donated assistance describes the act of aiding an indigenous actor engaged in a civil conflict without strings attached—without the intent or need to control the proxy's actions. The intervening state puts no effort into directing the actions of the local actor. In this sense, donated assistance involves any form of support, such as donating resources to improve an actor's capabilities in the intrastate conflict or exerting diplomatic influence to help improve an actor's standing in the target state and in the international system. The U.S. support of the mujahideen in Afghanistan provides a good example. Washington provided funds and weapons to enable the mujahideen to resist the Soviet invasion in the 1980s. Pakistan administered the distribution of U.S. support intended for the mujahideen, superseding America's ability to control the mujahideen's actions. This worked because the U.S. wanted to impede the Soviet invasion but had little concern about the duration or outcome of the conflict.[4]

Although similar in some ways to donated assistance, proxy war is different in two important ways. First, proxy war is a form of military intervention with the specific intent to intentionally influence the affairs of another state through the use (or threat) of violence.[5] Rather than intervening directly to influence the outcome of the intrastate conflict, an intervening state backs a local actor to do most of the fighting on the ground.[6] Second, the relationship between an intervening state and its proxy is hierarchical; the proxy subjugates its interests to that of the intervening state because of its inability to act on its own.[7] This does not mean that the proxy is not self-interested or acts purely in the interest of the intervening state. Depending on the conditions, a proxy may be more or less capable of pursuing its own objectives and taking advantage of the intervening state's support.

To narrow the focus of study, I define proxy war as *directing the use of force by a politically motivated, local actor to indirectly influence political affairs in the target state.* An indirect intervention demands that an intervening state's forces engage tangentially in the conflict as advisors or in a capacity that augments a proxy's ground forces (such as providing air power or intelligence) without participating directly in the fighting on the ground. Once the intervening state begins to use its own forces to engage in the fighting, the conflict becomes a direct intervention.

Although paying an additional actor that is not politically motivated to fight in the target state's civil conflict appears to fit into the basic definition of a proxy, I suggest that there is utility in separating the two phenomena. In this book, I separate out the use of mercenaries and focus only on indigenous groups that are politically motivated to alter the affairs of the target state.[8] Although Innes argues that private military companies fall under the definition of a proxy, the nature of a private military company's motivation alters the principal-agent relationship with the intervening state in a way that yields a similar, yet separate phenomenon.[9] I agree, however, that the use of private military companies as a means of indirect intervention warrants further study.

As mentioned, the nature of the relationship between a proxy and an intervening state provides important insights that lend specificity to the motivations behind this method of indirect intervention. In some ways, the relationship reflects something akin to an alliance. A consensus in the literature suggests that states form alliances to increase their own position; strategic partnerships provide greater resources to pursue security interests.[10] In this sense, more resources translates into three potential benefits: they can add critical skills that qualitatively improve a state's ability to influence a particular situation, they may provide the personnel necessary when commitments restrict a state's ability to use its own forces, and they should allow a state to conserve its resources in case they are needed elsewhere.[11] If a proxy can provide those capabilities, then an intervening state may benefit and subsequently choose to engage in a proxy war.

In his seminal work on alliances, Glenn Snyder finds that alliances can impose unwanted costs. One side may be dragged unwillingly into a conflict due to concerns that reneging on its commitment may justify similar behavior from other allies in the future.[12] Therefore, it stands to reason that partnering with a proxy could impose similar costs. If a state wants the ability to partner with nonstate actors in the future, Snyder's findings suggest that an intervening state may have to allow itself to get dragged deeper into a conflict. Although prominent scholars in the structural realist camp of international relations argue that alliances are not binding in this way, several alliance scholars provide empirical evidence indicating that states still often honor their commitments under undesirable conditions.[13] Evidence also shows that states make similar efforts to honor commitments in proxy wars. One example is how the U.S. provided asylum for Hmong refugees at the close of its proxy war in Laos.

Alliances built on mutual dependence can also impose costs. When one side abandons the other, the remaining state must bear the expense of continuing its effort or withdrawing and suffering a costly blow to its prestige. Alliances that involve states with large differences in their capabilities reduce the probability of abandonment but also transfer most of the costs to the stronger side.[14] History shows that partnering with a proxy typically avoids abandonment costs during periods of intense fighting, but in some cases (U.S.-Armas, India–Mukti Bahini, India-LTTE, Uganda-Rwanda/Alliance of Democratic Forces for the Liberation of Congo (AFDL), and U.S.–Northern Alliance) a proxy abandoned its commitment to the intervening state once it achieved some acceptable measure of security. Some alliance costs stem from a greater sense of commitment created when two actors work together and develop a concern for one another.[15] Alliances, unfortunately, do not accurately characterize all aspects of an intervening state's relationship with its proxy.

A principal-agent relationship fills in many of the gaps and expands our understanding of the relationship of the actors engaging in a proxy war: an intervening state (principal) contracts the services of a proxy (agent) to help intervene in the affairs in a foreign country. Agency theory complements explanations of alliance behavior because it concentrates on relationships when one side contracts the services of another rather than when two sides enter into a contract on more equal footing, such as an alliance.[16] Agency theory most aptly applies under the following three conditions: when a principal's (an intervening state's) goals conflict with those of its agent (proxy), when the uncertainty of the outcome increases the likelihood that each side will attempt to cheat the other, and when it is difficult to evaluate the other side's behavior.[17] Under most circumstances, an intervening state and its proxy will face at least one, if not all three, of these conditions. Costs associated with a principal-agent (intervening state–proxy) relationship (herein labeled *agency costs*) should apply to proxy war because an intervening state and its proxy, like a principal and its agent, will rarely have perfectly symmetrical interests and objectives. Therefore, an intervening state often must expend further resources—additional agency costs—just to keep the proxy under control.[18]

The two main benefits of a principal-agent relationship are that both parties share the costs of pursuing an objective and each side likely brings a unique set of skills that make attaining those objectives easier or more efficient.[19] In proxy war, an indigenous actor with knowledge of the local language and the ability to blend into the environment may not have adequate resources or skills to accomplish its objectives alone; an intervening state lacking these skills may still be able to accomplish its security objectives but at a significantly higher cost. Acting together, each side improves the chances of achieving their objectives and potentially reduces their costs. Understanding the relationship between an intervening state and its proxy allows for a better picture of what it takes to ensure the utility and efficacy of a proxy intervention.

HOW PROXY WAR FITS INTO A STATE'S CHOICE
TO INTERVENE INDIRECTLY

Explaining why a state intervened in another state's civil conflict is impossibly complex. There is no single smoking gun that explains the reason for an intervention. To aid in this analysis, I borrow Robert Art's convention for when states resort to the use of force: risk to *vital interests* and risks to *desirable interests*. The perception of risk to vital interests reflects a state's rational choice to sustain or improve its influence and security. Vital interests, therefore, represent systemically driven influences directly linked to the state's ability to survive and thrive in the international arena.[20] Vital interests, however, are insufficient for explaining foreign policy decisions. States have agency and the literature in the field of international relations has made a strong case that states act in a variety of ways that go beyond simple calculations regarding survival.[21] To account for such influences, Art recommends a secondary axis, which considers the relevance of risks to desirable interests on intervention decisions. Desirable interests reflect a state's concerns for how its actions (or inaction) may affect its ability to influence groups domestically and internationally. To pursue desirable interests, a government mixes elements of its hard and soft power to engage in policies that promote the welfare of its people at home and its partners abroad, protect human rights, advocate for free and fair governments, and build social connections with other states and international institutions.[22] Further, a state's identity also affects its desirable interests. Intervention decisions assessed based on the costs and benefits of pursuing either vital or desirable interests will ultimately determine a policy's efficacy.[23] Although combining these two different methods of looking at what drives intervention significantly complicates explanation, using both lenses provides a more robust investigation of the conditions that lead states to engage in proxy war.[24]

Looking at vital interests and desirable interests singularly makes it easy to conceive of a certain threshold for intervention. If a state perceives that an intrastate conflict outside its borders jeopardizes its survival or the security of its citizens (vital interests), then a direct intervention will occur. If a state perceives that an intrastate conflict outside its borders reduces its future prosperity or clashes with its espoused values such as human rights or democracy in some egregious manner (genocide, ethnic cleansing, a foreign government's use of chemical weapons in a civil war), then a direct intervention will occur. I argue that in some cases, the situation hits on both interests. For example, the United States' concern about losing Laos to the communist wave in Southeast Asia was the origin of its intervention in the Vietnam conflict.[25] Keeping communism contained in Southeast Asia was at stake—a serious interest related to America's interests abroad. Further, the United States wanted to demonstrate to Europe that it was committed to keeping communism at bay and would not cut and run if the Soviets attacked.[26] Under such conditions, vital and desirable interests compound to inspire a direct intervention. Using these concepts, I propose that states have an intervention threshold as reflected in Figure 2.1.

Nonintervention occurs when a state perceives that its capacity to act cannot overcome the barriers to any form of intervention. In such

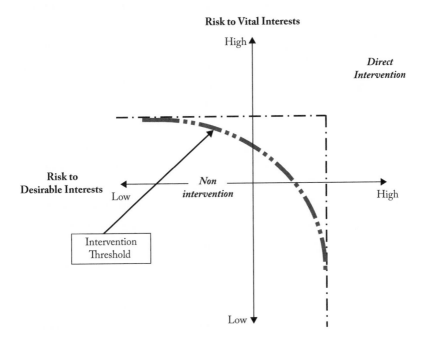

FIGURE 2.1 *Drivers for Intervention*

situations, there is usually very little at stake, or there is almost no concern about the outcome of an intrastate conflict. For example, the United States initially considered avoiding getting involved in the crisis in Bosnia in the early 1990s. The George H. W. Bush administration felt that the conditions on the ground in the Balkans would lead to another "Vietnam-style quagmire" and that the United States was not willing to engage in any form of intervention beyond diplomatically isolating the Milosevic regime. In 1995, however, President Bill Clinton kept true to his campaign promises to intervene in the Balkan crisis. The Clinton administration shifted America's perception of the importance of the Balkan conflict; the crisis did not jeopardize U.S. security, but it did raise the issue of the importance of humanitarian intervention in an international system clearly led by the United States. Washington perceived that it needed to intervene to influence the outcome of the conflict, despite the fact that the outcome had little bearing on national security.[27]

The perceived need for indirect intervention exists between direct intervention and nonintervention. Sometimes a government perceives pressure to "do something" about an intrastate conflict abroad, but directly intervening does not make sense. A state perceives the capacity to "do something," but how much it can do comes down to the barriers that prevent direct intervention. The ability to act somewhere in the space between the thresholds of direct and nonintervention, to indirectly intervene in an intrastate conflict abroad, is mostly a function of the intervener's relative capability vis-à-vis any opposition and the degree of competition in the international system (measured by the existing global order).

A NEW WAY TO THINK ABOUT PROXY WAR

The barriers mentioned previously that are associated with a state's capabilities and competition lead to the perception that there is an advantage in using an indirect intervention. However, *winning is not always the purpose of an indirect intervention*. Unlike a direct intervention that provides a visible display of a state's relative capability and potentially harms a state's ability to send credible signals about the willingness or ability to use force in the future, indirect interventions do not necessarily require a *win* to help an intervening state reach its objectives. To capture the broader range of objectives associated with indirect interventions, I offer four types of proxy war that states have used and will continue to use over time: *in it to win it, holding action, meddling,* and *feeding the chaos.* Each type has a specific purpose based on a state's perception of what is at stake and its commitment to the outcome.

Each of the four proxy war typologies reflects a different policy objective. Figure 2.2 maps each type of proxy war onto the intervention axis presented in Figure 2.1. All four adhere to the idea that a state perceives its situation falls between the thresholds of nonintervention and direct intervention. *In it to win it* should occur when a state perceives a greater need to influence the outcome of an intrastate conflict based on the connection to that intervening state's security and longevity, and therefore the intervening state will offer more support and a higher level of commitment to enable its proxy to win. An *in it to win it* approach should most likely appear in scenarios where the threat of a peer or near-peer competitor entering the conflict remains low. India's strong support of Mukti Bahini allowed it to sever Pakistan's use of East Pakistan (what is now Bangladesh) as a means of sustaining two fronts on India's borders and kept both the United States and the Soviet Union out of the conflict.

A *holding action* approach ought to come in when the stakes are sufficiently high to warrant indirect intervention, but the state perceives the actual outcome as less important or the desired outcome is unachievable. Most often, a secondary objective is driving the use of this kind of proxy war, such as when the intrastate conflict offers an opportunity to prevent or minimize the risks to a far greater interest in a nearby state. UNITA proved to be a credible force in Angola, but South Africa cared far more about the situation in South West Africa (Namibia), a country that shared a significant border, than it did about Angola. The civil war in Angola was just a way to tie up communist forces to prevent unfettered access to South West Africa (see Chapter 6). In some cases, the available proxy lacks the capability to actually win the conflict, but helping to prolong the civil war may improve the outcome in terms of the intervening state's interests. A good example of this is when the available proxy has little political capacity and correspondingly engenders only minute or no support among the target state's population. The Hmong in Laos best reflect this kind of situation (see Chapter 5). In this situation, extending the conflict reduces the opposition's claim to power, because it cannot control the violence within the borders, and may pave the way to greater concessions that do less harm to the intervening state's interests.

Meddling finds its place when an intervening state has little commitment to the outcome and the stakes in the target state are low. Gains would be nice but are not really needed to protect the intervening state's vital interests. Further, it would enhance the state's position without risking any loss in capability or prestige. If the risk of escalation with a peer or near-peer competitor is high or there are significant constraints (internationally and/or domestically) barring the amount of resources that can be made available to the proxy, then *meddling* offers a viable option. Arguably, the Soviet Union's support for the Sandinista regime reflects this kind of approach. Moscow recognized that the Western Hemisphere had a high risk for American escalation and believed that minor support would sustain the regime in Nicaragua considering that the Contras were not a very capable force.[28]

Lastly, *feeding the chaos* comes in when a state perceives that an intrastate conflict poses little threat to its vital interests but offers the potential

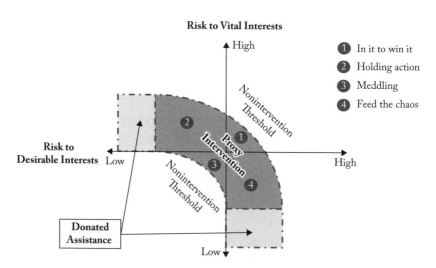

FIGURE 2.2 *Intervention Thresholds and Proxy War Types*

of denying another state the ability to attain its desirable interests. *Feeding the chaos* applies to a situation where an intervening state's desired outcome is to prolong the violence of an intrastate conflict and preventing the opposing side from winning. The intervening state does not want its proxy to actually win the conflict because it will likely inherit the problem in the future. Instead, prolonging the violence allows an intervening state to challenge or marginalize rival states. For example, Iran likely does not want the Houthis in Yemen to gain control of the government. Instead, keeping the fighting going in Yemen keeps its principal rival in the region, Saudi Arabia, distracted and engaged on its southern border. Without the ability to connect support to a specific interest or threat, *feeding the chaos* will often be conducted covertly to avoid international or domestic blowback.

SUMMARY

Proxy war is only one of two types of indirect intervention. Understanding the relationship between an intervening state and its proxy provides the primary mechanism for distinguishing between *donated assistance* and *proxy war*. The main difference between the two is that proxy war increases an intervening state's ability to influence *and* control the outcome of an intrastate conflict, whereas donated assistance offers only the ability to influence the outcome.

The decision to intervene indirectly stems from the perception of barriers to either direct intervention or nonintervention. In some cases, the stakes involved in another state's civil war demand that a state intervene directly to preserve its own security. In others, a state may not have a stake in the outcome of another state's internal conflict in terms of security, but the state has an interest in the outcome, perhaps to preserve or restore basic human rights, and therefore commits its own resources to achieve that outcome.

States do not, however, always intervene simply to help one side win an intrastate conflict. Therefore, the study of proxy war requires four different classifications: *in it to win it, holding action, meddling*, and *feed the chaos*. Each type of proxy war has a different aim and applies in a different

TABLE 2.1 *Summary of Non-state Proxy Wars, 1945–2001*

Intervening State(s)	Proxy	Location	Year	Type
China	Viet Minh	Indo-China	1949	Meddling
United States	Castillo Armas' Forces	Guatemala	1953	Meddling
China	Pathet Lao	Laos	1954	Meddling
United States	Hmong	Laos	1960	Holding Action
United States	Brigade 2506	Cuba	1961	Meddling
Soviet Union	Southwest Africa People's Organization (SWAPO)	SW Africa	1962	Meddling
Soviet Union	Zimbabwean African People's Union (ZAPU)	Zimbabwe	1962	Meddling
China	Zimbabwean African National Union (ZANU)	Zimbabwe	1963	Meddling
North Vietnam	National Liberation Front (NLF)	South Vietnam	1963	In It to Win It
Soviet Union	Popular Movement for the Liberation of Angola (MPLA)	Angola	1964	Meddling
India	Mukti Bahini	East Pakistan	1971	In It to Win It
China	National Liberation Front of Angola (FNLA)	Angola	1973	Meddling
United States	National Liberation Front of Angola (FNLA)	Angola	1974	Meddling
South Africa	Union for the Total Independence of Angola (UNITA)	Angola	1975	Holding Action
Syria	Lebanese Front (LF)	Lebanon	1975	Meddling
Syria	Palestine Liberation Organization (PLO)	Lebanon	1975	Meddling
Israel	South Lebanese Force (SLF)	Lebanon	1976	Meddling
Somalia	Western Somali Liberation Front (WSLF)	Ethiopia	1976	In It to Win It

Sponsor	Proxy	Year	Type
Somalia	Somali-Abo Liberation Front (SALF)	1976	In It to Win It
Pakistan	Mujahideen	1979	Feed the Chaos
South Africa	Mozambican National Resistance (RENAMO)	1980	Feed the Chaos
United States	Contras	1981	Meddling
India	Tamil Tigers (LTTE)	1983	Meddling
United States	Union for the Total Independence of Angola (UNITA)	1985	Meddling
Iran	Hezbollah	1997	Meddling
Uganda/Rwanda	Alliance of Democratic Forces for the Liberation of Congo (AFDL)	1997	Meddling
Uganda/Rwanda	Rassemblement Congolais pour la Democratie (RCD)	1998	Meddling
Liberia	Revolutionary United Front (RUF)	1998	Feed the Chaos
United States	Northern Alliance	2001	In It to Win It
United States/ NATO	Anti-Qaddafi Forces	2011	Meddling
Saudi Arabia	Pro-Hadi Forces	2012	Holding Action
Iran	Houthis	2013	Feed the Chaos
United States	Free Syrian Army	2014	Feed the Chaos

Note. Ambiguous cases of proxy war that do not have open-source confirmation have been omitted from this list (e.g., Soviet support of FMLN in El Salvador and American support of the KLA in Kosovo).

context. Looking at proxy war through these different lenses helps with the analysis and understanding of how and why an intervening state would choose it as a policy option.

Since the end of World War II, all types of proxy wars have been used. The states that have chosen proxy war vary in their degree of global influence and relative capability. The motives for choosing proxy war have also varied. Table 2.1 lists the nonstate proxy wars and their accompanying type as described in this chapter.

CHAPTER 3

THE EVOLUTION OF PROXY WAR SINCE 1945

ANY INTERVENTION presents risk. Regardless of time or technology, fueling existing violence as a means to intervene in the affairs of another state adds concerns about fog and friction. War has a way of confounding policy because it is so difficult to account for the myriad variables that influence its outcome. In addition, interventions have known second-order effects. A state may get drawn into the conflict deeper than it intended, even leading to a direct intervention. If the conflict breaks bad, domestic and/or political costs could skyrocket. A rival state may enter the fray and raise the costs or spoil the opportunity to achieve the desired objectives. For good or ill, these factors influence the outcome and duration of an intrastate conflict.[1]

In this chapter, I aim to shed some light on how the changing times have influenced the use of proxy war. I argue that the general reason states use proxies has not changed, but the structure of the world order and the underlying factors that accompany different types of order do influence a state's use of proxy war. More specifically, I develop a model that describes, and potentially predicts, the conditions under which a state will resort to proxy war.

Has proxy war changed? Richard Haass predicted at the end of the twentieth century that "the post–Cold War world promises to be a messy one where violence is common, where conflicts within and between nation-states abound, and where the question of US military intervention becomes more rather than less commonplace and more rather than less complicated."[2] Haass's prediction initially appears incorrect. Following the end of the Cold War, the number of armed conflicts and civil wars fell sharply, as did the duration of the civil wars that started afterward.[3] In the past few years, however, the number of armed conflicts has once again begun to increase.[4] Something has changed. Two potential explanations relate to alterations in the global order—often called "polarity" in the international relations literature—and variations in how states with regional or limited global influence intervene in the affairs of other states.[5] All states perceive limitations or barriers that restrain or constrain their foreign policy and the use of force. When concerns abroad warrant some effort to shape international outcomes, but those concerns fall below a threshold that would allow a direct military intervention (meaning the use of a state's own forces in another country), states (both past and present) have resorted to the use of a proxy to overcome the barriers that would otherwise hinder the pursuit of their objectives. The perception of barriers to intervention has arguably fluctuated over the past several decades. Accordingly, proxy wars have ebbed and flowed as well. How and why have states changed the practice of using proxies to influence the outcomes of intrastate conflicts?

Barriers continue to influence a state's decision to intervene in the affairs of another state, but the nature and interpretation of those barriers change as the structure of the world order changes. The need for proxy intervention remains, but the conditions under which such a tool of foreign policy operates have apparently changed. I am not arguing that the international order is *causal* in any of the changes, but looking at the changes from a systemic perspective offers some interesting insights. Based on these three insights, I ask three questions: (1) How does the order of the international system (bipolar, unipolar, quasi-unipolar) influence the use of proxy war? (2) How does a state's position in that order influence its use of proxy war? (3) How does a state's perception of the barriers to intervention under different conditions of international order and capability affect the choice to engage in proxy war?

WHEN IT COMES TO PROXY WAR, WHAT DRIVES CHOICE?

From a theoretical perspective, what drives a state's desire to intervene directly, indirectly, or not at all? In all three cases, the fundamental motivation stems from the perception that the state both needs to, and can, influence or control events in another state. Direct intervention requires the perception of significant need. The absence of that perception should result in nonintervention. Indirect intervention, however, indicates additional considerations that suggest the perceived need to intervene and the existence of conditions that limit the potential options of intervention. In some cases, states simply don't see an advantage in directly intervening based on the existing conditions—the benefit of intervening directly won't exceed the price. In other cases, states want (or some would say "appear to want") to abide by international norms that describe when intervention is allowed.[6] Proxy war has the potential to tip the balance of cost and benefit or to uphold appearances of adhering to international norms. Therefore, proxy war becomes a product of the motivation driving a state toward intervention and the perceived barriers to proscribe those options.

Using levels of analysis, I classify the drivers into three categories: individual, state, and system. I consider how each level of analysis influences the real and perceived barriers to intervention and how states perceive the utility of indirect intervention as opposed to direct intervention or nonintervention. Lastly, I include the presence of nuclear weapons as an additional consideration to a state's decision to intervene, given the subject and period of study.

Individual-Level Drivers

History provides numerous examples of powerful individuals influencing a state's policy. Napoleon, Hitler, and Mao all represent stark images of an individual driving a country's domestic and international relations. One of realism's core assumptions is that humans are flawed and that conflict stems from the human desire for power.[7] Increasing one's power may come from conquering other countries, as Napoleon and Hitler did, or it could be from seizing power inside the state, as Mao did. Regardless of regime type, individuals in a position to directly influence a state's foreign policy still have to answer to a domestic audience. People in power want to keep their seats.[8] Putting power aside, sometimes leaders have access to information that cannot be released publicly, especially if it compromises a state's sources and methods of intelligence operations. If leaders want to continue to rule or govern a state, they have to consider how the pursuit and justification of foreign policy will affect future prospects.

Barriers to intervention exist for both autocratic and democratic states. Under such conditions, acting through third parties can provide options to overcome some or all of those barriers. If an executive's ability to act remains relatively unrestrained, proxy war comes to the fore when it offers an added capability to conduct foreign military interventions. If an executive perceives constraints, either domestically or internationally, then a proxy may allow policy makers and decision makers alike to escape criticism.

The issue, however, is that individual choice is often difficult to separate from domestic politics. As Kenneth Waltz argues in *Man, the State, and War*, it is difficult (if not impossible) to separate actions taken at the individual level from those driven by state-level forces.[9] Was Indira Gandhi's decision to support Tamil militants driven by her desire to remain in power in India or was it necessitated by constituents living in the state of Tamil Nadu? Does it matter if state-level forces pushed her into a corner? I do not argue that the individual level is irrelevant. I simply argue that it is difficult to separate the causal factors that drive foreign policy. Therefore, I argue that it is more expedient to subsume the individual level of analysis into the state level when considering what drives the decision to engage in proxy war.

State-Level Drivers

States, regardless of regime type, are rarely free to make decisions regarding foreign policy, let alone when it comes to the use of force.[10] From a domestic politics perspective, the threshold for intervention stems from the government's ability to convince the relevant audiences at home that an intervention is necessary. Fundamentally, many of the same drivers operating at the international level also apply domestically—states will make the case that the intervention is needed to shore up their security. If a state predicts that intervention in any form will not garner the support necessary to avoid domestic (or international) penalties, it may attempt to circumvent restrictions through the use of covert action, but such choices are difficult to keep hidden from view and often come with significant blowback.[11] Further, covert action places additional burdens on the state, such as requiring support to go through third parties or taking additional risks with its own personnel.[12] Under such conditions, a proxy provides a means to lower the risk to the intervening state by reducing the need for its own personnel, but it compromises its ability to control the proxy with fewer observers or without being able to control the distribution of incentives.[13]

Governments can further justify an intervention policy based on the idea that costs and risks of the intervention will be shared with another actor (the proxy). Under some circumstances, a proxy allows the case to be made that an intervention is a moral obligation to protect the rights of people in the target country or to protect those people from an undesirable form of government. Lastly, vast increases in the availability of information, even in information-suppressed states, make it possible for domestic audiences to see responses from other states, both friends and rivals, and make judgments about the efficacy of an indirect intervention. Based on these considerations, all four barriers relate to domestic politics: the risk of escalation increases if a state directly intervenes, a lack of domestic support may risk the sustainability of the intervention, a lack of international support negatively affects the cost/benefit ratio of the intervention, and a lack of capacity makes direct intervention untenable.

System-Level Drivers
On one hand, the global order represents an impossibly complex and unwieldy variable. On the other hand, it significantly simplifies analysis, especially at the macro level. In the study of interventions and proxy war, I use the global order as a means of describing (and crudely measuring) international competition. I acknowledge that diminishing returns occurs quickly for less powerful states; the global order does a poor job of explaining intervention decisions for states with no capacity to rationally

intervene in other states. States with regional or global reach, however, logically consider global order (and their standing in it) when intervening militarily abroad.

The Cold War brought a bipolar world order with the United States and the Soviet Union representing the two poles, pulling equally against each other until the Soviet Union's demise in the early 1990s. In the aftermath, the United States stood alone as the world's lone superpower and brought forth a unipolar order—a single pole, unbalanced. Immersed in two conflicts, Afghanistan and Iraq, the unipolar order began to fray at the margins in the mid-2000s and drifted into what I describe as a quasi-unipolar order. The United States remains unmatched in any category of state influence, but the order has begun to wobble as increasingly influential regional powers push outward.

As it stands today, the international system remains quasi-unipolar. Under this system, proxy war will continue its current trend of occurring less than during the Cold War but more than when the system operated under a clear hegemon. Based on this research, I argue that the use of proxy war will increase as the world drifts further toward multipolarity. The reason is that complex interdependence and globalization—two phenomena with the perceived potential to improve a state's ability to compete in the international system—will make it necessary for global powers to compete on the margins without directly and overtly challenging one another (similar to the Cold War). The expanding influence of regional powers will create overlaps of interest with the United States and other regional powers. Proxy war will give global powers an excuse to pursue interests when attempting to influence events in another state's perceived sphere of influence. Proxy wars will also give regional or global powers an excuse to look away when their interests are not specifically challenged. In both cases, proxies will provide the means to manage unwanted escalation, including the continued avoidance of nuclear conflict where applicable. Lastly, proxy war will allow global powers the ability to circumvent institutional penalties and maintain the appearance of upholding institutional commitments.

I propose that when and how a state chooses proxy intervention stems from an interaction between a state's relative capabilities, the alignment and distribution of power in the international system, a state's perception of the importance of an intrastate conflict, and the barriers to direct intervention. More plainly, a state's decision is influenced by what the state perceives it can do to influence the affairs of another state and the barriers imposed on it by the international system and/or its own domestic audience. These factors influence a state's threshold for direct intervention, indirect intervention, and nonintervention.

INTERSTATE COMPETITION   States may respond to the international environment and often make choices, especially regarding the use of force, due to its relative capability vis-à-vis other states, the scarcity of resources available, and the desire for security.[14] In some cases, states act out of self-interest and seek to achieve gains in whatever way provides the greatest benefit.[15] States may view the choice to intervene as an opportunity and look for any means available to provide the greatest gain for the lowest cost.[16] A proxy may potentially serve these interests because it perceivably provides additional resources believed to extend an intervening state's capability to influence or control an outcome. A proxy may also be seen as a means to lower the amount of risk incurred from intervention, thus lowering the cost and increasing the benefit.

In addition to the pursuit of additional gains in terms of resources and security, states may logically perceive the need to intervene based on the actions of other states. Because states do not always, or often, explain their intentions when it comes to foreign policy and national security, other states must fill in the gaps. Such speculation leads to a security dilemma and understandably creates tension between states. Under such circumstances, states may intervene as a countermove to actions perceived as being aggressive or threatening.[17] In this situation, a proxy provides a state with the opportunity to conserve its own resources, should they be needed later, and thereby extends the state's ability to pursue its interests.

Despite the negative aspects of international competition that can lead to armed conflict, states still cooperate. Over time, international institutions have increased in number and scope, causing states to increasingly seek to protect their reputations and improve their influence. Because of these developments, reputation has become an important means of a state's influence.[18] Further, as globalization knits a more interdependent world, direct intervention potentially works against a state's ability to influence other international actors and thrive in the international system.[19] Under these conditions, a proxy offers a state the means to intervene in the affairs of another state with the hope of protecting its reputation, avoiding institutional penalties, and keeping the costs of entering into cooperative agreements with other states manageable. Put more simply, a proxy offers the possibility of circumventing institutional constraints. In cases where the character of the proxy raises eyebrows from institutional partners because of their brutality or politics, a state may seek to engage covertly in a proxy war.

Although rationalist and realist explanations for why states might resort to proxy war appear logical in many instances, states have also engaged in proxy war to protect others from the persecution of abusive governments or to provide people with a better form of government.[20] Under such circumstances, a state may hope for some form of gain such as a new ally or trading partner, but the primary motive may be to just help humanity.[21] A proxy war selected for this reason would be used to avoid all of the proposed barriers: the risk of escalation increases if a state directly intervenes, a lack of domestic support may risk the sustainability of the intervention, a lack of international support negatively affects the cost/benefit ratio of the intervention, and a lack of capacity makes direct intervention untenable.

When it comes to interstate competition and the use of force, nuclear weapons should add a sobering dose of sensibility.[22] The existential threat of destroying the world as we know it adds the ultimate counterbalance to any perceived gains attained through intervention. Under such conditions, any state that perceives the possibility of nuclear escalation will look for options to indirectly intervene or skip intervention altogether. So long as a state's perception of the stakes or its commitment to the outcome of an intrastate conflict remains below what it might accept in terms of risk when considering direct intervention, something less than direct intervention should occur.

THE CONCEPTUAL INFLUENCE OF THE WORLD ORDER   The pecking order in the international system significantly influences competition and a state's perception of the options available to influence events outside its own borders. Changes in the global order influence how states perceive the threshold for intervention. The combination of global order and a state's position within it—based largely on its relative capability, its identity, and the perceived relationship with other actors—affects a state's decision to intervene directly in the affairs of another state, to intervene indirectly, or to forgo intervention entirely.[23] Different polarities, meaning different orderings of the international system, should influence a state's decision to intervene.

The alignment of power in the international system already has well-established categories, with the three most common being multipolar, bipolar, and unipolar. In each case, the poles are defined by their significant advantage in terms of relative capability that allows them to influence global affairs. The Concert of Europe is often considered the benchmark example of a multipolar system. A bipolar structure created the conditions that led to the Cold War era forcing two superpowers—the United States and the Soviet Union—to engage in a global, ideological competition.[24] With the fall of the Soviet Union, unipolarity emerged as the United States remained the only state in the system with global reach and influence.

Tracing changes in the global order provides a convenient and effective starting point to understand the changes in the use of proxy war as a means to pursue interests without having to directly intervene. Proxy war has been around for a long time, and the reasons for using proxies to indirectly intervene in another state have not fundamentally changed. For example, prior to World War I, under a multipolar order, proxy wars were used by great powers to avoid direct confrontation that might lead to a large-scale war.[25] The Concert of Europe helped ensure that alliances shifted to maintain the balance of power, pushing great power conflict to play out in small countries and distant regions. Russia did not want to challenge Great Britain directly in South Asia but instead engaged the British in the Great Game fought in the Northwest Frontier.[26] During the interwar period, European states were exhausted and the United States moved toward isolationism. Two regional powers, Germany and Russia, engaged in a proxy war in Spain to test one another, rather than engaging in a conflict neither state could manage overtly because each lacked the resources and wanted to avoid drawing in other states.[27]

Bipolar   Bipolarity should see the two poles doing the majority of the interventions with only minimal interventions by peripheral states. The two poles have the resources, interests, and reach to meet any challenge by an opponent. Further, the two poles will look for opportunities to gain an advantage on their primary adversary. States on the periphery will have been forced to choose between the two poles and will defer to the chosen superpower when it comes to intervention because any action taken may cause a response by the opposing superpower. In addition, independent intervention decisions may incur retribution from the aligned superpower.[28]

Under a bipolar order, proxy war serves as a way to manage escalation between the superpowers. The intense competition of a bipolar order also suggests that domestic factors should play a smaller role in intervention decisions. Intrastate conflicts would only be opportunities to make small gains on the margins that would not threaten the balance of power. As long as the competition at the fringe of each pole's sphere of influence did not become an overtly obvious sign of commitment or interest, competition could remain limited.[29] Neither superpower should commit to a direct intervention, and they should rarely commit to a proxy war to win because of the risk of escalation and the perception that its influence was waning—something that might overtly signal commitment or interest. Holding action, feeding the chaos, or meddling should be the primary focus of proxy wars in a bipolar structure. As an added measure of protection, interventions that suggest high levels of interest, regardless of how they are pursued, would be pursued covertly.

Unipolar   Unipolarity should result in a single pole, the hegemon, doing most of the interventions. States that see the unipolar system as a benefit to their own security will ally themselves to the hegemon and should not undertake actions that might undermine that system.[30] Other states operating in ways that challenge the hegemon's established order or in areas that fall within the hegemon's interest should reduce direct interventions, less they incur a check on their action.[31] From a systemic perspective, the hegemon should feel less constrained and its threshold for direct intervention should increase. A hegemon's concerns about the stakes should revolve around the need to sustain the unipolar order, and its commitment to the outcome in intrastate conflicts should focus on maintaining stability and ensuring that other states observe its power and willingness to use it.

Under a unipolar system, restrictions on a hegemon's ability to sustain the system it has created are few. A hegemon's prestige is the coin of the realm, and a hegemon's ability to entice rather than coerce other states to accept its position and the system it offers lowers costs and increases benefits.[32] A hegemon should engage in a proxy war only when interventions may harm the unity among regionally powerful states and the concordant international institutions that have adopted and uphold the hegemon's system.

Under such conditions, a hegemon's use of proxy wars intended to meddle should predominate. States beneath the hegemon with the ability to intervene outside their own borders, however, have more restrictions. Escalation considerations from the hegemon or regional competitors could drive the need for proxy war. In addition, states may also seek indirect, proxy interventions to avoid reprisals from international institutions to which they belong. States will want to maximize their capabilities; therefore, proxy wars may provide an opportunity to avoid institutionally driven penalties. Under such conditions, regional powers should engage in all four types of proxy wars to gain or maintain a competitive edge within their specific region of influence.

Quasi-Unipolar   A quasi-unipolar order represents a point when only one state in the international system possesses the relative capability to operate on a global level, yet its regional influence in areas with strong states gets increasingly tested. As the single global power makes more and more concessions to regional powers, the unipolar system drifts into unknown territory. Revisionist states that desire to challenge the weakening hegemon become regional powers with increasing reach.

Many of the same logics operating in a unipolar system should continue to broadly influence state behavior under a quasi-unipolar system.

The hegemon retains the ability to intervene globally and continues to use its influence to uphold the system that provides its power and advantage. The difference, however, is that the hegemon's influence has shrunk while other states have made significant gains. The hegemon no longer possesses the overwhelming distribution of power in the international system, causing the hegemon to go to greater lengths to avoid actions that look overly aggressive or tyrannical that might lead bandwagoning states to balance against it.[33]

The waning of the hegemon's relative capability in comparison to other would-be challengers of the unipolar order should create incentives to avoid direct intervention in areas that do not clearly suggest a direct threat to the hegemon's security. Proxy war, under this condition, could offer the hegemon an opportunity to influence, or even control, events in areas of interest without appearing overly oppressive. Under these circumstances, proxy wars intended to prevent gains by regional actors (holding actions) and meddling should occur. A hegemon should not logically engage in proxy wars intended to feed the chaos because it could undermine the legitimacy of the current international system. Intrastate conflicts that have moderate stakes and in which the hegemon feels some sense of commitment to the outcome should result in direct intervention.

Regional powers sense a greater flexibility to intervene and expand their spheres of influence. Other states seeking to disrupt or unmake the hegemon's system (known as revisionist states in the international relations literature) will seek opportunities to expand their relative capability and improve their lot in the international system.[34] If a regional power possesses nuclear weapons, the state may perceive an added incentive to be more adventurous and bet on the hope that the hegemon will not want to risk an inadvertent nuclear incident for something that is not clearly a risk to its national security.[35] Given these opportunities, regional powers should be likely to engage in proxy wars intended to provide gains (in it to win it), or further dismantle the unipolar order (meddling and feeding the chaos).

States with even less relative capability might be more willing to risk interventions, especially proxy interventions, that the hegemon will see as stretching its commitments needlessly in an increasingly competitive

TABLE 3.1 *Relevance of Barriers to Intervention that Might Lead to Proxy War*

World Order (Polarity)	Relative Capability	Risk of Escalation	Domestic Support	International Support	Lack of Capacity
Bipolar	Superpower	High*	Low	Low	Low
	Regional Power	High	Low	High	High
Unipolar	Global Hegemon	Low	Moderate	Moderate	Low
	Regional Power	Low	Low	Low	High
Quasi-unipolar	Global Hegemon	High*	High	High	Low
	Regional Power	High*	High	High	Low
	Other States	High	Low	Low	High

*Indicates nuclear weapons highly influence concerns about the risk of escalation.

international system. Based on that logic, lesser powers should engage in proxy wars to make small gains (in it to win it) or reduce the capability of local competitors (meddling and feeding the chaos). In both cases, holding actions will likely prove too expensive and be perceived as a direct challenge to the hegemonic system.

CASE STUDIES

In this section, I apply the concepts presented in the first part of the chapter to selected cases that represent different aspects of the arguments presented. Table 3.1 contains a breakdown of the different ideas under investigation. Different periods, relative capabilities, and the effects of different barriers will all be applied to see if states choose proxy war based on the logic presented. For each type of global order and the cases selected from those periods, I consider the following questions:

1. How did/does the order of the international system—bipolar, unipolar, quasi-unipolar—influence the use of proxy war (column 1)?

2. How did/does a state's position in that order influence its use of proxy war (column 2)?

3. How did/does a state's perception of the proposed barriers to intervention under different conditions of international order and capability affect the choice to engage in proxy war (columns 3–6)?

For question 3, I focus on the proposed barriers to proxy war: risk of escalation, lack of domestic support, lack of international support, and lack of capacity. The cases selected for each period reflect one specific type of proxy war. The unipolar order presents one exception, because none of the proxy wars I have found fit the types for "in it to win it" or a holding action.

I do have two limitations in the cases used in this chapter. Because a holding action occurs infrequently, I use two abbreviated versions of the cases presented in Chapters 6 and 7 (U.S. intervention in Laos and South African intervention in Angola).

The Cold War and Bipolarity's Influence on the Use of Proxy War
During the Cold War, the number of states engaged in civil wars increased dramatically compared to the period preceding World War II. Intrastate conflicts most often ended with one side declaring victory and tended to last longer. Negotiated settlements were rare. The presence of external support made it easier for antagonists to keep fighting, likely causing the two sides to cling to the belief of total victory rather than settling for some power-sharing agreement.[36] In light of such intense competition and with such high barriers to direct intervention, the superpowers (the United States and the Union of Soviet Socialist Republics [USSR]) engaged widely in proxy war to compete at the margins—Africa, Latin America, and Southeast Asia—to avoid direct confrontation and the possibility of unwanted escalation that could lead to nuclear war.

In this section, I apply my proposed model described earlier and the theoretical and empirical considerations connected to the Cold War. I present cases that represent all four typologies: the United States in Nicaragua (in it to win it), South Africa in Angola (holding action), India in Sri Lanka (meddling), and Pakistan in Afghanistan (feeding the chaos). US support of the Contras in Nicaragua in the 1980s challenges the idea that a superpower should commit to win an intervention when the stakes remain relatively low in terms of how the intrastate conflict threatens its national security and how domestic restraints can significantly impact an interventionist policy. South Africa's support of UNITA resembles a regional power operating on the periphery and explores how a state with limited reach (compared to the superpowers) used a proxy war to mitigate the potential threat of a superpower encroaching on its border. India's intervention in Sri Lanka in the 1980s provides another case of a nonsuperpower engaging in proxy war, this time based on a combination of concerns about the potential of superpower states aligning with the Sinhalese government, the desire to prevent an independent Tamil state from emerging, and the need to mollify the interests of the influential Tamil ethnic group needed to sustain a domestic, political coalition. Lastly, Pakistan's intervention in Afghanistan did not seek a specific political solution. Instead, Islamabad wanted to keep Afghan militias relatively equal to prevent the emergence of a single faction capable of unifying and leading the diverse groups of anti-Soviet forces, yet still capable of keeping Soviet forces bogged down on the west side of Afghan-Pakistan border.

Unlike the period before World War I and the interwar period, the international system during the Cold War reflected a bipolar order. The character of a bipolar international system derives first from the presence of only two powerful rivals—superpowers—whose relative capability would remain largely unaffected by alliances with lesser powers.[37] According to the theories presented, a bipolar order creates an intense desire to remain relatively equal in capability, forcing each side to stay sharp and vigilant. Kenneth Waltz argued in 1964 that these three factors would continue to feed the stability of the bipolar system and prevent the Cold War from ever turning hot.[38] The two superpowers should have competed in every facet of the global arena—if one gained an advantage, the other would commit the required resources and efforts to catch up. Any intervention in Africa or Latin America by the United States should have caused a counterintervention by the Soviet Union—the reverse also being true. Soviet direct support to Cuba and America's support of proxies in Angola both support the proposed theory.

Although some instances followed this logic, on some occasions the superpowers did not behave accordingly. In both Rhodesia and South West Africa (Namibia), the Soviet Union supported a proxy to sway the outcome of those intrastate conflicts, but the United States steered clear. The chief adversaries in both cases were the white-dominated, repressive governments in those countries and the Republic of South Africa. In Latin America, the Soviet Union passed on backing a proxy to counter U.S. efforts to remove socialist, anti-American regimes in Guatemala and Nicaragua. In Southeast Asia, the Soviet Union also passed on supporting the communist Pathet Lao in Laos, despite U.S. support for Hmong forces and, to a lesser extent, the Laotian government in Vientiane. On the U.S. side, the lack of support for two repressive regimes suggests that domestic barriers to intervention may have played a role. Adding to this idea, the United States engaged in a covert proxy war to influence events in Angola in hopes of stalling Moscow's efforts to expand its influence in southern Africa.[39]

During the Cold War, most other states in the international system picked a side. An ally of one of the superpowers intervening in another state was often seen as an attempt to gain an advantage for that side against the other. The perceptions of East versus West, or the North Atlantic Treaty Organization (NATO) versus the Warsaw Pact were just manifestations of the competition between the United States and the Soviet Union. There were, however, some exceptions. The United Kingdom intervened directly against Argentina in the Falkland Islands without an armed response from the Soviet Union. The United States, however, made it clear that it would sit on the sidelines for the most part.[40] Both Syria and Israel engaged in proxy interventions in neighboring Lebanon during the mid-1970s, without causing a counterintervention from either of the superpowers.[41] Somalia (a state aligned with the Soviet Union) used a proxy to attempt to capture the Ogaden region from Ethiopia (a state also aligned with the Soviet Union). When Somalia's efforts stalled, it severed its relations with the Soviet Union and asked the United States to intervene on its behalf. America rebuffed this request, and Moscow shortly thereafter threw significant support behind Ethiopia. Soundly defeated, Somalia not only failed to gain the Ogaden but also lost its military superiority in the Horn of Africa.[42]

Lastly, there were a few instances where a nonsuperpower with significant regional influence engaged in proxy war. Per the theory, regional powers should have engaged in indirect interventions only in areas that were outside a superpower's sphere of influence because even indirect intervention would have sparked an unwinnable competition with a superpower. Pakistan's support of the mujahideen in Afghanistan created a serious impediment to the Soviet Union's intervention in Afghanistan. South Africa's support of proxies in Rhodesia, Angola, and South West Africa (Namibia) in the 1980s and 1990s challenged Moscow's influence in Southern Africa. India engaged in two different proxy wars— supporting Mukti Bahini in East Pakistan in 1970 and the Tamil Tigers in Sri Lanka in the 1980s—with the intent to intervene in its neighbors' affairs without incurring a superpower response; in both cases India managed to avoid sparking a counterintervention.[43] Why did the United States and the Soviet Union both sit on the sidelines?

From this systemic look at proxy war, it appears that there is a link between geography, the perception of stakes involved in an intrastate conflict, a state's commitment to the outcome of an intrastate conflict, and the barriers that determine the spectrum of intervention options. Africa and South Asia fell mostly within the Soviet sphere of influence, while Latin America and Southeast Asia fell within America's. The word *mostly* is important here. Except for Angola, it appears that superpower efforts, when constrained by indirect intervention, succeeded in staving off a counterintervention by the other superpower. The fact that regional powers managed to sustain proxy interventions against a superpower suggests that the use of proxy war effectively avoided unwanted escalation.

In the remainder of this section, I present four cases (one for each type of proxy war) that provide anomalies to the presented logic. A communist beachhead in Latin America would have been a landmark accomplishment for the Soviet Union, but Moscow failed to counter the proxy intervention by the United States. Further, America was committed to deciding the outcome in Nicaragua, but its efforts seemed more constrained by its domestic politics than by the possibility of a clash with the Soviet Union. South Africa used proxy war as a holding action in the border region between Angola and South West Africa (Namibia) without being subjected to an untenable counterintervention by the Soviet Union. India meddled in Sri Lanka's affairs without backlash from either superpower. Pakistan challenged a direct Soviet intervention, feeding the chaos in Afghanistan to ensure that Moscow could not achieve victory, without an overwhelming Soviet response.

IN IT TO WIN IT: U.S. INTERVENTION IN NICARAGUA   As the competition between the Soviet Union and the United States intensified in the early 1980s, the presence of a socialist regime in the Western Hemisphere open to Soviet influence was an anathema to the Reagan administration. The American public, however, continued to resist a policy resembling a limited intervention in the Third World based on the shadows of the Vietnam War.[44] When the Sandinista government first came to power in 1979, the United States immediately recognized the new regime and offered aid to the troubled country. Although the new Nicaraguan regime openly stated that it desired good relations with the United States, the Sandinista government mostly rejected U.S. overtures and instead moved closer to Cuba and the Soviet Union.

In 1981, the Reagan administration directed the Central Intelligence Agency (CIA) to begin covert paramilitary operations to interdict arms transfers from Cuba and Nicaragua to insurgencies in Central America. In 1982, Congress enacted the Boland I Amendment to prohibit the use of public funds aimed at bringing down the Sandinista government. In the same year, Walter Raymond Jr., a veteran CIA officer experienced in covert operations, was moved to the National Security Council to resume pressuring Nicaragua's government to stop working against U.S. interests.[45]

Between 1982 and 1986, Soviet military assistance increased significantly, fueling the Reagan administration's concerns about the dangers of the Sandinista government. The Soviet Union repeatedly claimed that the United States was trying to unseat Nicaragua's elected government, but Moscow also appeared to believe that the Sandinista government would prevail in the conflict.[46] Congress, however, did not seem to share President Ronald Reagan's view of the stakes involved and continued to impede the administration's efforts. After the CIA's mining of Nicaraguan harbors became public in 1984 (an effort designed to overcome the Contras' ineffectiveness), Congress enacted the Boland II Amendment, which specifically denied funding in fiscal year 1985 to "the Central Intelligence Agency, the Department of Defense, or any other agency or entity of the United States involved in intelligence activities that may be obligated or expended for the purpose or which would have the effect of supporting directly or indirectly, military or paramilitary operations in Nicaragua by any nation, group, organization, movement or individual." This language left the door open for the National Security Council to remain involved with the Contras.[47]

In response to Congress's decision, members of the National Security Council created a covert program to resume funding the Contras.[48] The funding, however, proved inadequate. In 1986, President Reagan persuaded Congress to reinstate significant military support for the Contras totaling $70 million.[49] Shortly thereafter, Congress found out that the United States had been selling arms to Iran to fund the Contras. Although Congress had already approved $100 million in aid, it firmly stated that it would provide only humanitarian aid in the future. The nature of the operation apparently protected the White House from long-lasting domestic disappointment. After eight months of news coverage on the Iran-Contra affair, only 54 percent of the people in the United States knew that the United States supported rebels trying to overthrow the government in Nicaragua.[50] President Reagan's approval rating dropped from 63 percent to 47 percent after news of the Iran-Contra affair had been made public; it remained relatively low throughout the next two years but rebounded back to 63 percent at the end of his presidency.[51]

In 1986, the International Court of Justice (ICJ) found that the United States, having mined Nicaragua's harbors and promoted civil dissent, had violated international law. Despite the ICJ's ruling, the United States ignored the ICJ's order to pay reparations and continued supporting the Contras.[52] Operations reached their peak in 1987 as ten to twelve thousand Contra insurgents conducted attacks against the Sandinista government. In early 1988, the Contras and Sandinistas agreed to a cease-fire and began negotiations. By the end of 1988, operations promptly ceased and the Contras fled to neighboring countries. In 1989, the Sandinistas honored their agreement to allow the Contras to return to Nicaragua and to hold open elections. In 1990, the Sandinistas lost the presidential election, and after the new president took office the Contras demobilized. In 1991, Nicaragua informed the ICJ that it no longer wanted to pursue the case against the United States, relieving Washington from any obligation to pay Nicaragua reparations.[53]

HOLDING ACTION: SOUTH AFRICAN INTERVENTION IN ANGOLA   There are only two cases of a holding action in the Cold War era, both of which are detailed case studies in this book (Angola and Laos). A detailed description of this case can be found in Chapter 4. I do, however, include a discussion in the summary of this chapter of how the South Africa/ UNITA case informs the ideas and concepts presented earlier and in the previous chapter.

MEDDLING: INDIAN INTERVENTION IN SRI LANKA   India's intervention in Sri Lanka is interesting due to New Delhi's leading role in the non-aligned movement. It demonstrates how proxy war served more than just the superpowers during the Cold War. A more detailed description of this case can be found in Chapter 5. I include discussion in the summary of this chapter of how the India/LTTE case informs the ideas and concepts presented above and in the previous chapter.

FEEDING THE CHAOS: PAKISTANI INTERVENTION IN AFGHANISTAN   The Soviet invasion of Afghanistan presented two serious threats to Pakistan. First, the rapidly increasing number of refugees threatened to overwhelm Islamabad's domestic security. Second, Pakistan's buffer from communist pressure had been removed. To avoid unnecessarily provoking Moscow and to keep its domestic situation under control, Islamabad sought to disguise its involvement. In addition, Pakistan wanted to create the ability to strongly influence Afghanistan's domestic politics to ensure that it did not jeopardize Pakistan's security.[54]

Pakistan's geographical position made it the logical distribution hub for the substantial amount of aid flowing in from the United States and Saudi Arabia. Islamabad used its position to control the mujahideen groups, giving greater support to those more in line with Pakistan's strategic objectives. Pakistan also allowed the mujahideen, either tacitly or deliberately, to engage in illicit operations such as gun running and drug trafficking to further finance their operations.[55] Allowing these illicit activities, however, later caused problems for Islamabad as the mujahideen groups became more self-reliant and more resistant to government control in Pakistan's Tribal Areas.[56]

Pakistan made extensive use of Inter-Services Intelligence (ISI), its intelligence service. ISI personnel operated mujahideen training camps, distributed U.S. intelligence, and directly participated in mujahideen operations. Most importantly, the ISI managed to foster cooperation and discord between mujahideen factions in a way that maximized Pakistan's benefit. Pakistan's objective was not only to harass Soviet operations in Afghanistan but also to keep mujahideen groups sufficiently weak to prevent the emergence of a dominant faction that could challenge Pakistan's control. The tenacious and adaptable mujahideen fighters proved highly capable, but most importantly, they were fiercely independent and prone to factionalism. These qualities enabled Pakistan to manipulate the mujahideen. By 1982, the ISI had managed to reduce the number of mujahideen groups from over forty to just seven. This allowed Pakistan to keep closer tabs on mujahideen operations and to monitor the relative strength of each group.

When the Soviets withdrew in 1989, Pakistan fueled the civil war that ensued. In the short term, Pakistan's efforts paid great dividends and allowed Islamabad to continue to influence Afghanistan's domestic politics. The policy, however, also fostered greater unrest and resistance in the Tribal Areas.

Bipolar/Cold War Summary
During the Cold War, all four types of proxy war occurred (see Figure 3.1). The U.S. government, under the Reagan administration, resorted to a proxy (Contras) to usurp a leftist government in Managua. The threshold for direct intervention had not been crossed, considering that the Sandinista regime was elected into office and both Congress and the American public still wanted to avoid another quagmire in the Third World. Undoubtedly, President Reagan and his national security team felt that a Soviet satellite in Central America jeopardized America's security. Domestic limits to influence the outcome of the intrastate conflict

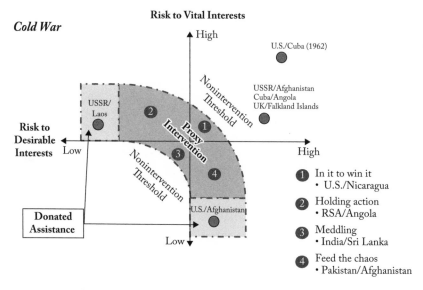

FIGURE 3.1 *Cold War Intervention Axis*

in Nicaragua challenged Washington's efforts, but the presence of the Contras as a proxy combined with covert support enabled the indirect intervention. Further, the fact that the Contras struggled militarily resulted in an escalation of U.S. efforts, to include the mining of Managua's harbor—a point that demonstrates the Reagan administration's commitment to the conflict. What is interesting, however, is that Moscow remained on the sidelines. Even Cuba, which was willing to engage in an intrastate conflict in Angola, elected to essentially sit out the civil war in Nicaragua. This suggests that the world order had exceptions on the rules of the road when it came to intervention and that the United States had the right to intervene in Latin America without a counterintervention or a threat of escalation from the Soviet Union.

South Africa's support for UNITA upends the notion that a regional power would not challenge a superpower, even in an indirect intervention. The Soviet Union did respond, as did Cuba, but neither state was able to amass sufficient military capability to break South Africa's proxy. In this situation, a regional power achieved a stalemate against a counterintervention from a superpower. This suggests that holding actions provided an effective type of proxy intervention. It also suggests that South Africa's proxy and the management of that proxy may have been superior to Moscow's. Pretoria managed to control its proxy and did not let its objectives go beyond keeping communism from reaching into Southwest Africa. Equally important, South Africa did not let UNITA drag it into a deeper commitment in Angola; Pretoria cut its ties when its proxy no longer served its interests.

In Sri Lanka, meddling was an effective means of intervention to avoid attracting unwanted attention from either superpower. The need for Tamil support domestically, however, hurt India's ability to avoid deeper commitment. Adding to this, India's desire to serve as a regional power led to a direct intervention that further entrenched New Delhi in the Sri Lankan crisis and ultimately ended in an unwanted, direct intervention.

Pakistan challenged a direct Soviet intervention without suffering overwhelming conventional escalation. Using a "feeding the chaos" method of indirect intervention in Afghanistan ensured that Moscow could not achieve victory and maintained Islamabad's desire to have an unstable government in Afghanistan. This raises questions about why the Soviet Union intervened directly in Afghanistan and why it avoided shutting down Pakistan's support of the mujahideen. The United States did participate through donated assistance, sending the signal that it would risk competing with Moscow in South Asia. Events suggest that the Soviet Union lacked the capacity to bring Afghanistan under control—an outcome that history all but confirms.

Post–Cold War and Unipolarity's Influence on the Use of Proxy War
When the global order transitioned to a unipolar order, external support for intrastate conflicts decreased sharply. "Immediately after 1991, the number of civil war onsets declined, whereas terminations went up. These two trends converged to produce a decline in the number of ongoing civil wars in the post–Cold War period."[57] Further, civil conflicts during the unipolar era ended in victory far less often—from 58 percent during the Cold War to 13 percent between 1989 and 2009. Negotiated settlements also jumped by 30 percent (from 10 percent to 40 percent) after the Cold

War. Lastly, "more conflicts ended in the 15 years after the fall of the Berlin Wall than in the preceding half-century. The proportion of countries fighting civil wars had declined to about 12% by 1995."[58]

The change in the global order also coincided with a change in how interventions were justified. In 1992, the UN Security Council authorized the use of "all means necessary" to restore security in Somalia.[59] Similar guidance was given to restore security in Bosnia and Herzegovina.[60] Humanitarian interventions during this time also increased.[61]

Regionally influential states that perceived the flexibility to intervene, especially in areas of significant concern, were decisively put in check. Iraq's intervention in Kuwait in 1990 illustrates this best. Although the United States pulled together a broad coalition of states to counter Iraq's attempt to annex Kuwait, the United States provided the overwhelming preponderance of capability. States with significant relative capability vis-à-vis the rest of the world, such as the United Kingdom, were demonstrating their commitment to the newly established world order led by the United States. Lesser power states, such as Saudi Arabia, were simply bandwagoning.[62] Other regionally powerful states such as Russia, China, and India sat out the conflict and did not attempt to counter.

Some cases of direct intervention and nonintervention—essentially negative cases of indirect intervention—during the early stages of the unipolar era are also instructive. For almost two years, President George H. W. Bush's administration avoided intervening in the intrastate conflicts in Bosnia and Somalia. Both conflicts were considered humanitarian crises. Little gain would come from intervening in places with so little at stake. After avoiding intervention in Bosnia and Somalia for over a year, the United States decided to directly intervene in Somalia to curb the humanitarian crisis caused by internecine violence because it was considered the easier of the two conflicts. Although Somalia was still perceived as an enormous challenge for direct intervention, the Bush administration changed its position to change the opinion that it was callous to human suffering.[63] What is interesting is that the United States felt no restriction to intervention other than the operational challenge of trying to influence the outcome of bitter tribal conflict. Restrictions on intervention that would have driven an indirect approach were absent.

Despite the direct intervention and the use of highly trained soldiers, the United States found its forces stalled and taking unwanted losses in the streets of Mogadishu. The prospect of the United States looking incapable of accomplishing its objectives against an uncoordinated and relatively untrained adversary, as well as sacrificing the lives of its personnel with no real threat to its homeland, revived the belief that Washington should continue to ignore such squabbles.

Not long afterward, the genocide in Rwanda in 1994 found the United States committed to sitting on the sidelines. President Clinton, who had campaigned on the need to intervene in the humanitarian crisis in Bosnia, put off intervening there for two years. The extent of the genocide and America's refusal to weigh in to stop it created the impetus for recalculating the threshold for direct intervention. In 1995, the United States directly intervened in the humanitarian crisis in Bosnia, and a few years later in Kosovo. All three of these cases suggest that something changed. From the perspective of states with the capability of intervening in other countries, the perceived utility or need for indirect intervention, especially via proxy, apparently evaporated after the end of the Cold War.

The observed change lends strength to the theoretical notion that the hegemon in a unipolar order should feel less constrained. Further, the inefficiency associated with using a proxy to intervene directly and the overwhelming capacity enjoyed from its extreme advantage in relative capability should dissuade the hegemon from using proxies. A hegemon's desire to promote its desired world order, however, could alter the threshold for intervention.

The fact that the United States is a republic further complicates the calculation and highlights the relevance of domestic politics. Without an external, existential threat, the notion that politics stops at "the water's edge" begins to fall apart. The prevailing view during the Cold War was that America could be partisan and divided domestically, but foreign policy enjoys widespread bipartisan support. Leading up to the end of the Cold War, and especially thereafter, partisan politics began to complicate foreign policy; parties began to use foreign policy to influence domestic political races. Executives and representatives had to consider how their support for different interventions (or noninterventions) could affect their political position. Such considerations pushed policy makers to alter their intervention decisions.[64]

In this section, I apply my proposed model to the period after the Cold War. I present only cases that represent two of the four typologies: Uganda/Rwanda in Zaire/the Democratic Republic of the Congo (meddling) and Liberia in Sierra Leone (feeding the chaos). During this period, there are no examples of proxy wars where a state is in it to win it or engaged in a holding action.[65] Both cases represent examples where small, regionally influential states use proxy war to indirectly intervene. They are interesting because they address the notion that Africa may have been less important to the United States, allowing small levels of competition among neighboring states without incurring an admonishment from the hegemon.[66] The cases also demonstrate that states, especially the hegemon, can be moved to intervene directly when the stakes are lower but the desire for a particular outcome (cessation of violence) is higher.

MEDDLING: UGANDAN/RWANDAN INTERVENTION IN DRC   For years, Zaire had poor relations with Rwanda and Uganda. In 1996, President Mobutu Sese Seko ordered the Banyamulenge (ethnic Tutsis) to leave Zaire's territory. In retaliation, Rwanda and Uganda provided advisors, weapons, and regular forces to help the AFDL bring down the Mobutu regime.[67] The AFDL's role was critical because it kept Uganda's and Rwanda's involvement from looking like an occupation to Zaire's people. Internationally, the combination of Mobutu's reputation as a harsh, tyrannical leader and the support of an indigenous insurgency provided sufficient political cover.[68] With considerable help from Rwanda and Uganda, AFDL's forces led by Laurent Kabila took control of the capital in Kinshasa in May 1997 with relative ease. The insurgency was largely welcomed by Zaire's population after they had suffered under Mobutu's regime for over thirty years. Kabila, once in power, renamed the country the Democratic Republic of the Congo (DRC).

Kabila's ties to Uganda and Rwanda were strong immediately following his ascension to power. Kabila granted both Uganda and Rwanda access to DRC territory for the purpose of pursuing terrorist groups that had retreated from their countries inside DRC borders. Kabila also allowed Uganda and Rwanda to position regular forces in DRC territory to help them root out terrorist camps.[69]

The ties to Kabila's patrons, however, became problematic—most Congolese citizens chafed at the presence of high-ranking Ugandan and Rwandan advisors in Kabila's government and military.[70] In response to domestic pressure, Kabila removed Ugandan and Rwandan Tutsis from office and ordered Ugandan and Rwandan forces to leave DRC territory.[71] Although both countries were still allowed to pursue hostile groups in Congolese territory, both countries complained that Kinshasa was incapable of stopping terrorists from invading their borders and also charged that Kabila was allowing genocide of Banyamulenge living in eastern Congo.

In the middle of 1998, relations between Kinshasa, Kampala, and Kigali soured. Kinshasa began complaining that Uganda and Rwanda were stealing the DRC's resources, and Uganda and Rwanda began supporting a Banyamulenge insurgency to remove Kabila from power.[72] Kabila's decision to limit Rwandan and Ugandan influence in his country convinced both countries to remove Kabila's regime from power. The disaffected Tutsi officers that Kabila had forced out of their government positions formed the Rassemblement Congolais pour la Démocratie (RCD). Uganda and Rwanda saw the RCD as another opportunity, similar to Kabila's AFDL, to intervene in their neighbor's affairs.

The RCD, along with a significant number of Rwandan regular forces, made gains quickly against Kabila's forces and would have taken Kinshasa had Angola and Zimbabwe not sent expeditionary forces to stop them. As a result, RCD's progress (supported by Rwandan regulars) quickly stalled. Rwanda's difficulties increased when the United States, its main supplier of military aid, decided to cut off its support in retaliation for Rwanda's involvement in DRC. To prevent a collapse in Rwanda and damage to the regime's domestic prestige, Uganda's president sent forces to assist RCD and Rwandan forces.[73] Although both Uganda and Rwanda attempted to conceal their activities, a UN Security Council report confirmed that both were involved.[74]

Under international pressure, Uganda and Rwanda signed a cease-fire agreement with DRC. Rwanda and RCD, however, continued to conduct insurgency operations in an attempt to gain control of DRC's natural resources.[75] The split between Uganda and Rwanda led to a falling-out between the two countries and divided the ranks of RCD. Later, Ugandan and Rwanda forces began fighting against each other. The UN Security Council enacted Chapter VII powers to the UN mission in the DRC. In 2001, both Uganda and Rwanda, under international pressure, began removing their troops from inside DRC's borders. Both countries, separately, signed a peace agreement with Kinshasa in 2002.[76]

FEEDING THE CHAOS: LIBERIAN INTERVENTION IN SIERRA LEONE   Liberia's notorious president Charles Taylor had a close relationship with the leaders of the Revolutionary United Front (RUF), an insurgency group operating in Sierra Leone.[77] In October 1998, the RUF launched an offensive against Sierra Leone's government and captured Freetown (the capital of Sierra Leone) the following January. Liberia provided weapons, funding, and sanctuary to the RUF. Taylor wanted an RUF-led government in Sierra Leone to reduce his political isolation and to gain control over the country's lucrative diamond mines.[78] Although Taylor tried to keep his support secret, numerous reports revealed Liberia's involvement. In addition to gaining influence in Sierra Leone, Taylor's regime used the RUF to probe the limits of the United Nations' willingness to intervene in his affairs in West Africa.[79]

When the RUF first began its insurgency operations in Sierra Leone in 1991, its habit of conducting wanton violence and terrorizing the population distanced the movement from the rural population.[80] In this respect, RUF strategy differed significantly from most insurgency operations; there was no attempt to gain the support of the population but only to terrorize it into submission. During the 1998 offensive, President Taylor directed the RUF to commit atrocities, believing that this would lead the international community to push for a settlement rather than further subject innocent civilians to the torturous and murderous acts of the RUF.[81]

In response to the RUF capturing Freetown, the Economic Community of West African States Monitoring Group (ECOMOG) intervened. Led by Nigeria, ECOMOG quickly took back the capital and reinstalled

Sierra Leone's previous regime.[82] The European Union (EU) also took action and withheld a $53 million aid package intended for Liberia.[83]

Unfortunately, the costs of the peacekeeping operation quickly surpassed Nigeria's and the UN's available resources. To avoid having to pull the peacekeeping forces out before a cease-fire had been initiated, the United States pushed for a settlement. The RUF agreed to halt its operations in exchange for the creation of a unity government and amnesty for its members. Under both international and domestic pressure, Sierra Leone agreed. The settlement left the RUF with a considerable hold on the country, especially over the diamond-producing areas. Surprisingly, the RUF was in many ways rewarded for its brutal policies. In addition to getting amnesty, RUF members received incentive packages, job training, and reintegration benefits from Sierra Leone's government.[84]

President Taylor used his position to profit from the diamonds being smuggled out of Sierra Leone by the RUF.[85] Although Taylor seemed to benefit in the short term, increasing pressure from the international community and a waxing domestic insurgency in his own country forced him to step down in 2003. Taylor, however, escaped to Nigeria, where he was offered sanctuary. After three years, Nigeria agreed to release Taylor to Sierra Leone to stand trial; he has been charged with crimes against humanity for his support of the RUF by the UN-sanctioned Special Court for Sierra Leone.[86]

Unipolar/Post–Cold War Summary

The post-Cold War period reveals a shift in the intervention axis. The space for indirect intervention shrank compared to the period during the Cold War. The threshold for direct intervention decreased as the relative capability of states became extremely lopsided, favoring the United States as the global hegemon (see Figure 3.2). The willingness of the United States to engage directly in civil wars abroad also appears to have deterred other countries from using proxies or crossing the threshold for direct intervention. As long as small, regional proxy wars did not get too violent and did not grossly cross the boundaries of human rights—at least under the unipolar system led by the United States—they avoided any kind of check from the hegemon. This makes sense because a hegemon's desire to maintain the system will lead it to intervene in the affairs of states only when those affairs threaten the global system it supports.[87] Gains that did not threaten the status quo and employed lower levels of violence to accomplish objectives, such as when Uganda and Rwanda backed the AFDL in 1997, meant that the United States and the international institutions that supported its interests were willing to forgo intervention. Charles Taylor used the RUF to probe the limits of the hegemon's tolerance. In the face of wanton violence, a regional institution (ECOMOG) and Nigeria intervened; their efforts, however, stalled without support from the United States or the UN Security Council. Restoring the former regime in Sierra Leone appears to have been enough to prevent an American intervention. Liberia obliged the United States and agreed to settle the conflict but managed to hold on to its significant gains in Sierra Leone.

Regional powers, especially those attempting to influence events in geopolitically important areas, find proxies useful when they want to avoid direct intervention because of international barriers. Uganda and Rwanda were concerned that a direct intervention would anger ethnic Tutsis in Zaire. The AFDL took control of Zaire with little resistance from the domestic population or the international system. The RUF provided just enough international cover to allow Liberia to get what it wanted from Sierra Leone.

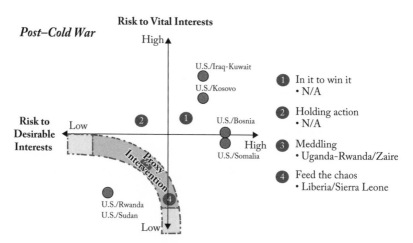

FIGURE 3.2 *Post-Cold War Intervention Axis*

In both cases, widespread violence and human rights violations, however, attracted the hegemon's attention. When Rwanda and Uganda
blurred the line between direct and indirect intervention, the United
States and the UN Security Council began to pressure the two countries.
Additionally, the UN Security Council enacted a Chapter VII operation to stop the violence and forced the antagonists to settle the conflict.
Charles Taylor was eventually extradited back to Sierra Leone for his
atrocities.

Post-9/11 and the Drift Toward Quasi-Unipolarity
Following the terrorist attack on 9/11, the United States began contem-
plating options to defeat Al Qaeda and its leader, Osama bin Laden.
The Taliban government in Afghanistan was given the option to give up
the network and its leadership or suffer the consequences. When Mul-
lah Mohammad Omar refused, the United States intervened. Although
Washington had broad international and domestic support, the George
W. Bush administration elected to use the Northern Alliance to decrease
the footprint of American forces. In a sense, it was a choice of efficiency
over effectiveness. Why would the United States feel so constrained in a
unipolar order with a mandate to intervene?

When presented with intelligence that Saddam Hussein's regime in
Iraq might have connections to Al Qaeda, the Bush administration felt
less constrained. Although the desire was to avoid a large-scale intervention similar to the one under Bush's father in 1991, the United States
still intervened directly to topple Iraq's regime, an operation that would
later suffer the challenges of occupying a country torn apart by sectarian violence. As the situation in Iraq became more violent, U.S. involvement suffered a bitter sentiment in the American public and in many
countries worldwide. President Barack Obama campaigned on a promise to withdraw from Iraq and refocus America's efforts on Afghanistan.
Within four years after the promised withdrawal, what had once been an
Al Qaeda affiliate in Iraq morphed into the Islamic State.

It was also around 2005 when interventions for humanitarian reasons required greater justification. The term *responsibility to protect* (RtoP)
emerged in 2001 and was endorsed by the World Summit in 2005, but

the content of RtoP "essentially provided that the Security Council could authorize, on a case by case basis, things that it had been authorizing for more than a decade."[88] The U.S./NATO intervention called on RtoP to justify its intervention in Libya in 2011.[89]

The rising competition presented by regionally powerful states to the U.S.-driven world order has created space for small-level competitions among lesser powers—interests have diversified from being on one side or the other (Cold War) and from the concern of U.S. intervention (Somalia, Bosnia, Kosovo, and Iraq). Smaller states are making plays for regional hegemony—a signal of a waning unipolar world. Regional challengers started expanding aspirations. Russia intervened in Georgia in 2004. North Korea has ramped up its nuclear weapons development and continues to improve its rocket technology. Iran was on a similar path but accepted the lifting of sanctions in exchange for increased monitoring of its nuclear program and promises that it will cease weaponization. China's efforts to expand its influence in the Indian Ocean, Africa, and the South China Sea further mark the transition. Russia's seizure of Crimea, intervention in Ukraine, support for the Assad regime in Syria, and interference in U.S. elections exemplify the drift from unipolar to a more quasi-unipolar structure. Although Iran has curbed its nuclear aspirations for now, it has continued to expand its influence in the Middle East, causing other regional actors such as Saudi Arabia and Israel to respond. How the drifting quasi-unipolar system of today manifests later will most likely continue to influence how proxy wars are used in the future.

In this section, I apply my proposed model and the theoretical and empirical considerations connected to the post-9/11 world. I present cases that represent all four typologies: the United States in Afghanistan (in it to win it), Saudi Arabia in Yemen (holding action), the United States/NATO in Libya (meddling), and Iran in Yemen (feeding the chaos).

IN IT TO WIN IT: U.S. INTERVENTION IN AFGHANISTAN   Following the tragic events of September 11, 2001, the United States enjoyed overwhelming international and domestic support for Operation Enduring

Freedom. NATO ratified Article V and pledged its support. The authorization for the use of military force passed easily through the U.S. Congress. The Taliban's refusal to extradite Al Qaeda leaders and broad support for U.S. retaliation led Washington to seek a regime change in Kabul. Afghanistan's isolated, landlocked territory, however, lacked a feasible location for deploying ground forces, and Afghanistan's neighbors offered relatively poor options as well.[90] Further, Afghanistan had earned worldwide notoriety as an exceedingly difficult place to conduct military operations, persuading Washington to look for other options.[91]

The United States saw an opportunity to use the Northern Alliance, a coalition of three anti-Taliban factions, as a proxy ground force. The Northern Alliance provided a capability that allowed the United States to avoid the expense of deploying a sizable US force, conserved its equipment and manpower, and prevented Washington from having to expend an enormous amount of political capital to carve out a staging area for its forces. To accomplish its objectives, the United States embedded Special Forces and CIA operators with Pashtun warlords and Northern Alliance forces to provide them with highly effective air and space assets. Although the fighting got off to a slow start, the Taliban quickly fell to the combined forces of the United States, its NATO allies, and the Northern Alliance. As a result, the American people and the international community remained overwhelmingly supportive of Washington's policy.[92]

The quick victory over the Taliban, however, also brought some unexpected costs. First, the United States overestimated the loyalty and ability of its proxy forces. Al Qaeda leaders slipped out of the Tora Bora region and into Pakistan because of insufficient support and commitment, dashing U.S. hopes of capturing Osama bin Laden and his lieutenants.[93] Second, factional leaders of the Northern Alliance reestablished their fiefdoms shortly after the Taliban had been removed from power. American desires for a strong central government that could deny sanctuary to transnational terrorist networks would remain an elusive goal, especially after the United States provided factional leaders with the material resources necessary to resist Kabul's authority.[94] Third, the United States faced a significant challenge in bringing an ethnically fragmented Afghanistan under the control of a predominantly non-Pashtun government. Although the Taliban proved remarkably easy to remove from power, the United States found itself drawn deeper into the conflict.

HOLDING ACTION: SAUDI ARABIAN INTERVENTION IN YEMEN   After the fall of the Soviet Union, the current state of Yemen merged the Yemen Arab Republic (YAR) in the north, supported by the United States and Saudi Arabia, and the People's Democratic Republic of Yemen (PDRY), previously supported by Moscow, in the south. The ruler of the YAR since 1978, Ali Abdullah Saleh, gained control of the newly unified state. Despite unification, Saleh's reach was confined mostly to area around the capital in Sana'a. Yemenis in the south and the Houthis in the north felt underrepresented and fought against Saleh's rule. Making things even more complex, Al Qaeda in the Arabian Peninsula took root in central and southern Yemen.[95]

Although the United States offered limited support to the government in Sana'a after the bombing of the USS *Cole*, Saleh's widespread corruption, domestic backlash, and international pressure convinced Saleh to step down. The Gulf Cooperation Council (GCC), supported by the United States, enabled Yemen's vice president, Abed Rabbo Mansour al-Hadi to become the interim president. Unfortunately, Yemen was unable to reach an agreeable political situation, leaving Yemen essentially ungoverned. Military forces loyal to Saleh joined the Houthi movement—a Zaydi Shi'a group. Other military forces remained supportive of Hadi. Because the turmoil created opportunities for intervention, the two local powers—Saudi Arabia and Iran—expanded their regional competition.[96]

Houthis, supported by Iran, managed to seize much of Sana'a in September 2014. Hadi fled Yemen and sought refuge in Saudi Arabia. Riyadh perceived that a Houthi-dominated state would present a dangerous and hostile neighbor on its southern border. The Houthis' connection with Iran made its removal an imperative. Therefore, Saudi Arabia responded to Houthi advances with an air campaign to assist pro-Hadi government forces and Sunni southern tribesmen reinstate Hadi in Sana'a. Pro-Hadi forces, with support from Saudi airstrikes and a Saudi naval blockade, regained control of Aden a few months after Hadi's exit.[97]

Indicative of the way intrastate conflicts played out during the Cold War, the duration of the conflict in Yemen continues well past where the sides would have likely been exhausted and willing to negotiate.[98] As of March 24, 2017, the United Nations claims that there were over thirteen thousand civilian casualties in the previous two years.[99] The UN has warned that the crisis in Yemen will create an epic humanitarian disaster. The conflict in Yemen jeopardizes most of the necessary functions that enable the people there to survive.[100]

A resurgent Iran spooks Saudi Arabia and the GCC. Supporting pro-Hadi forces in Yemen has enabled Saudi to intervene in Yemen without incurring significant costs from other international states. The Houthi threat has not reached a level that drives the stakes high enough for direct intervention, and Riyadh isn't committed enough to the political outcome in Yemen to directly intervene either. Lastly, Saudi Arabia's capacity to directly intervene on the ground and put Hadi back in control is questionable. As long as the government in Yemen does not become a puppet of Iran, the Saudis will likely continue to support its proxy and fuel the intrastate conflict. No victory in Yemen for the Houthis is almost as good as reinstating Hadi. As the conflict in Yemen continues, the reality that the world continues to slip away from a definitively unipolar to a quasi-unipolar order becomes more apparent. Under such conditions, intrastate conflicts fought by regional players in areas of higher geopolitical importance will likely pop up more often and last longer.

MEDDLING: U.S./NATO INTERVENTION IN LIBYA   Libya, from a geopolitical perspective, was of relatively minor interest. Muammar Gaddafi's ascension to become the ruler of Libya in 1969 was unremarkable in a period of intense competition between the United States and the Soviet Union. Libya did, however, become of interest in 1986 when it was discovered that Gaddafi's regime sponsored a terrorist attack on a German nightclub and killed American personnel.[101] Gaddafi's notoriety worsened with the attack on Pan Am Flight 103 in 1988, an action that incurred a UN Security Council resolution prohibiting member states from selling military equipment or supporting previously purchased items, selling or servicing aircraft, denying overflight of aircraft originating or terminating in Libya, and denying entry to Libyan citizens suspected of terrorist activity by any other state.[102]

Gaddafi did regain some international favor in 2003 when he took responsibility for the attack on Pan Am Flight 103 and turned over the perpetrators to international authorities, but the Arab Spring in 2011 pushed his regime to brutally repress the pro-democracy rebellion. The African Union pleaded against the enforcement of a no-fly zone over Libya but acknowledged that the violence should stop. On March 12, the Arab League and the GCC asked the UN Security Council to impose a no-fly zone over Libya, and the council complied five days later with a vote of ten in favor and five abstentions (Brazil, Russia, India, China, and Germany).[103] The council approved "all means necessary" to protect the citizens of Libya.[104] The United States facilitated the resolution and called on the "responsibility to protect" norm as the justification.[105] In relatively short order, Libya was freed from Gaddafi's tyranny.

Publicly released figures put the cost of the campaign to protect Libya's people at "$1.1 billion for the United States and several billion dollars overall . . . a fraction of that spent on previous interventions in the Balkans, Afghanistan, and Iraq."[106] The operation in Libya definitely confirms some long-held beliefs about proxy war: that it lowers risks and costs. The Libyan opposition successfully ousted the country's dictator. During the conflict, NATO maintained firm control of the execution of the conflict. The United States, the United Kingdom, France, and Italy all provided advisors on the ground to help rebel forces.[107] All aspects of this case fit into the definition of proxy war, but the type is questionable: does this case reflect an example of meddling, or was the US/NATO "in it to win it"?.

The resounding military success of the campaign in Libya and the commitment of the fourteen NATO member states suggest that they may have been "in it to win it." Such a case is interesting and further supports the idea that the world order may have not yet changed to a quasi-unipolar order, especially considering that revisionist states like Russia and China elected to abstain rather than challenge NATO's efforts. Two things, however, raise questions about the indirect intervention in Libya.

First, why intervene indirectly? Second, why work so hard to bring about the end of the Gaddafi regime and then walk away?

The answer to the first question is likely as simple as the fact that the costs didn't warrant the benefits of intervening directly. Interventions in the Middle East had already been viewed with suspicion by the domestic audiences of the NATO states. The stakes were simply insufficient to warrant a direct intervention. Further, the fact that NATO had no political stake in the outcome suggests that it was not really committed to any outcome other than the ousting of Gaddafi. Based on that observation, the indirect intervention most closely resembles meddling. What the United States and NATO likely wanted was to get rid of Gaddafi *and* promote the idea that the unipolar order led by the United States would not tolerate such horrific suffering. Both objectives could be accomplished through meddling. Going any further, however, would have likely incurred a costly occupation. Further, another bitter civil war amid a U.S./NATO led occupation would further cast doubt about the benefits of the unipolar order. To stave off a sharper decline toward multipolarity, it makes sense that the U.S. and NATO cut their losses and declared their mission to protect the Libyan people a success.

FEEDING THE CHAOS: IRANIAN INTERVENTION IN YEMEN Is the Houthi-Saleh coalition in Yemen really an Iranian proxy? Building on the background offered in Saudi-Arabia's proxy war in Yemen, this case explores the notion that the Houthis, a Zaydi Shi'a sect, is Iran's proxy in Yemen. Based on the limited evidence available, a reasonable conclusion is that Iran is engaged in an indirect intervention in Yemen. On several occasions, weapons shipments attributed to Iran have been seized during transport to Houthi forces.[108] Peter Salisbury challenges the possibility that Iran is conducting a proxy war, citing personal interviews with Houthi leaders that claim that the majority of its revenue and capability come from tax collections in Houthi-controlled areas and that weapons are mostly purchased from Saleh supporters on the black market.[109] Thomas Juneau makes a similar claim but acknowledges that Iran has steadily increased its support. Juneau argues that despite these increases, Iran's support has not "reached significant levels" to confirm Iran's hold over the Houthi-Saleh coalition.[110] Juneau's question gets to the heart of this book: does Iran have a hierarchical relationship with the Houthi-Saleh coalition? Juneau's principal argument is that Iran is intervening in Yemen indirectly through the use of *donated assistance*. The question that remains is whether Iran controls, or at least is attempting to control, the Houthi-Saleh coalition or is just donating its assistance.

Iran has likely avoided directly intervening in Yemen for fear of backlash from the international system, especially from the United States. America's relative capability to influence affairs in the Middle East remains significant. Iran's release from the crippling sanctions in exchange for deescalating its nuclear program also provides a significant carrot to avoid intervention. Lastly, the United States has already backed Saudi Arabia's efforts in Yemen and would predictably take Saudi's side if Iran were to directly intervene. Put simply, the projected benefit of intervening in Yemen directly does not warrant the cost. These factors also suggest that Iran may not indirectly intervene in a way that would significantly challenge Saudi Arabia's position on the peninsula, meaning Iran isn't "in it to win it." The conflict in Yemen could reflect a holding action if there were an Iranian interest that needed protection, similar to the way that South Africa used UNITA to keep communism from gaining direct access to its border. This leaves the question of whether Iran is meddling or feeding the chaos.

Iran opposes the current world order. Iran tends to support conflict where it challenges the existing status quo in the region rather than pushing for the expansion of Shi'a Islam.[111] Because Iran is a lesser power with revisionist intentions, pushing conflict provides it with opportunities to persuade other states that the current system is undesirable.[112] This behavior best reflects the desire to use proxy war to feed the chaos; the objective is not to influence the outcome of the political situation in specific states but rather to create as much havoc as possible to hobble greater powers and increase Iran's freedom of movement in the region.

If the quasi-unipolar order remains, Iran should only be committing to feeding the chaos. The United States has already shown that it is willing to provide some donated assistance to support the Arab coalition's efforts to roll back the Houthis.[113] If the quasi-unipolar moment is fading, it signals a further drift toward multipolarity and the waning influence of the United States. Iran may perceive this to be the case. There is evidence that Houthi supporters report having been flown to Iran for training in civil affairs.[114] If true, this demonstrates that Iran may have different plans for the Houthis and may actually be meddling, providing political capacity to its Houthi proxy in the hopes of eventually gaining an ally on the Arabian Peninsula.

Quasi-Unipolar, Post-9/11 Summary

The descent from a unipolar to a quasi-unipolar order has opened the doors to the full complement of proxy war (see Figure 3.3). The restrictions on direct intervention remain, but the ability to indirectly intervene in regions where multiple states have significant interests shifts the political terrain. Both internationally and domestically driven cost/benefit calculations have placed a premium on using indigenous forces to aid interventions. Regional powers use proxies to offset international costs, and global powers, including the remaining hegemon, use proxies to offset domestic and international costs.

One paradox in the U.S./Afghanistan case is why the United States, still clearly and overwhelmingly the dominant state in the international

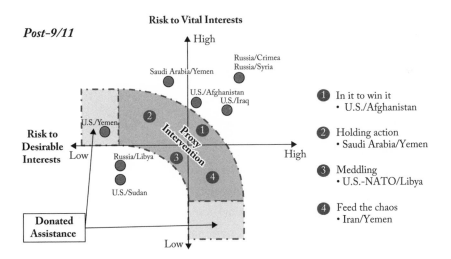

FIGURE 3.3 *Post-9/11 Intervention Axis*

system, felt constrained from a direct intervention. The United States, as mentioned, enjoyed broad domestic and international support. Washington's view in some ways reflects that of an unleashed hegemon. NATO's offer of support was nice but unnecessary.[115] The Afghan Model was initially touted as an unqualified success but has since fallen from that pinnacle.[116] Perhaps America's overconfidence in proxy war and the lessons learned from Operation Allied Force in Kosovo led to the operational failure that prevented the capture of Osama bin Laden. Perhaps the United States started to perceive the need for efficiency and a light touch to sustain its unipolar position—a notion that captures the transition to a quasi-unipolar system.

The Iran/Saudi Arabia/Yemen cases suggest that the types of proxy war and the states that use them may evolve over time. As they both stand now, they reflect barriers indicative of a unipolar order. If the world order shifts more toward multipolarity, the Yemen conflict could potentially change as Saudi and Iran view the stakes of the conflict in Yemen going up. Unlike the cases in the DRC and Sierra Leone, the United States has actually contributed to the duration of the conflict, again showing a change in the system. Under a strictly unipolar order, I would expect the United States to pressure the actors in much the same way it did Uganda, Rwanda, and, to a lesser extent, Liberia.

CONCLUSION

Civil wars decreased somewhat after the end of the Cold War, and the duration of intrastate conflicts markedly shrank. The unipolar order appears to have curbed proxy interventions in many areas, with regions likely deemed a lower interest such as central and western Africa as exceptions. The threshold for superpower intervention appears to follow the suggested model until the 9/11 terrorist attacks against the United States in 2001.

Intrastate conflicts are on the rise in the international system, and one of the main constraints against external intervention appears to be weakening—the unipolar order. The recent increase in interventions and the return of the diversity of the types and users of proxy war suggest that the unipolar order reflects more of a quasi-unipolar order. Proxy war continues to provide states with the ability to intervene indirectly when conditions do not cross the threshold of direct intervention. If globally minded regional powers are able to use proxy wars to their advantage, it may further erode the unipolar order and lead the international system into multipolarity. If that is the case, intrastate conflicts will continue to increase as the competition between global powers finds its balance.

Looking at the use and types of proxy wars used in the Cold War, it appears that the two superpowers conceded certain regions—Southeast Asia and Latin America to the United States and South Asia and Africa to the Soviet Union. Competition in those areas remained limited, but it appears that the superpowers took their adversaries' use of a proxy as a means to look the other way in certain areas. As long as the proxy sustained a thin veil of cover, each superpower was freed from the threat of unwanted escalation.

In a multipolar order with multiple states possessing or about to gain nuclear weapons, I expect similar divisions of interest to occur. The reason is that complex interdependence and globalization will make it necessary for global powers to compete on the margins without directly and overtly challenging one another (similar to the Cold War). Proxy war will give global powers an excuse to look away when their interests are not specifically challenged and will provide the means to manage escalation to avoid nuclear conflict. Proxy war will also allow global powers the ability to circumvent institutional penalties and maintain the appearance of upholding institutional commitments.

As it stands today, the international system remains quasi-unipolar. Under this system, proxy war will continue its current trend of occurring less than during the Cold War but more than when the system operated under a clear hegemon. China and India will compete for dominance in the Indian Ocean—a region where proxy wars could certainly heat up. China will likely receive acknowledged dominance in Eastern and Southern Africa but will be challenged by the United States in the Horn of Africa. The Middle East will continue its current trajectory as a hot bed of intrastate conflicts fed by external states using proxies to gain an advantage.

States currently are limited in their choices of proxy war. States with higher degrees of relative capability can find all four types of proxy war useful. If the world order drifts further away from unipolarity, regional powers will be able to expand their selection of proxy war types to best fit their needs as well. Proxy wars are here to stay, but they are likely to become a lot more popular in the near future.

Given the apparent drift away from unipolarity, I expect to see the United States increase its use of the rhetoric of "responsibility to protect" to justify increased reliance on indirect interventions, especially when the stakes are low but the commitment to the outcome is higher (humanitarian interventions being the most likely case). Much like the Cold War, in confrontations with regional powers, especially when they possess nuclear weapons, the United States will avoid direct interventions that do not clearly threaten its homeland. Instead, Washington will look for proxies that challenge the influence and reach of those regional powers. For example, if Iran increases its support for the Houthis and gains a significant advantage over Hadi's forces, I expect to see covert support (likely brokered through Saudi Arabia) to begin.

If the world shifts completely to multipolarity, Washington will keep the pressure on states such as North Korea and will likely signal a willingness to directly intervene to prevent Pyongyang's aggression. In other areas, such as non-NATO states in Europe (Moldova being one possibility), the United States will seek a holding action via proxy to tie up Russian resources. Meddling will occur in Africa or Latin America if needed. The polarization of America's domestic political landscape, however, will prevent the use of proxies to feed the chaos.

CHAPTER 4

A THEORY OF PROXY WAR

CHANCES ARE, a proxy war policy will go ahead despite suboptimal conditions. Regardless of how well the proxy appears to fit the need, the reliance on another to pursue interests and objectives means that the intervening state must prepare for the additional costs and challenges associated with working through a third party. The previous chapter focused on how to think about proxy war during deliberations and how best to present the risks and rewards of choosing such an option. Here I offer a theory of how best to think about, plan for, and structure a proxy war policy after the decision has been made.

This chapter explores the conditions and methods that lead to maximizing a proxy's utility and efficacy. Utility, in this sense, answers the first question—can a particular proxy do what we need it to do? It refers to the idea that a proxy can do what is needed—that it can perform the tasks necessary to carry out the intervention. Utility, as applied here, should be regarded with a short-term perspective that focuses on whether a proxy intervention is even possible. Efficacy, on the other hand, relates to the question—can a particular proxy get us what we want? It describes the proxy's ability to enable the intervening state to accomplish its desired objectives. Therefore, efficacy represents a long-term perspective.

To be clear, this chapter does not offer a theory to cover every facet of proxy war but rather attempts to break down the constituent elements of proxy war into manageable pieces to reveal the ways in which a proxy intervention can bring both utility and efficacy to foreign policy. The effort is purposely oversimplified because the complexity of proxy war, like any social interaction, quickly overwhelms the capacity of the human brain. Ultimately, a good policy requires a deeper yet manageable understanding of the issues at work once a proxy war is underway.

FRAMING A PROXY WAR POLICY

Framing colors how we describe the situation or policy and how the situation or policy is perceived by decision makers.[1] Framing a proxy intervention policy should center on the proxy's role in the policy and how it influences the utility and efficacy associated with the different frames. For example, deliberating the strengths and weaknesses of a proxy intervention policy based on the context in the target state should occur separately from decisions about how best to employ the proxy in the target state. Putting the two together risks framing the policy in a way that could cause those doing the analysis and working on recommendations to overprioritize the capabilities of a potential proxy; creating a plan based on such a myopic view of the situation may neglect more important factors that should be considered. Starting with finding the right questions rather than the right actions will help curb policy myopia.

Framing also requires asking the right questions to avoid concept stretch—the tendency to widen the scope of a policy beyond its intended purpose to chase economy of scale. Framing, much like good strategy, explores what *should* be done rather than what *can* be done. Equally relevant, questions should focus on the *intent* of the policy. A question like "How do we make this proxy work?" puts a different spin on analysis than "How will using a proxy help us achieve our policy goals?"

In his work on foreign policy formulation and analysis, Alexander George highlights the importance of factors beyond relative capability and power; a state's domestic conditions, its strategy, its desire to bargain, and its understanding and perception of an adversary hold considerable sway when choosing a foreign policy.[2] Because decision makers will want to weigh their decisions based on more concrete facts, strategists and policy analysts need to wrestle with the more uncertain aspects of a potential policy to better prepare them for discussions with decision makers. Framing the situation properly will help decision makers see a more complete picture. Additionally, framing provides clearly identifiable pieces that make up the very complex situation—the clearer the frame, the easier it is to explain how the different aspects of the frame fit into the policy's calculus.

An infinite number of factors contribute to the context surrounding any potential proxy war, and none of those conditions act independently—every contextual condition has the potential to directly affect some aspect of the utility and/or efficacy of a policy. Like all things of this nature, ignoring any contextual condition is a gamble; the recommendations offered here are intended to serve as a framework for policy analysis but are neither a panacea nor a substitute for critical thinking. Because no policy is made or executed in a vacuum, numerous factors will influence the choice of proxy war as a course of action and the utility of proxy war as a means of pursuing interest or accomplishing objectives. For example, globalization draws states and policies into an even tighter orbit; behaviors and outcomes can be coupled in ways that create unintended or inconceivable second-order effects that make prediction challenging, if not impossible. Considering the pressure and complexity of using force abroad, narrowing down conditions to the most likely and relevant becomes an imperative.

To that end, I suggest considering four aspects that frame a proxy war policy: time, domestic influences, international influences, and the proxy itself (see Figure 4.1). Each aspect remains highly complex, but there are important differences that require consideration. To aid in framing each of these four categories, I break down each aspect into smaller elements and separate them into two broad categories: immutable and mutable. Immutable conditions largely represent those that an intervening state must work around during the implementation of its policy. Immutable conditions remain relatively constant while policy options are being formulated and implemented. Mutable conditions, on the other hand, represent areas that can potentially be altered during the execution of the

TABLE 4.1 *Framing a Proxy War Policy*

Frame	Considerations	Immutable?
Time	Perception of Urgency	No
	Short-Term vs Long-Term Focus	Yes
Domestic	Domestic Opinion	Yes (short-term)
	Degree of Freedom for Executive	No
	Bureaucratic Politics	Yes
	Strategy	No
	Commitment	No
	Secrecy	No
International	Interstate Competition	Yes
	International Opinion	Yes
	International Institutions	Yes
	Secrecy	No
Proxy	Character of the Conflict	Yes
	Proxy's Capabilities	No
	Objective Convergence/Divergence	No
	Degree of Isolation	No

policy. Knowing which conditions to work around and which conditions to shape helps focus information gathering and policy design.

The Time Frame

Time plays a role in framing every policy. The key to this frame in policy formulation, however, is to separate out the issues or factors that alter the importance of time on a policy. If a situation becomes dire, then the policy might be framed based on what can be done within the perceived timeline; such a frame can lead to poor policy choices. In dire situations when time feels like the driving factor, look at the issues that make time such an important consideration. The driving issues, whatever they may be, should be made explicit. If a horrific event occurs that has domestic and international audiences crying out for a response—yet those demands fall short of providing cause for direct intervention—throwing support to a proxy might come to the fore. At that point, consideration should be given to providing rhetorical caveats to the support that will limit commitment and decrease the connection between the intervening state and its proxy. For example, the United States may elect to throw more support behind Syrian rebels following the chemical weapon attacks in April 2017. If that were to occur, the president should openly state that greater support is being offered to Syrian rebels to even the playing field and allow them a more serious opportunity to determine the future of Syria. The United States should not say it stands behind the Syrian rebel groups; that would be a rhetorical corner that could overcommit the United States to the rebels' cause.

Aside from the urgency of the situation, the time frame keeps the focus on the utility and efficacy of a proxy intervention. The short-term question of whether the proxy can help an intervening state get what it wants keys in on a proxy's utility; it informs deliberations on the merit of proxy war at the outset and answers the question "Is it even *possible* to get what we want supporting this proxy?" Second, time should be framed to help consider the efficacy of proxy intervention and the long-term question of how the context of the situation hinders or helps the use of a proxy over time and answers the question "Will supporting this proxy help us accomplish our objectives?" With any foreign policy, it is wise to consider how utility and efficacy may change during the implementation of a specific policy.[3] Executed well, framing time in this way should help prevent circular conversations about the utility and efficacy of a proxy war policy and prevent a short timeline from driving the decision.

The Domestic Frame

When threats to national security or risks to national interest do not warrant the mobilization, or even the deployment, of the state's armed forces, it stands to reason that domestic influences hold even greater sway. States that must respond to domestic influences are generally considered "weak" because the strength of a state's society does not allow an executive to make decisions in isolation.[4] Weak states have a wider range of actors participating in policy decisions and therefore must incorporate or adjust to more diverse interests.[5] An executive's decision to use force correlates strongly to his or her standing in public opinion polls.[6] Given that, it makes sense that the use of proxy war may carry extra weight in a decision maker's mind to ensure greater latitude in foreign policy options.

Democratic states rarely make foreign policy in isolation; forces at work inside a state, as well as outside, influence those decisions. This frame focuses on the influences at work inside the state. The idea that states are not unitary actors is a cornerstone of one strand of liberal theory; liberal scholars argue that states are complex social structures with competing interests that influence policy formulation and outcomes.[7] The domestic costs and benefits of foreign policy usually depend on whether the public perceives the policy as necessary and legitimate.[8] Whether a policy is necessary and legitimate, however, is not the only factor that decides a policy's efficacy. For example, if a policy conflicts with the public's sense of acceptable behavior, then the public is likely to reject the policy, even if it appears that the gain will exceed the cost.[9] The response of Israel's people to the South Lebanese Force's massacre of four hundred Palestinian prisoners reflects this—the Israeli public stopped supporting Tel Aviv's proxy policy in Lebanon and convinced the government to withdraw.

If decision makers want to stay in office, they often must balance what they think they should do against what they think the people will tolerate and support.[10] This gets complicated because decision makers often have more information and a better understanding of potential threats than can be related to the public.[11] Two logical reasons for this are: the need to protect intelligence sources and the cumulative level of the public's understanding of complex foreign policy issues is going to be less than those who devote their full attention to such matters. Foreign policies that include the use of force are particularly dependent on internal consensus to sustain military operations.[12]

DOMESTIC OPINION   Democratic states cannot really dictate domestic opinion within their own borders. Although an intervening state's government plays a part, the public—or at least those that give political authority to elected or established leaders—has the freedom to decide how it will respond to different policies.[13] Negative domestic opinion can inflict costly penalties on a policy, even though it produces significant benefits in theater.[14] Policy analysts and strategists need to consider how the domestic audience will view a proxy war policy; this requires a realistic assessment of how well decision makers can articulate the need for such a policy. For example, the Tet Offensive of 1968 clearly demonstrated the benefits of U.S. policy in Southeast Asia; U.S. forces overwhelmingly defeated North Vietnam's incursion into South Vietnam and permanently crippled Hanoi's proxy (the National Liberation Front). In the United States, however, the Johnson administration failed to articulate the successes associated with the Tet Offensive, a fact that marked a major turning point in the American public's support for the war.[15] Decision makers should articulate to the public that there is a threat to the state's interests and that support is being given to a group fighting to achieve those interests. In cases where governments have communicated this connection, costs attributable to domestic willingness remained relatively low.[16]

A proxy war policy can become particularly unwieldy when there is a strong connection between an intervening state's domestic public and the chosen proxy. India's costs skyrocketed because of the connection between its domestic audience and the Sri Lankan Tamils; those costs became even more inflated because of the government's political vulnerability to the Tamil population. The connection between Indian Tamils and India's proxy adversely affected India's ability to implement control measures on LTTE's actions. Tamil sympathy inside India contributed to LTTE's independence from support from the Indian government and left New Delhi without the leverage necessary to force LTTE to agree to the proposed settlement or comply with the Indo-Lanka Accord.

If decision makers sense that the public will not support getting involved in an area they deem vital, then they can attempt to persuade the public that the intervention is worth the cost. The use of a proxy in this case offers two potential benefits. First, supporting a proxy gives the appearance that the state's costs will be low—the proxy's people will be risking their lives and contributing their resources. South Africa managed to maintain its (white) people's support for operations in Angola because UNITA provided much of the personnel, allowing South Africa to avoid unacceptable numbers of casualties. Second, a decision maker may also claim that the state has an obligation to support a proxy that is suffering human rights violations as an attempt to overthrow a repressive regime.

Justifying the support of a proxy based on moral arguments, how-ever, potentially carries a corresponding cost. A proxy intervention policy based entirely on the cause and not on the cost could make it politi-cally difficult to drop the policy. Although there are no proven historical cases of this happening, decision makers might overstretch the state's re-sources to avoid losing face with their constituents, losing office, or being punished.[17]

DEGREE OF FREEDOM FOR EXECUTIVE AUTHORITY   A president's perfor-mance in the formulation and execution of foreign policy can certainly help with reelection. More importantly, a president must sustain domestic popular support to maintain the desired freedom of action abroad to pur-sue national interests.[18] When domestic opinion may not support direct intervention and the use of force, proxy war becomes an interesting policy. In such cases, the pressure to give the president what he or she wants can trickle down to the analyst level. Analysts perceive domestic pressures just by living in society. Presidential speeches or executive communication to the public will suggest desired courses of action. These types of influences can hinder the objectivity of analysis. I discuss the effects and ways to al-leviate the negative effects of those influences later in this chapter.

From a policy maker's perspective, the utility of a proxy is based on what it can do for a state desiring to intervene in another country with-out sufficient provocation. Presently, the United States finds itself dealing with situations abroad that seem to demand proxy interventions based on the American public's antipathy to get immersed in another protracted conflict. For example, the resistance to put boots on the ground in Syria to support the Free Syrian Army against the Assad regime or in Iraq to stop the advance of the Islamic State of Iraq and the Levant (ISIL) has made it difficult for the Obama administration—neither of those groups perceivably poses a direct threat to the United States.

A lack of sufficient provocation, however, does not necessarily mini-mize the desire to act. The executive of a democratic state may wish to act because of considerations for reelection or the desire to get other legisla-tion through the government; this desire is made even more complicated by the fact that the government will likely oppose any such action out of a desire to remain responsive to its citizens.[19] Even in autocratic states, political leaders often remain beholden to the groups that put them in power.[20] In either case, a proxy potentially offers the government an opportunity to act without alienating those who put them in power.

An additional complication related to domestic politics comes from the fact that when political leaders are forced to explicitly state their preferences with some precision, those preferences often conflict.[21] For example, Governor Bill Clinton walked a very fine line during his election campaign in 1992 when he explained that abortion should remain a legal right for women but that the government should not fund abortion because so many Americans think it is wrong.[22] In terms of proxy war, leaders attempt to manage the desire to do something with the desire to remain, or at least appear to remain, uninvolved or minimally involved. Using a proxy provides the appearance of remaining on the fence but still having some influence over the potential outcome. What is often more difficult for political leaders is that they often feel obliged to act before they have even had the luxury of defining their preferences in a situation.[23] President Obama's remarks in 2012 about a "red line" associated with the use of chemical weapons in Syria best reflect this sentiment; he wanted to prevent the Assad regime from using chemical weapons, but his actions in 2013 indicate that he did not really want to have to compel Assad to stop. A proxy can provide some breathing room and act as a stopgap while decision makers figure out what they want to do—this concept applies at the international level as well.

STRATEGY   A policy's strategy is particularly important because it provides the guidance for turning policy into reality.[24] As a mutable condition in proxy war, strategy will, or at the very least should, drive how and to what end the intervening state uses its proxy. Strategy is inexorably linked with objectives and forms the basis for how a policy will be operationalized. More specifically, strategy influences how a state supports its proxy, influences how efforts will alter or mitigate immutable conditions, and shapes other mutable conditions that strongly affect the policy's efficacy.

A deeper study of proxy war reveals three conditions that have a profound effect on the utility and efficacy associated with how a state supports its proxy: resource dependence (an immutable condition that must be converted into a mutable condition), operational autonomy, and incentive structure. The importance of these three conditions leads to their use as the primary elements of control over a proxy; they are discussed in greater detail later in this chapter.

COMMITMENT   For any intervention, commitment will logically come to the fore.[25] Commitment, in this sense, means the degree to which an intervening state will commit its own personnel to advise proxy combat operations and monitor the proxy's use of material support, as well as the conduct of proxy-led operations. For the intervening state, too much commitment can lead to unwanted, yet publicly forced, escalation in two ways. First, the domestic audience can develop a sense of responsibility/ debt to a proxy that will later require the government to commit additional resources. For example, India's government felt compelled to intervene directly when ethnic Tamils in Sri Lanka did not abide by the peace accords. Second, if the level of commitment attracts the attention of other peer, or near-peer competitors, then the proxy may need additional resources. For example, Cuba's support of FAPLA in Angola sparked additional resources for the FNLA and UNITA.

Commitment is mutable because when it comes to the degree of participation in these areas, an intervening state has a choice. If a proxy's behavior, survival, or success carries little weight in terms of domestic or international opinion, then commitment is manageable—support can be dropped without significant penalty. If not, the intervening state needs to monitor its proxy carefully to ensure that it behaves appropriately and receives the necessary support. Monitoring a proxy's behavior greatly depends on objective alignment and the proxy's dependence on the intervening state. If the objectives are aligned or if the proxy is highly dependent on the intervening state's support, then it will likely behave appropriately. Monitoring a proxy's survival and success depends heavily on the proxy's capability; if an intervening state wants to ensure that its proxy does not get annihilated, it must have its own experts on the ground making assessments about whether the proxy's ambition matches its operational capability. Poor monitoring can lead to unsustainable losses. For example, the battle over the Plain of Jars in Laos became a sustained war of attrition for America's Hmong proxy. The Hmong did not have an inexhaustible supply of men with which to fight. Although American support helped the Hmong sustain their fight against the Pathet Lao, the war of attrition compromised the Hmong's ability to endure. American advisors should have seen the futility of the Plain of Jars campaign and sought other lines of effort. Monitors must also ensure that the proxy is fulfilling its assigned tasks. With too little monitoring, proxies may pursue their own interests (especially if each side's objectives do not closely match up) or perform tasks in ways that may undermine public opinion and support among the supporting state's citizens.

Although proxy war requires some degree of monitoring by the intervening state, there is a corresponding danger to having too much. An intervening state must carefully balance its involvement to avoid the slippery slope that could result in direct intervention. A larger number of personnel committed to areas of fighting increases the risk of casualties. If the state loses some of its own personnel, public or political pressure may force additional support—causing a potential surplus of support and a corresponding control problem as mentioned earlier—or it may force direct involvement and undermine the original intent of the policy. The United States fell victim to this slippery slope in South Vietnam in 1964. Hoping to keep its involvement limited, Washington sent advisory teams to help the government in Saigon defeat the communist insurgency. As the South Vietnamese government faltered in its efforts, America's policy of containment would not allow North Vietnam to prevail. U.S. involvement expanded exponentially over the next four years and led to a large-scale, direct intervention.

SECRECY   If a strategic partnership with a proxy is expected to fail to engender public support, then a decision maker may choose to keep an intervention secret, or at the very least plausibly deniable.[26] The benefit of keeping the policy secret or deniable, however, carries at least three domestic costs. First, it may be costly to keep the proxy quiet. The U.S. proxy in Angola hired a lobby group in Washington, D.C., and directed it to inform Congress of the secret support it was receiving from the CIA in hopes of gaining greater amounts of aid.[27] Second, secrecy, as I mentioned earlier, jeopardizes relative superiority in the battlespace because it limits the type and amount of support an intervening state can provide. Third, if the policy becomes public, competing parties or coalitions within a government may use it to their advantage in future elections.[28] Although I have cast these costs as a response to a secret proxy war becoming public, these costs could also apply to overt uses of proxy war that had purposely or accidentally misled the public.

In the United States, covert action is closely monitored by intelligence committees in Congress.[29] From a strategic or operational perspective, oversight of covert action is relatively robust. During the tactical execution of a covert policy, however, oversight will likely be very difficult and the government may not have a full understanding or control of the actions being taken because of the need for secrecy and deniability. The challenge of ensuring that tactical efforts adhere to the intent of the policy can adversely affect the coherence and efficacy of the policy overall.

The International Frame

International actors can influence a state's behavior based on their ability to exact penalties for unwanted behavior.[30] From an international perspective, a proxy's utility comes from its ability to prevent direct confrontation or escalation and from its ability to minimize costs associated with international partners exacting penalties. For example, South Africa's apartheid government used proxies to avoid economic sanctions from its primary trading partners in the West (see Chapter 6).

By its very nature, foreign policy takes place on the international stage. States, multinational corporations, nonstate actors, and international institutions all operate at this level and have corresponding effects on foreign policy choices. When a state chooses to intervene via proxy in the affairs of another state, these actors can all influence the overall efficacy of the policy. At the international level, three factors warrant consideration in every case: interstate competition, international institutions, and international opinion.

INTERSTATE COMPETITION   The way in which the international system is organized reflects a strong influence on the behavior of states. Adding to this, the international system remains state-centric. Numerous arguments can be made that the international system has become increasingly globalized and that interdependence has begun to erode the primacy of states. Although there are certainly indications that the influence and power of states may be waning, states remain the most capable and influential actors in the international system.[31] Considering the primacy of states in the current and foreseeable future, three factors that are interrelated and contribute to both conflict and cooperation between states are interstate competition, a state's desire to survive, and the desire for interdependence. Competition between states can lead to conflict because nearly every material resource on the planet has an associated level of scarcity. Resource scarcity varies across the globe; some states have more than enough fresh water, while others are desperate (compare Norway to India). When states perceive those resources as critical and their ability to acquire those resources becomes threatened, states may justify some form of military intervention.

Proxy war becomes a possible policy choice to offset some of the costs of an intervention driven by competition. If a state can formulate a policy that lowers the costs of an intervention—intervention being the state's effort to compete for resources—then the policy becomes more desirable. For example, Russia intervened in Ukraine/Crimea in 2014 using Russian nationalist militias and disguised Russian military personnel to gain permanent access to the port of Sevastopol. Avoiding direct intervention with Russian armed forces likely provided Moscow with the belief that it would lower the costs of intervening. If Russia had foreseen the price of oil dropping and the negative effect of sanctions on its oil and natural gas industry, the intervention might not have occurred. Proxy war also comes into consideration as a policy when the competition perceived between states falls below a threshold that can be communicated as something that puts survival at risk (a point I make in Chapter 2). In such cases, states desiring to intervene must either attempt to keep their activities secret or attempt to justify their actions to international and domestic audiences.

INTERNATIONAL INSTITUTIONS   In today's competitive environment, states must cooperate to survive and prosper.[32] Interstate cooperation has led states to form dense webs of associations in areas such as politics, economics, diplomacy, security, and the environment.[33] The growing density of global networks and the ever-increasing speed at which information travels make it virtually impossible for states to conduct foreign policy in isolation.[34] Although states clearly benefit from cooperating with one another, sustained benefits depend on both parties keeping up their end of the bargain. If one side cheats, the other side pays—at least in the short term.[35] The potential for cheating is a particularly difficult problem for interstate cooperation because there is no overarching authority to ensure that states fulfill their contractual obligations—a concept known as anarchy in the field of international relations.[36] The necessity of interstate cooperation and its inherent uncertainty highlight the importance of international institutions and a state's reputation.

Institutions are "persistent and connected sets of rules that prescribe behavior roles, constrain activity, and shape expectations."[37] Institutions facilitate interstate cooperation in three major ways. First, institutions help states avoid having to engage repeatedly in lengthy, costly negotiations about the terms of cooperation.[38] Second, once states have gone through the trouble and expense of creating an institution, states will not easily risk their investment to make small immediate gains by cheating on one or two transactions.[39] Third, institutions provide valuable information to states about the behavior of other states with regard to interstate cooperation. Institutional rules offer states a much clearer picture with which to evaluate the cooperative behavior of other states.[40] Further, a state's ability to benefit from one international institution often depends on its compliance in others.[41] A misstep in one institution carries the possibility of sanction in another. For example, when Iraq invaded Kuwait on August 2, 1990, the UN Security Council first invoked economic sanctions cutting off all trade, including Iraq's oil supplies, and the European Community froze Iraq's financial assets in its members' countries.[42]

Reputation refers to how a state's past patterns of behavior affect its current and future relationships.[43] Reputations, like institutions, strongly influence cooperation. Reputation facilitates cooperation because states tempted to cheat and reap benefits in the short term fear the long term costs of being labeled a cheater.[44] A good reputation increases a state's ability to influence others and encourages other states to expand their interaction with that state.[45] Supporting a proxy may trigger institutional and reputational costs because, under most circumstances, states are not supposed to intervene in the domestic affairs of another state.[46] Further, supporting a proxy could have a ripple effect, causing an intervening state to suffer in trade, diplomatic, and security relations unrelated to the proxy war.

If an intervening state perceives that a proxy will not justify its involvement enough to avoid institutional or reputational costs, then a proxy also provides a necessary front through which it can secretly intervene in a target state or, at the very least, offers the benefit of plausible deniability. If the international community cannot definitively prove that the intervening state acted unlawfully, this decreases the chance that the intervening state will incur institutional or reputational costs and lowers the potential for inviting unwanted escalation. U.S. involvement in Laos provides an excellent example of both. Numerous countries suspected but could not substantiate Washington's involvement in Laos; America's ability to deny its activities avoided institutional and reputational costs and prevented Soviet retaliation.

Plausible deniability provides a benefit in another way. Proxy war gives outside states the ability to look the other way, especially under conditions where cooperation with the intervening state provides enormous benefit. For example, the United States is a lucrative market for many states. If the United States uses a proxy, it enables states with domestic publics opposed to foreign intervention to continue trading with America without suffering domestic political consequences.

INTERNATIONAL OPINION   Potential problems due to negative perceptions of the proxy or of an intervening state using a proxy to forward its own interests can come from the international arena as well. States, much like individuals, often have established opinions about certain types of behavior.[47] Perceptions of inappropriate behavior by the proxy and/or transgressions against established international norms regarding intervention can negatively influence the utility and efficacy of a policy. Ensuring that a proxy adheres to accepted norms of behavior during armed conflict can mitigate some of the negative effects.

If a state perceives that its survival is in jeopardy, then intervention becomes more justifiable and more likely.[48] Under such conditions, states are willing to accept higher costs for the simple benefit of surviving. Proxy war becomes part of the discussion under these circumstances when the ability to succeed in an intervention becomes questionable or when escalation becomes untenable. An example in the first sense would be Pakistan's use of Lashkar e Taiba (LeT), a Pashtun tribal militia, in Kashmir. Pakistan's need for security has driven the state to use LeT to keep India from gaining undisputed control of the Jammu/Kashmir area.[49] Pakistan lacks the ability to directly invade the region and take it back with force, but Islamabad's perspective is that maintaining Kashmir is a strategic priority.[50] In the second case, nuclear states must be careful to manage escalation when pursuing objectives to protect national security; the possibility of nuclear escalation strongly influences intervention policies.[51] For example, both the United States and the Soviet Union relied heavily on proxies in conflicts in Asia and Africa during the Cold War to avoid a direct clash. In either of these instances where survival is connected to competition, many of the issues associated with proxy war at the international level diminish because extreme measures, even desperate measures, become more acceptable to states outside the conflict.[52]

Conversely, a proxy may justify an intervening state's involvement; supporting an indigenous actor in a way that does not deviate from what other states consider acceptable behavior largely avoids institutional and reputational costs. For example, India justified its support of Mukti Bahini in East Pakistan because the government crackdown caused millions of refugees to seek shelter inside India's border. As a result, other states in the international system stood by as India supported East Pakistan's secession and significantly weakened Islamabad's strategic position. Yet overtly supporting a proxy may also invite additional costs to an intervening state because it could justify a rival state supporting the opposition. For example, both South Africa and the United States incurred additional costs when supporting UNITA in Angola because the Soviet Union backed the MPLA.

Treat domestic and international opinions/connections as immutable conditions during policy formulation; the execution of the policy, however, should include plans to cultivate, gain, and sustain support over time. If the policy is estimated to be too contentious to at least gain tacit approval abroad, then some consideration should be given to accept the risks associated with keeping the policy secret or, at the very least, plausibly deniable. In such a case, further deliberations should be taken to structure the policy and prepare decision makers for the likely event that the policy becomes public.

The Proxy Frame

Think of a proxy as an entity that needs help and will therefore put its own interests aside to recruit outside help. A state becomes willing to enlist the assistance of a proxy because it offers some sort of benefit. The type of proxy and the quality of the benefits it provides depends on several factors listed in the following sections.

THE PROXY'S CAPABILITIES   Some argue that relative capabilities determine a policy's outcome; the more capable side always achieves its desired outcome.[53] This suggests that in a proxy war, the capabilities of an intervening state, its proxy, and their adversary drive the proxy's utility up or down. This view, however, ignores many other factors that can affect the policy's efficacy. Discussions of a proxy's relative capability and the intervening state's material ability to influence the situation in the target state are important topics; they should be discussed, but strategists and policy analysts must avoid becoming overly focused on them.

CHARACTER OF THE CONFLICT   Ethnic and/or ideological factors found at the source of a conflict define what I call the *character* of a conflict. Paying attention to the character of the conflict yields important information about the motivation of a proxy and informs an intervening state about the scope of its objectives and the potential need for additional control measures. If there are doubts or unknowns about the character of a conflict, serious consideration should be given to avoiding a proxy option no matter how enticing it may appear. Whether the conflict is based on ethnic or ideological differences, however, should be considered immutable. Ideological wars center on a competition for the loyalty of the people, and ethnic wars focus on a competition for territory; both ultimately represent a competition for control of the state.[54]

Ethnic conflicts can increase resource and commitment costs because they reduce the willingness of the two sides to negotiate—a point shown specifically in the India-LTTE case. The ethnic character of the conflict in Sri Lanka raised India's resource costs because it prolonged the conflict and lowered its prestige as the regional hegemon because it struggled to bring the two sides to an agreement. As I mentioned previously, competing proxies may provide an additional measure of control, but only if the intervening state maintains the ability to play one off the other. LTTE's elimination of rival Tamil militant groups ultimately limited India's ability to control it.

Ethnic and ideological conflicts have different effects when an intervening state desires a negotiated settlement. Ethnic conflicts are not easily (cheaply) resolved via bargaining. Neither UNITA nor LTTE was involved in the bargaining process that "ended" the two conflicts, and both groups, unsatisfied with the outcome and distrustful of the other side, continued to fight. Although South Africa did not incur costs due to UNITA's decision to continue the conflict in Angola, India suffered heavy costs due to its commitment to the negotiation process and the Indian government's decision to provide peacekeeping forces to enforce the Indo-Sri Lankan Accord. Ideological conflicts have more room for compromise. If the proxy wants to be a part of the government and has the capability—militarily and politically—to pressure the existing government to concede to its participation, then the conflict should cost less. The U.S.-Hmong case demonstrates the folly of backing a proxy in an ideological conflict without the ability or desire to influence the political process. When backing a politically weak proxy, an intervening state should realize that any long-term solution is not going to involve its proxy and there should be no intention of influencing affairs in the target state beyond the short term.

OBJECTIVE CONVERGENCE/DIVERGENCE   Strategists and policy analysts should pay attention to situations when an intervening state and its proxy have convergent objectives in only one area. Even if a common objective overlaps with the intervening state's overall objective, this can lead to a quick decision for short-term gains and can result in long-term losses. An additional complication is that a proxy may not be truthful about its objectives. Although a proxy's objectives are somewhat mutable in the sense that incentives can alter those objectives, an intervening state should objectively consider its ability to steer a proxy's objectives and efforts throughout the course of the policy.

Looking at military alliances as a concept that closely mirrors many aspects of proxy war, one of the most difficult challenges is managing the objectives of alliance members, especially over time and as conditions change.[55] Alliance members bargain over which objectives will take priority. Although proxy war involves a stronger form of hierarchy than alliances, negotiations on objectives are still required; the degree to which the established objectives serve the proxy's interests and potentially hinder the intervening state's objectives should strongly be considered.

History shows that the alignment of objectives in a proxy war tends to change over time.[56] Further complicating the issue, a proxy's success or failure can often work at cross-purposes with those of the state supporting it. For example, a proxy's ambition often grows as it experiences success against its opponent. If the supporting state seeks limited objectives, such as creating favorable conditions from which to bargain with the target state, then it will likely struggle with restraining the desires of its proxy. In the 1980s, the seven major mujahideen militias in Afghanistan wanted more than to preserve Pakistan's strategic depth or to bleed the Soviet army dry; they wanted control of Afghanistan, proven by the violent civil war that ensued after the Soviets pulled out and American and Saudi funding stopped flowing.[57]

An intervening state's objectives change based on the degree of its public's support or when state competitors get involved in the conflict. In the United States, two important determinants of public support are whether a policy produces some sort of observable progress and whether the policy appears to align with American values.[58] If there is little progress, decision makers may elect to increase support for the proxy. Although providing additional support can potentially increase progress in a measurable way, it can also produce undesirable effects. First, it can further entrench a state in a conflict where only limited involvement was desired. Second, increasing a proxy's capability can lead to a point where the proxy's ambitions grow and then begin to challenge the intervening state's own objectives. Third, throwing additional support into a conflict that appeared to be a rather stable stalemate runs the risk of escalation by potentially inviting competing states into the conflict. If a proxy's behavior or the purpose for which a state chooses to support a proxy does not perceivably match the values of the state's public, the state may either withdraw its support (threatening its ability to influence events in the target state) or elect to hide its support. Covert action can present a significant problem if the proxy seeks legitimacy and desires overt political support from the intervening state because the intervener will deny its involvement. In addition, covert action carries certain risks for decision makers and presents significant challenges to the execution of the policy (a possibility that will be explained in greater detail shortly).

Changes in a proxy's ambition, domestic public support, or the degree of escalation all may lead to corresponding changes in objectives that have a significant effect on a proxy war policy's efficacy. In most cases, costs to the intervening state (as well as costs to the proxy) go up with such changes. For example, Rwanda and Uganda supported the AFDL, led by Joseph Kabila, in 1996. The original objective was to bring down Mobutu's regime in Zaire after he ordered all the ethnic Tutsis to leave the country. With both outside and domestic support, Kabila's AFDL forces defeated Mobutu's regime with relative ease. Rwanda and Uganda wanted to maintain control of Kabila after he was in office in Kinshasa to enable them to deal with insurgents hiding outside their own borders. Kabila, however, received significant criticism from his primary patrons for having Rwandan and Ugandan officials in his government. Kabila, desperate to hold on to power in the newly named Democratic Republic of the Congo (DRC), expelled these foreign advisors and ordered all Rwandan and Ugandan forces out of the DRC. After this perceived betrayal, Uganda and Rwanda formed a new proxy, the Rassemblement Congolais pour la Démocratie (RCD), to bring down Kabila's regime and restore their access to the DRC. Kabila's ambition and the change in popular support in the DRC created the need for a new proxy and another war.[59]

If proxy war becomes the policy of choice, then a serious debate about the convergence and divergence of objectives between the state and its proxy should precede any action. Limiting policy objectives is recommended if there are doubts about the veracity of the proxy's stated objectives or if the political and cultural context of the conflict remains murky and poorly understood. Changes in objectives or in the degree of support require a reevaluation of the policy and its corresponding strategy.

DEGREE OF ISOLATION   A proxy's isolation or, more specifically, the ability to shape a proxy's isolation is the third mutable condition that warrants consideration. In an alliance, members bargain with one another to decide which objectives take priority (a topic discussed previously). The relative bargaining power of each state depends on its need for the other. In an alliance, need depends on three elements: "a state's need for military assistance, the degree to which the ally fills that need, and alternative ways of meeting that need."[60] A proxy has significant need of military assistance. A proxy's willingness to subjugate its interests (at least to some degree) to an outsider establishes the fact that it needs help. Likely in a desperate situation, the proxy will take what assistance it can get and will, rhetorically at least, acknowledge the superiority of the supporting state's interests. The third element—alternative ways of meeting its needs—lends strength to the importance of cultivating a proxy's isolation. If an intervening state wants some assurance that its proxy will not stray from the desired objectives, then the state must assess its proxy's isolation and look for ways of increasing that isolation to ensure that the proxy has no other ways of meeting its needs. With no other means of support, a proxy must subjugate its interests until another means of support—from either an outside source or an overabundance of support from its patron—materializes.

A THEORY FOR HOW TO FIGHT A PROXY WAR

Considering that states do not always intend for a proxy to win, meaning to gain (insurgency) or regain (counterinsurgency) control of the country engaged in civil war, the utility and efficacy of proxy war covers a broad spectrum. An intervening state's objectives, therefore, determine how and when a proxy war serves its interests. As explained in Chapter 2, I organize proxy war into four categories: *in it to win it*, *holding action*, *meddling*, and *feed the chaos*. Although these are four different types of proxy war with four different objectives, there are some commonalities among them when it comes to maximizing utility and efficacy of a proxy war.

In a perfect world, an intervening state benefits most from proxy war when it supports a proxy with similar objectives, when the proxy remains highly capable with respect to its adversary, and if the proxy maintains a high degree of dependence on an intervening state's support. Under such conditions, the proxy's agency—its ability to shirk or cheat on its commitments—has few, if any, negative effects. Proxy war conditions, however, are never perfect. Despite this, a proxy can still provide a useful means to assist a state desiring to intervene in the affairs of another state. Understanding how and when conditions can be adapted or overcome in ways that will allow the proxy to fit the needs of the intervening state will make or break the utility and efficacy of a proxy intervention.

Two conditions that can be adapted to enhance the utility and efficacy—conditions I define as mutable—are a policy's coherence and the intervener's control over its proxy. An effective proxy war policy blends coherence and control. Maintaining a coherent policy at all levels (proxy, international, and domestic) and maintaining control over the proxy, simultaneously, provide the best method for engaging in a conflict through an association with an indigenous group. Coherence refers to the degree to which all aspects of the policy contribute to the intervener's desired objectives. Coherence also refers to the policy's ability to adapt to changing conditions. To *formulate* a coherent policy, a strategist must consider how to create and coordinate interactions in three different areas: with its proxy, the international arena, and the domestic arena. To *sustain* a coherent policy, strategists must predict and manage their leaders' changing expectations, understand and work through how the uncertainty associated with proxy warfare will affect the policy over time, and deal with conditions—those self-inflicted as well as those beyond control—that hinder policy coherence.

In proxy war, one of the primary sources of unexpected challenges—a concept military theorists often call *fog*—are due to proxy actions and interactions. An intervening state engaged in proxy war must assess its ability to control its proxy and limit its objectives commensurate with that ability. Control over a proxy depends largely on three conditions: *compatibility of objectives, capability of a proxy*, and *the dependence of a proxy on outside support*. Understanding how proxy war challenges coherence and how the interactions between a proxy, an intervening state, and external audiences influence an intervening state's ability to control its proxy will help put policies in place to enhance the utility and efficacy of a proxy.

Coherence

Coherence, when it comes to policy, reflects the synergy of different actors and diverse efforts to accomplish an objective under complex conditions. More specifically, in their work on the effects of OECD policies to improve development efforts, Kichiro Fukusaku and Akira Hirata suggest that policy coherence has four distinct elements":

1. Internal coherence: the consistency between goals and objectives, modalities and protocols of a single policy or program carried out by an OECD government in support of development (e.g. aid).

2. Intra-country coherence: the consistency among several aid and non-aid policies of an OECD government in terms of their combined contribution to development.

3. Inter-country coherence: the consistency of aid and non-aid policies across several OECD countries in terms of their aggregate contribution to development.

4. Donor–recipient coherence: the consistency of policies adopted by rich countries collectively and poor countries individually or collectively to achieve shared development objectives.[61]

Looking at coherence this way allows for a better breakdown of the relationships and activities that can affect a policy. Slight modifications to the definitions of those elements provide a useful way of looking at the coherence of a proxy war policy. I use similar categories but have altered the specific definition of each (and added one) to better reflect a proxy war policy.

1. Internal coherence: the consistency of the intervening state's objectives with the policy, strategy, operations, and tactics used by all contributing agencies and departments when carrying out the proxy intervention.

2. Intrastate coherence: the policy and supporting actions that reflect the political and military situation on the ground in the target state.

3. International coherence: the consistency of support, or the degree of adversarial support, among states that influence those involved in the proxy intervention.

4. Domestic coherence: the consistency of support and/or opposition among parties inside the intervening state that influence the conduct of the proxy intervention.

5. Proxy coherence: the consistency of policies used by the intervening state to employ and control the proxy to achieve objectives.

Using this model, coherence requires two necessary elements. First, the context of the policy must be sufficiently framed (as discussed in the previous section). Proper framing promotes a deeper understanding of the actions required both in the execution of the proxy war and in the dense network of relations that surround any state operating in a foreign country. Second, the actions taken to support the proxy demand deliberate and well-coordinated interactions in the five areas. In most cases, something should be accomplished in each area and the effects of one often bleed over into others. Historically, it has been difficult for an intervening state to maintain a high level of coherence across all five areas. This chapter takes these considerations and describes how an intervening state should either adapt to conditions or manipulate the conditions in its favor.

INTERNAL COHERENCE   From an internal coherence perspective, strategists must consider how to balance the expectations of decision makers regarding the proxy intervention with other foreign policy areas. Managing utility and efficacy once the proxy war has begun becomes challenging because the policy will take on an inertia of its own. Decision makers who were previously skeptical about the potential of a policy may become overconfident about the efficacy of that course of action after the decision has been made, even though the circumstances have not changed.[62] In a proxy war scenario, decision makers who chose proxy war because it appeared to be the "least bad" option could misread initial tactical successes and assume they had underestimated the efficacy of the proxy intervention policy. Such beliefs could lead to the slippery slope of providing more support (to increase the proxy's utility) and either becoming more entrenched in the conflict or losing the balance between support and control—an outcome that can have significant negative consequences.

Striking this balance helps ensure the efficacy of the proxy intervention policy. Focusing too much on the utility of the proxy can damage the policy's efficacy. For example, India wanted to mollify ethnic Tamils living in Tamil Nadu and therefore had to provide sufficient support to allow the Tamil Tigers to make gains in Sri Lanka. Empowering the Tamil Tigers, however, allowed LTTE to consolidate its power by eliminating other nationalist Tamil groups operating in Sri Lanka. India's support also made the Tamil Tigers impossible to control. Unintentional consequences and second-order effects created by the proxy intervention can influence other policies. India had to directly intervene to tamp down Tamil operations and try to convince the group to negotiate. When LTTE refused to negotiate, India had to step in and act against its proxy to deliver stability within its sphere of influence (see Chapter 5).

INTRASTATE COHERENCE   Intrastate coherence focuses on how the situation on the ground in the target state affects the proxy war policy. Political conditions in the target state provide the motivation and the opportunity for an intervening state to get involved. Political conditions also determine the actors that can serve as a proxy and define the relationship between antagonists. Typically being some form of insurgency or counterinsurgency, proxy wars almost always entail a battle to win the local population's favor. Therefore, the underlying character of the existing conflict in the target state should significantly affect a proxy war's utility and efficacy. According to Chaim Kaufmann, civil conflicts are predominantly either ideologically or ethnically driven.[63] Kaufmann does not consider the possibility that a civil conflict can also be about greed. In two of the cases discussed in Chapter 3—Liberia/RUF and Uganda-Rwanda/RCD—the character of the civil conflict was more about greed than ethnic or ideological differences. Liberia and the RUF wanted control of Sierra Leone's diamond mines; the ethnic issues were a much lesser issue. Uganda and Rwanda wanted access to territory in the DRC to exploit the state's rich natural resources. The ethnic issues that involved Kabila's government allowing Congolese Tutsis to be harassed and terrorized came after Uganda and Rwanda began supporting RCD's efforts to overthrow Kabila. Although this situation is rare, states considering proxy intervention should consider it a possibility.

Kaufmann claims that outside assistance in ideological conflicts is rarely decisive because the determining factor "is the relative political competence of the competing factions" because the battle centers on gaining control of the government. Kaufmann further argues, "more massive involvement does not necessarily produce better results than a lesser involvement, and may actually reduce the chances of the local client."[64] In fact, an intervening state's involvement may sour its proxy's ability to gain popular support. If the intervening state plays too large a role in assisting its proxy, it may incur the unintended cost of spoiling its proxy's domestic legitimacy.[65] Ethnic conflicts, however, center on controlling territory and involve one group bent on secession. There is no competition for loyalty because each side is committed to its own cause based on its ethnic affiliation. Therefore, an intervening state does not have to pay the additional costs of ensuring that its proxy gains public support. Ethnic conflicts, on the other hand, are more often a test of the relative military strength between competing factions and rely less on political competency because ethnicity rather than political views divide the two sides.[66] Therefore, an intervening state can dramatically tip the balance in its proxy's favor by providing the resources and training necessary to defeat the adversary militarily. A proxy war that takes place within an ethnic conflict may still have high costs, but the corresponding benefits should also be much higher.

Kaufmann's assessment suggests that involvement in an ideological conflict could reduce the policy's efficacy, yielding little return for the investment unless its proxy is politically competent and well received among the target state's people. If the proxy does enjoy widespread popular support in the target state, then it stands to reason that the target state's population would shoulder some of the burden of supporting the proxy and reduce the amount of resources coming from the intervening state. If not, the intervening state will be forced to invest significant resources to bolster its proxy's political competency—a condition an intervening state will find extremely difficult to influence or improve considering that outside support can compromise a proxy's political/ideological legitimacy.[67]

INTERNATIONAL/DOMESTIC COHERENCE   Domestic and/or international condemnation can severely hamper a proxy war's utility and efficacy because it affects an intervening state's ability to support its proxy and can negatively reflect on decision makers. In 1975, the Clark Amendment impeded the utility of a proxy war policy because it constrained the United States' ability to support the FNLA and UNITA in Angola based on UNITA's affiliation with the apartheid government in South Africa. Although this situation did not hurt President Reagan's popularity, the lack of funding and support eliminated the policy's efficacy because it allowed the Soviet-backed proxy (MPLA) to defeat one of the U.S. proxies (FNLA) and push the other, UNITA, back toward the border of South West Africa (Namibia). Without domestic support, coherence becomes challenging, if not untenable. International condemnation can hurt foreign relations and trade or, more locally focused, can spark a counterintervention on the side of the adversary. An intervening state must structure involvement to prevent other states from offering support directly to the proxy; if the proxy manages to pull other supporters into the conflict based on the perception that it is undersupported, then the intervening state will struggle with control and/or coherence.

One factor that occurs at the international level that interferes with a policy's coherence is when another actor gets involved. Regardless of which side the international actor gets involved with, an intervener will have to make some adjustments. If an additional state joins in support of the proxy, its objectives will likely differ in some way; this jeopardizes control because it opens up the possibility that the proxy will have the ability to play one supporter off the other. An additional supporter may also harm an intervener's ability to justify intervention or sustain support if it is considered a pariah. In the early 1970s, China had to abandon the FNLA in Angola after the United States began providing support. If the policy drives the will for a rival state to get directly involved or to throw support behind its own proxy, then the entire conflict escalates and potentially risks greater confrontation. America's support of FNLA and UNITA instigated both: the Soviet Union backed the MPLA, and Cuba deployed its regular forces to counter Washington's proxy war.

Keeping the proxy war secret can mitigate both issues. Blowback is an obvious problem for an intervener from international and/or domestic audiences. Yet even if the policy remains secret, it has the potential to create an additional problem for coherence from a domestic, internal perspective. Secrecy, especially in the form of covert operations, imposes significant barriers to policy transparency. Covert operations demand a high level of autonomy due to the requirement to ensure that operations remain plausibly deniable. Even with government oversight, the policy may lose its coherence from the strategic level to implementation at the operational and tactical levels.

PROXY COHERENCE   Although coherence at domestic and international levels depends in part on the reasons an intervening state chose the proxy war route as opposed to direct intervention or nonintervention, interveners are still forced to uphold—at least in appearance—standards similar to those that would have applied if they had deployed their own forces. A proxy's behavior and the means by which the intervening state supports its proxy should remain in sync with international norms regarding conduct in war or domestic hostilities. Although an intervening state may not be strictly liable for the misconduct of its proxy, connections to an actor performing atrocities or violating accepted laws of war can damage its reputation and/or its relationships with other state and nonstate actors.[68]

An intervening state ought to consider how a policy articulated to earn or sustain the support of international and domestic audiences may influence its relationship with its proxy. Proxies live in constant fear of being abandoned—a reason that further leads them to pursue their own agenda as much as possible out of fear that if they commit to the intervening state's objectives and methods, they may get left with nothing should the intervening state lose interest. Intervening states should be aware of how an articulated proxy war policy that does not engender confidence in its proxy could affect the overall coherence of the policy. A proxy that continuously believes it will be abandoned will likely fail to contribute to the policy's coherence.

To maintain coherence with a proxy, an intervening state must balance a high degree of control over its proxy's actions with allowing enough autonomy to avoid being dragged into a direct intervention. Matching the type of support, outcome-based or performance-based, offers its proxy the capabilities needed to achieve the desired objectives in the target state. This is why *control* becomes an element of coherence. The concept of control, however, represents a separate discussion.

The proxy's ability to accomplish desired tasks, in all aspects and phases, depends mostly on its capability vis-à-vis the adversary. Because perceptions about proxy war typically center on the use of violence to achieve objectives, a proxy's worth tends to revolve around its ability to militarily defeat its adversary as a means to accomplish an intervening state's objectives; this is also why operationalizing such a policy tends to revolve around how to get the proxy the necessary training and weapons to do so.[69]

Conventional wisdom surrounding proxy war typically focuses on combat skills—make the proxy more combat effective and success is right around the corner. For example, discussions about rebel efforts in both Libya (2011) and Syria (2013) focused on their ability to militarily defeat the seated governments; there was little discussion about how to support the broader objectives of bringing stability to those two countries. An intervening state must strongly consider how well its proxy matches up to its adversary in terms of combat skill. A proxy's relative military capability vis-à-vis the adversary, however, only applies to limited objectives such as executing a holding action or as a means to gain increased leverage at the bargaining table. In many cases, a proxy needs additional capabilities. For example, the MPLA served as the Soviet Union's proxy in Angola for nearly twenty-five years. Soviet weapons, training, and advisors provided the MPLA with a distinctive edge early in the conflict, but the MPLA did not have the political capacity to rally the other ethnic groups to support its cause. In most cases, therefore, the relative capabilities between a proxy and an adversary require consideration beyond kinetic, military capability. Like any policy, the connection between objectives, strategy, operations, and the realities present in the conditions surrounding the conflict must knit together to produce a coherent plan of execution.

Domestic and international connections or opinions regarding the proxy can influence this aspect of the policy's coherence. External audiences that have a connection to the proxy can be used by the proxy to lobby against the government of an intervening state—which becomes a means to undercut policies that the proxy finds unappealing or confining with respect to its own interests and can disrupt the coherence of an intervening state's policy. External connections can also make it difficult politically to manage support to the proxy, similar to the way that nepotism can make it difficult to control certain employees because they are the son or daughter of a powerful person in the organization. For example, India supported the Tamil Tigers in Sri Lanka because Indira Gandhi needed the Tamil vote domestically to stay in power. The Tamil Tigers capitalized on that need to wrest more freedom and more support from India, a situation that made the Tamil Tigers uncontrollable and an obstacle to India's foreign policy. In such cases, the intervening state must look for these types of connections and incorporate their potential effects into its pursuit of a coherent policy that sustains its control over the proxy.

A coherent policy finds a way to balance the objectives of the intervening state with the objectives of the proxy. India's support of Mukti Bahini in the early 1970s represents a positive example. India wanted to cut off Islamabad's control of East Pakistan and weaken Pakistan's position in the region. Mukti Bahini wanted to conduct a successful insurgency against Pakistan's government, allowing it to secede and become its own country. India provided the capability for its proxy, Mukti Bahini, to challenge Islamabad's control in East Pakistan. India knew that Mukti Bahini and the new government in East Pakistan (now Bangladesh) would soon become a new neighbor and did not want a strong military next door that could cause problems. India also knew that Mukti Bahini, without significant stores of weapons and training, would never be militarily strong enough to defeat Pakistan's forces alone and would therefore require some form of intervention. Intervention, however, would likely spark some sort of international interference that could potentially prevent India from accomplishing its objective and also cast India as a bully. Therefore, India covertly concentrated on the command and control of Mukti Bahini's efforts, ensuring that the proxy did not engage in atrocities that would provide outsiders with an excuse to stop a case of impending secession. India's covert support and tight rein on Mukti Bahini ensured that Pakistan would appear to have started the conflict and avoided any impetus for other states to intervene to stop East Pakistan's secession. India's attention to how Mukti Bahini pursued secession contributed to India's ability to help wrest East Pakistan away from Islamabad's span of control.

A final point regarding coherence is that all five elements demand significant consideration about *how* a proxy accomplishes specific tasks rather than simply *whether* it accomplishes those tasks. This relates to the popular dictum "win the battle and lose the war." An intervening state does not have the luxury to make an isolated assessment of how its proxy's efforts affect each arena individually; they all have an influence on the others, and interveners should work hard to forecast the effects of proxy actions across different arenas. The intricacies of proxy war and the importance of how different objectives are achieved mean that the coherence of the policy is strongly connected to an intervening state's ability to control its proxy.

Control
Control refers to the intervening state's ability to direct and coordinate the support to, and the actions of, its proxy. To gain complete control,

an intervening state would have to become so deeply entrenched in the conflict that it would likely be more effective for the state to use its own forces and thus obviate the need for a proxy in the first place. The proxy, on the other hand, lacks the resources and influences to achieve its desires alone and must therefore cede some degree of its autonomy to the intervening state. Control is tricky, however, because it relies so heavily on the alignment of an intervener's and its proxy's objectives. Making matters even more complicated, an intervening state's efforts to support a proxy can compromise the state's ability to control it; if the proxy believes it has the capability to pursue its own desires, it most likely will. In a principal-agent relationship, both parties are self-interested and only grudgingly give up the autonomy to drive efforts toward their desired end.[70] The real challenge in this area stems from the fact that each side, in one way or another, needs the other.

Military efforts to achieve political objectives and/or increase the leverage with which to bargain in a particular target state require the use of disciplined and restrained violence. Using James Fearon's idea that war is a means of bargaining, the use of a proxy could be considered as a way of gaining leverage.[71] In the end, the intervening state would rather negotiate than commit its own forces and engage in a war. Leverage, however, has to entice the target state to negotiate; a proxy run amok and committing atrocities would likely have the opposite effect. The use of a proxy, more specifically the ability to control the proxy's actions in combat, must be weighed against the use of the intervening state's own forces.

In the armed forces of most modern states, discipline and obedience provide the means to control large numbers of personnel and coordinate them toward a common purpose or action. Discipline ensures that members of the force act in the desired way and minimizes the chance that fear will dictate behavior. Obedience ensures that members stay true to goals of the state, even when it means that an individual must sacrifice his or her life to help accomplish the state's desires. For those in command, disciplined and obedient forces mean control. That control and the ability to restrain violence when necessary, however, fall apart without discipline and obedience.

The need for control in proxy war is no different than the need for control in any other type of conflict, yet the barriers to control are significantly different. Because a proxy is somewhat disconnected from the intervening state's interests and does not share a common identity, a divide exists between what each party desires. The intervening state provides the means to use violence and intends it to accomplish some objective; the proxy, however, does the lion's share of the fighting and dying but is required to put the intervener's interests before its own desires. For these reasons, intervening states and their proxies are not allies or partners—there is no loyalty or affiliation beyond two actors brought together through mutual need and some overlap in intention. The proxy is not fighting for the intervener's cause, and the intervener is not necessarily wedded to the proxy's cause. The distance an intervening state maintains in its vicarious participation in the conflict helps it maintain its focus on the need for disciplined and restrained violence during the conflict. The proximity of the proxy to the conflict means it is more likely to get emotionally involved in the conflict and has significantly more at stake. The differences in the stakes and desired outcomes for each party highlights why control plays such an important role in proxy war.

Above all else, an intervening state intending to engage in a proxy war must assess its ability to control its proxy and limit its objectives commensurate with that ability. Thinking in terms of control enables an intervening state to focus on how best to engage with its proxy. To guide this thinking, three general factors underpin an intervening state's ability to control its proxy: *objective compatibility*, *the proxy's capacity for autonomy*, and *the proxy's resource dependence*. Each factor should be fully understood prior to engaging in a proxy war and carefully managed during its conduct. Understanding how these three conditions affect the relationship between an intervening state and its proxy determines the level of participation and the degree of support required to accomplish the desired objectives.

Three accompanying maxims enable a better understanding of the three identified factors and guide the execution of such a difficult endeavor as proxy. The first maxim is *know your enemy, but know your proxy even better*. Initially, the most important aspect of this maxim is assessing the degree to which the intervener's objectives are compatible with the proxy's. If the policy calls for more ambitious objectives than the conditions warrant, then the intervening state must consider employing more robust control mechanisms and risk being drawn deeper into the conflict. Knowing your proxy, however, goes much deeper and includes an understanding of the type of conflict the proxy is fighting (ethnic, ideological, or some combination of the two), the proxy's motives and objectives, and the extent of its connections to outsiders (diasporas, religious or ethnic affiliations, etc.). The second maxim, *let the proxy lead, but only so far*, addresses issues connected to a proxy's self-interest and its autonomy. Autonomy must be managed carefully because of proxy self-interest; if able, the proxy will naturally tend to apply resources toward its own ends—a phenomenon that increases as autonomy increases. The third maxim is *cultivate proxy dependence*. This maxim highlights the critical relationship between a proxy's resource dependence and an intervener's ability to gain and maintain control over its proxy. The desire to survive *and* attain its own objectives will drive a proxy to find additional means and resources. If an intervening state provides an excess of resources or a proxy finds external sources of support, it will use the excess to achieve its own ends. If an intervening state carefully manages donated resources to prevent overages and actively prevents a proxy from obtaining outside sources of support, it has the best opportunity to maintain control of its proxy.

As mentioned previously, there are some things in an intervention an intervening state can control and some things it cannot. In addition, there are many things for which it is extremely difficult to prepare—the adversary gets a vote, the fog and friction of war, imperfect information, and so on. Adding the complexities and uncertainty of a proxy makes the job of an intervening state that much more difficult; knowing how to control a proxy mitigates some of that difficulty. The remainder of this section will derive in further detail the connection between an intervening state's three primary sources of control and the maxims presented in the previous paragraph designed to help guide control efforts.

OBJECTIVE COMPATIBILITY: KNOW YOUR ENEMY, BUT KNOW YOUR PROXY
EVEN BETTER   Objective compatibility underpins the first of my three
proxy war maxims: *know your enemy, but know your proxy even better.*
Knowing your proxy includes an understanding of the type of conflict
(ethnic, ideological, or some combination of the two), the proxy's motives
and objectives, and the extent of its connections to outsiders (diasporas,
religious or ethnic affiliations, etc.). Intervening states should limit their
objectives to a degree commensurate with their lack of knowledge and
understanding of the proxy and the degree to which the objectives on
both sides diverge. If the policy calls for more ambitious objectives than
the conditions warrant, then the intervening state must employ more robust control mechanisms and risk being drawn deeper into the conflict.

A proxy war policy demands an in-depth study of a proxy's motivations. Be wary of situations where an intervening state and its proxy have
convergent objectives in only one particular area; this can lead to a quick
decision for short-term gains and can result in long-term losses. A state
must realistically evaluate its objectives and compare those to the objectives of its proxy; objectives are not likely attainable with an uncooperative proxy. The more closely those objectives are aligned, the more likely
that costs are going to decrease because it allows less stringent control
and monitoring measures, lowers the possibility that a proxy will pursue
methods or means that can harm the intervening state's interests, and
makes bargaining more feasible.

If the proxy's objectives closely match those of the intervening state,
then costs are likely to be low and benefits high—there is no incentive for
the proxy to cheat, the intervening state does not have to offer incentives
to get the proxy to do something it does not really want to do, and the
intervening state saves the cost of having to implement strict measures to
monitor and control its proxy.

A second aspect of this maxim that goes hand-in-hand with objective
compatibility is the proxy's perception of the intervener's commitment
to the conflict and, more importantly, the proxy's cause. Robert Axelrod
established that trust is only necessary for effective cooperation for short-
term interactions; when interactions will predictably occur over the long

term, then those involved realize they stand a much better chance of getting what they want when they cooperate.[72] Proxy war, however, is typically a short-term endeavor, and those externally involved are never going to match the commitment of individuals who will remain in the region long after the intervener has left.

A third aspect of this maxim is answering the question of how well an intervening state knows and understands its proxy. What is the proxy fighting for? What has pushed the parties involved to resort to violence? The greater the divide, the more likely that misperception and poor communication will drive the relationship. Another aspect along this line of thinking that an intervening state should also be aware of is the tendency to believe that undesirable behavior is based on the actor's motives rather than attribute the behavior to the conditions under which the behavior occurred.[73] An intervener should get to know its proxy and its proxy's relationship with the surrounding environment. Lastly, an intervener should understand how the proxy perceives the relationship. A decision maker not only needs to understand the adversary, he or she needs to understand how the adversary sees them.[74] This applies to proxies as well. As an intervener, you should know how your proxy thinks about you. What does the proxy believe you are fighting for? Understanding a proxy's doubts can spawn efforts to mitigate those concerns and inspire more confidence in the proxy—a behavior that should engender greater control.

PROXY AUTONOMY: LET THE PROXY LEAD, BUT ONLY SO FAR   On the surface, autonomy in a proxy seems like a fantastic trait. The intervening state gets what it wants without having to get involved beyond providing the means; it's like getting an army without having to supply the people. This idea and the relationship between proxy autonomy and an intervening state's ability to maintain control of its proxy leads to my second maxim: *let the proxy lead, but only so far.* In most cases, a proxy must be able to fight and win. A capable proxy that has the ability to lead its movement/forces and engage an adversary with relatively minimal assistance ensures that an intervening state can minimize the material costs of its involvement. The main objective of a proxy war, however, is rarely to minimize material expenses. Because the proxy is self-interested, it will naturally tend to apply resources toward its own ends; this phenomenon increases as autonomy increases. Therefore, autonomy must be managed carefully. The greater the divergence in objectives, the more likely the proxy's operations will drift away from the intervening state's desired outcome.

As mentioned in Chapter 2, war by proxy requires the creation of a hierarchical structure between an intervening state and an actor selected to serve as a proxy. Both sides will have their own desires and agendas, but the proxy's need for support and the intervening state's ability to provide that support creates a hierarchical relationship that places its desires above those of the proxy. If an intervening state doesn't get what it wants out of the relationship, it usually has the option to take its support elsewhere. An intervening state must understand the dynamics of these challenges—known in social science as the principal-agent problem—to have the best opportunity of successfully executing a proxy war under suboptimal conditions.

Why do two parties enter into a principal-agent relationship? The two main benefits are that both parties share the costs of pursuing perceivably common objectives and each side likely brings a unique set of skills that make attaining those objectives easier and more efficient.[75] In proxy war, an indigenous actor with knowledge of the local language and the ability to blend into the environment may not have adequate resources or skills to accomplish its objectives alone; an intervening state lacking these skills may still be able to accomplish its security objectives but at a significantly higher cost. Acting together, each side improves the chances of achieving their objectives and potentially reduces their costs.

Barriers to control associated with a principal-agent relationship can be broken down into three categories: moral hazard, adverse selection, and Madison's dilemma. Moral hazard refers to the principal's inability to see and understand the actions of its agent. Two ways moral hazard manifests into a barrier are when the agent is shirking (not doing all that was contracted) or doing the task in an undesirable way.[76] A good example of shirking is when Northern Alliance forces (the U.S. proxy in Afghanistan) allowed members of the Taliban and Al Qaeda to escape across the Afghan border into Pakistan. An example of costs associated with undesirable behavior is how Israel's international and domestic costs skyrocketed after its proxy, the South Lebanese Force, summarily executed four hundred Palestinian prisoners and caused Israel's domestic audience to stop supporting the government's efforts.

Adverse selection occurs when the agent does not have the qualities and capabilities it professed to have, and when the principal does not have the expertise necessary to notice.[77] Somalia, for example, used the SALF to help gain control of the Ogaden region. The SALF shared a common ethnicity with a large group of people living in the Ogaden and had been recruited to gain popular support for Somali efforts to reclaim the region. The SALF, however, chose to terrorize the population, preventing the necessary mobilization of the Ogaden people against Ethiopian control.

Madison's dilemma refers to the costs created when "resources or authority granted to an agent for the purpose of advancing the interests of the principal are turned against the principal."[78] Costs stemming from Madison's dilemma are easy to imagine because a state-proxy relationship is often based on convenience rather than deeper ties that promote and sustain amity between the two actors. Uganda's and Rwanda's support for the AFDL provides an excellent example of this phenomenon. Uganda and Rwanda had terrible relations with President Mobutu in neighboring Zaire. When Mobutu ordered ethnic Tutsis to leave Zaire, Uganda and Rwanda decided to support AFDL with advisors, weapons, and some of their own regular forces under the leadership of Laurent Kabila. Kabila succeeded, renamed the country the Democratic Republic of the Congo (DRC), and initially maintained strong ties to Uganda and Rwanda. Once in power, Kabila began to have problems similar to those of Mobutu; the Congolese wanted the Tutsis out. Within a year, Kabila pushed the Tutsis out and tacitly allowed the genocide of Tutsis living in eastern Congo to stay in power. Uganda and Rwanda threw their support behind another proxy, the RLC.[79] In this case, however, the proxy had to fight a stronger and better-equipped group under Kabila. In the end, both Uganda and Rwanda were sanctioned by the international community for their actions, and Kabila remained in power.

Having a proxy that can lead is desirable, but it requires limits. An intervening state must cultivate its proxy's ability to lead both politically and militarily, while at the same time restricting its proxy's opportunity to lead in areas that can damage or hinder the desired objectives. For example, if an intervening state is open to a negotiated settlement, the intervening state should not allow its proxy to participate or lead negotiations. Further, the intervening state should ensure that it has the control necessary to prevent the proxy from committing some atrocity that makes it impossible for the adversary to settle.

RESOURCE DEPENDENCE: CULTIVATE PROXY DEPENDENCE   The third maxim, *cultivate proxy dependence*, highlights the necessity of a proxy's resource dependence. A proxy must be able to fight and win. How well it fights is often a function of resources, and intervening states often make the mistake of thinking the best way to support its proxy is to provide it with the means necessary to win. The point here is that a proxy capable of winning a war against its adversary does not necessarily keep an intervening state's support costs to a minimum or allow it to achieve its desired objectives. A proxy's desire to survive *and* attain its own objectives will drive it to find additional resources. If an intervening state provides an excess of resources, a proxy will use that excess to achieve its own ends. If an intervening state carefully manages donated resources to prevent overages, the proxy will pursue outside sources of support. Isolation can have a significant impact; a proxy that is too isolated—geographically and socially—to establish and/or capitalize on outsides sources of support is easier to control. For these reasons, a proxy's dependence must be cultivated and managed in a way that promotes control and capability simultaneously.

An intervening state must balance efforts to support and control its proxy. Too much support and the proxy may become too independent, a condition that likely leads to greater self-interest, higher costs, and less control. Too little support and the proxy may fail to accomplish the intervening state's objectives. Overcontrolling the proxy may lead the state to overcommit and lose the benefits of using a proxy—the option no longer carries the benefits of an indirect approach. Undercontrolling the proxy may lead the state's proxy to find other ways to sustain or support its efforts; it may also allow the proxy to engage in activities that undermine the intervening state's interests. Knowing how much support and control is needed requires a great deal of insight about the target state, the proxy, the intervening state's role in the international system, and the intervening state's domestic public. Admittedly, an accurate and unbiased understanding of those four factors is difficult, but engaging in proxy war without that understanding could prove disastrous.

SUMMARY

A coherent policy emphasizes the aspects that enable an intervener to maintain control of its proxy. Control ensures that the proxy's efforts do not detract from an intervener's desired intentions in the target state or cause conflicts with the audiences that could have a negative influence on an intervener's policy. Strategists, therefore, must pay particular attention to conditions that may cause conflict between efforts to formulate and sustain policy coherence with efforts to maintain control over a proxy. The means with which the proxy can most easily accomplish a particular task may have negative effects both inside and outside the target state. Supplying the proxy with more costly or more potent means can strain the intervening state's ability to maintain coherence and control. For example, China supported the Pathet Lao in the mid-1950s in response to growing U.S. influence in Laos. China initially supported Pathet Lao activities but did not want those activities to escalate the conflict based on Beijing's relatively weak position. When the Pathet Lao took control of a significant U.S. outpost in Laos (Nam Tha) in 1962, the Chinese curtailed its support in hopes of spurring further U.S. intervention. Instead of increasing the numbers of weapons or military support, China pushed Mao's revolutionary model on the Pathet Lao as the primary means to take control of the country; the Pathet Lao rejected this model because of its poor fit among the diverse groupings of Laotian people. What the Pathet Lao wanted was the ability to militarily defeat its opponents, so it turned to the government in Hanoi, which offered military support in exchange for protecting supply routes running between North and South Vietnam.[80] China's proxy policy failed because it lacked the coherence to connect how its support would contribute to its ability to both control and sustain the Pathet Lao's efforts. Coherence and control are inextricably linked—one often affects the other. Understanding these two aspects individually, however, is a critical step to creating a better policy overall.

The guidance offered in this chapter provides a conceptual framework with which to formulate a general proxy war policy and emphasizes the need to take the actions necessary to sustain that policy for the duration of the conflict. The argument proposed here is that coherence and control in proxy war are a necessity. In the same way that policy deliberations regarding proxy war (presented in the previous chapter) should revolve around three different audiences—the proxy, the domestic, and the international—so should the concept of coherence and control. Each different audience and each condition has the potential to create synergies and barriers.

A coherent policy takes into account what an intervening state wants and how it wants its proxy to accomplish those desires—the method of accomplishment significantly affects coherence. At the international and domestic levels, there are reasons pushing a state to engage in a proxy war, many of which were presented in the previous chapter. External connections—even if they come from the intervener's own population—can challenge a proxy war policy's coherence. In addition, the behavior of the proxy can disrupt the policy's coherence at international and domestic levels. In many cases, a proxy requires a tight leash, especially in situations where the connection between the intervener and its proxy is completely overt.

At the proxy level, the convergence or divergence of the intervener's and its proxy's objectives provides a necessary baseline for what is possible or impossible. Further, an intervening state must manage the support it gives to its proxy to keep efforts moving in the intended direction. In many cases, a hands-off approach would make an intervener's policy more effective with regard to domestic and international audiences but would likely lose coherence as the proxy used the provided resources to pursue its own ends. This is why control is so inextricably linked to coherence.

Agency theory aptly describes the *proxy-specific* conditions that are most conducive to a proxy war policy. A highly capable proxy with similar objectives that remains dependent on the intervening state for support favors an intervening state's ability to maintain control and increases the likelihood of sustaining a coherent policy across all three audiences. Although a proxy may be capable, it may lack certain resources to enable its activities; this is how capability and dependence differ. Therefore, an intervening state must carefully manage support and dependence—a sustainable proxy war policy requires the right mix of each to ensure that the proxy can accomplish the necessary tasks and does so in a fashion that does not get in the way of the intervener's intentions.

At a minimum, if the proxy's objectives closely match those of the intervening state, there is no incentive for the proxy to cheat, the intervening state does not have to offer incentives to get the proxy to do something it does not really want to do, and the intervening state saves the cost of having to implement strict measures to monitor and control its proxy. This, however, rarely happens. A high level of proxy dependence provides the means to control a proxy and counteract the negative effects of having divergent objectives. In such a case, proxy autonomy should be as high as possible. If not, then the resources required to reduce proxy autonomy are worth it—these measures will be discussed in further detail in the next chapter. Ultimately, states must continually think about how to sustain coherence and control throughout the conflict.

CHAPTER 5

AMERICA'S PROXY WAR IN LAOS

THE PATH TO PROXY WAR

Following France's defeat at Dien Bien Phu, the Geneva Conference convened and led to the creation and signing of the Geneva Accords on July 21, 1954. The Accords split the country of Vietnam at the 17th parallel, required communist forces to leave the countries of Laos and Cambodia, and required free elections in the following year. The accords directed the establishment of a coalition government in Laos that included all political parties: conservative, neutral, and communist. The accords opened the door for communist influence, giving two northern provinces—Phong Saly and Sam Neua—to the communist Pathet Lao.

As the communist threat increased in the years following World War II, the United States started its strategy of containment—to keep communist forces hemmed in and prevent a communist wave from overwhelming weak states in the Third World.[1] Following the armistice on the Korean peninsula, America's concerns about communist expansion meant that Laos, a small and landlocked country with little infrastructure and difficult terrain, posed a significant threat to U.S. interests in Southeast Asia. The United States feared that the fledgling country might fall to communist expansion and that should Laos fall, the remainder of Southeast Asia would follow shortly thereafter.[2] The Eisenhower administration worried that a coalition government, as mandated by the Geneva

Accords, would have negative effects on the administration of President Ngo Dinh Diem in South Vietnam.[3] The situation in Laos did not create an existential threat to the United States. Washington had no illusion of creating a strong partner, economically and militarily, in Laos. Instead, the Eisenhower administration looked at the conditions on the ground and elected to limit America's involvement to denying communist efforts to claim a country that could pose a serious threat to America's strongest ally in the region, Thailand.

The primary political aim of the Royal Lao Government (RLG) from 1954 to 1958 centered on reunification and incorporating the Pathet Lao into the government rather than thwarting communist expansion. American interest in Laos focused on preventing communism from taking root and spreading uncontrollably to the rest of the region. Conversely, the Soviet Union, China, and North Vietnam all supported the expansion of communist ideology throughout the region.

The accords explicitly prevented Washington—or any other country—from sending armed forces into Laos. Although the United States did not sign the accords, it acknowledged its desire to avoid overtly breaking them. Washington wanted to make sure it had the latitude to continue its fight against the spread of communism in Southeast Asia, but also desired to avoid damaging its relationship with Britain and France.[4] Instead, Washington flooded Laos with money to bolster the country's economy and strengthen the RLG's domestic support against communist advances.[5] The infusion of aid, however, only fueled elite corruption and increased the Lao people's enmity for its government.[6]

Inside Laos, widespread distrust between the different ethnic groups and the lack of meaningful connections in terms of communication and transportation prevented the formation of a singular effort to keep communist forces at bay.[7] The situation in Vientiane proved equally divisive, which resulted in the development of three separate factions. The conservative faction, made up of social elites controlling most of the country's wealth and power, wanted to maintain control of the RLG. The elites strongly opposed communism and rejected the mandate within the Geneva Accords that required the inclusion of all political parties in the government. The communist faction—the Pathet Lao—followed a Marxist-

Leninist ideology, rejected the elites' self-proclaimed right to rule Laos, and sought political and economic reform. The neutral faction, largely consisting of lower-class elites heavily involved in politics and government, believed it could solve the political problems in Laos without foreign assistance or intervention through a policy of national reconciliation that addressed the grievances between the haves and have-nots.[8]

Despite American warnings about the extreme likelihood of communist subversion, the RLG in Vientiane believed that there was nothing to fear from the Pathet Lao because they were "Laotians first and Communists afterward."[9] The free elections held in 1958, however, saw nine of the twenty-one available seats in the national government go to the political wing of the Pathet Lao and four to its allies in the neutral faction.[10] This greatly concerned the Eisenhower administration and led to increased efforts to strengthen the conservative faction.

In 1959, U.S. support enabled the right-wing faction led by Phoumi Nosavan to gain control of the RLG from the neutral Souvanna Phouma and declare that Laos had fulfilled its commitment to the Geneva Accords and "was no longer bound by its provisions." The RLG directed the Royal Lao Army (RLA) to purge members of the Pathet Lao from the state's armed forces, imprison the leader of the Pathet Lao political organization, and declare the Pathet Lao illegal.[11] In response to this order, the Pathet Lao organized its forces and launched an offensive against the RLG.[12] Immediately, Vientiane claimed that Hanoi had sent forces to support the Pathet Lao, but further evidence failed to confirm the claim. The United States did, however, believe that the Pathet Lao had received both moral and materiel support for the attacks and that those accusations would raise ample motivation to boost American support.[13]

In August 1960, RLA captain Kong Le seized control of the RLG from Nosavan in a successful coup d'état and subsequently reinstated the neutralist Souvanna Phouma. The United States tacitly accepted the change in government but continued to agitate for a noncommunist agenda in Vientiane by continuing to support Nosavan's military activities against the RLG. This drove Phouma to entreat with the Pathet Lao and seek assistance from Peking and Moscow. America's efforts pushed the RLG away from its desired direction.[14]

To prevent superpower confrontation, the states interested in the conflict in Laos signed a new set of accords in 1962. The new Geneva Accords reaffirmed the objective of maintaining Laos's neutrality, removed Laos from the protection of the Southeast Asia Treaty Organization (SEATO) Treaty, and charged that all states were to refrain from intervening in Laos's affairs.[15] The RLG returned to politically neutral footing under the leadership of Phouma, which did little to assuage U.S. concerns about the communist threat.

Between 1961 and 1975, the political situation in Laos remained relatively static. The neutral faction stayed in control of the RLG because Hmong and Thai irregular forces kept the Pathet Lao occupied in northern Laos. The RLG and RLA refused to commit themselves wholeheartedly to upholding democracy and fighting against the Pathet Lao. As the Vietnam War ended, U.S. interest in Indochina waned and the Americans began a slow withdrawal from Laos. Despite U.S. assistance, the RLG failed to gain adequate public support, ultimately causing its defeat at the hands of the North Vietnamese and the Pathet Lao. The communist wave, however, stalled and Thailand sustained its connection with the United States.

What Were the Barriers to Direct Intervention and Nonintervention?
Still keenly aware of its failure to keep China out of the Korean War and concerned about the rapid escalation that would occur should Americans directly confront Soviet forces, Washington avoided getting directly involved in Laos.[16] For the United States, nonintervention was not an option. Both Dwight Eisenhower and John F. Kennedy were staunch anticommunists committed to containing any communist threat.[17] Although military advisors such as Admiral Arleigh Burke recommended direct U.S. involvement, the strategic situation in Laos did not support getting overtly bogged down in a landlocked country devoid of a competent military and plagued with little infrastructure or access.[18] From an international perspective, the Geneva Accords of 1954 did not afford the United States the ability to get directly involved without exposing itself to strong international criticism. France and Great Britain both pushed for a neutralist and nonmilitary solution. China's and North Vietnam's

proximity to Laos offered both countries easy access. Based on these issues, the United States elected to intervene indirectly.

Indirect intervention, especially using a policy of donating assistance, proved troublesome. The RLG refused to acknowledge the need to protect itself from the rising threat of communism during the first four to five years of the conflict. Most Lao statesmen maintained a neutral stance and remained committed to the idea that the danger associated with the Pathet Lao was an internal matter.[19] Without sufficient support from Lao political leaders, U.S. efforts to strengthen the RLG's capacity and credibility within Laos failed to produce positive results.

Washington faced the difficult task of supporting a government that did not perceive any danger from the Pathet Lao and remained unwilling "to shed blood in its own defense."[20] Both the Eisenhower and Kennedy administrations viewed the RLG and Laotians in general with contempt.[21] Considering the difficult political and geographical terrain surrounding an intervention in Laos, the Eisenhower administration elected to forgo deploying its own forces.[22] Instead, the initial policy involved donating assistance to the sitting government in Vientiane, and then later to right-wing factions when Phouma's neutralist government refused to cooperate with the United States. The neutralist stance and the reluctance of the RLG also denied the RLA the leadership it needed to provide an effective defense force against communist advances.[23]

The situation on the ground in Laos made implementing the policy untenable. Although the State Department, the Defense Department, and the CIA were all committed to "preventing a communist takeover, diplomats, military officers, and intelligence operatives often proposed and pursued contradictory actions in the field. The culmination of US disunity occurred in the second half of 1960, when officials in Vientiane, the DoS, and the pentagon and CIA HQ held three different viewpoints about policy in Laos." They were working against each other, and "by the time a more defensible policy emerged, covert American military trainers were combatants in Laos, the USSR was directly engaged in the conflict, and the US was propping up a politically weak, militarily incompetent government."[24]

Indirect intervention did, however, provide some preliminary advantages. Although the use of international norms to defend U.S.

involvement did not prevent outside states from intervening and escalating the conflict, it did arguably reduce the degree of escalation. China refused to fight directly and only sent its forces to protect Chinese personnel sent to build roads. The Soviet Union predominantly stayed on the sidelines until the late 1950s. The corruption of the RLG and the elites' tendency to abscond with U.S. funds intended to build public support, however, negated the potentially beneficial effect and led Washington to abandon its policy of donating assistance.

Why Did the United States Choose a Proxy War Policy?

Although the conflict in Laos contained some ethnic issues, it was predominantly an ideological conflict. Conservative, neutralist, and communist factions all maintained different ideologies about how Laos should be governed.

Concerns about Soviet and Chinese involvement kept the United States from intervening directly. Donating assistance to the RLG to keep communist influence at bay, however, also backfired. Although the policy of donated assistance enabled Nosavan's right-wing government to take a strong anticommunist stance to replace Phouma's neutralist government, Nosavan damaged the RLG's appeal to Laos's diverse population. The corruption of the RLG and the Lao elites' tendency to abscond with U.S. funds intended to build public support negated Washington's hope of engendering widespread public support. Nosavan's conservative government failed to establish political control in non–Pathet Lao areas and foster the support and leadership necessary to enable the RLA to defend against the Pathet Lao and NVA regulars. Making matters worse, Le's successful coup and his reinstatement of Phouma returned the RLG to a neutral stance.[25]

The United States hoped that secretly bolstering the Lao economy with outside funds would generate enough support for the RLG that it could stop Pathet Lao advances on its own. In addition, Washington took the necessary action to install a conservative government in Vientiane to curb support for the Pathet Lao and to provide better justification for expanded U.S. involvement. After Nosavan and Boun Oum ousted Phouma, the RLG formally requested support. The situation intensified when the

Soviet Union began conducting air support operations to assist communist forces.[26] Admiral Harry D. Felt, commander in chief of the Pacific Fleet, and Admiral Arleigh Burke, chief of naval operations, feared Laos would soon fall to the communists and advised an American response.[27]

The perception of increasing pressure from the Soviet Union and the failure of the policy of donating assistance to produce a regime in Vientiane that could unite the Laotian people and forestall communist influences led the United States to change its policy of simply donating assistance.[28] In 1959, the United States started Operation White Star; its mission initially focused on using American special forces personnel to train RLA units to fight the Pathet Lao. After two years, poor leadership in the RLA ranks led Washington to adapt White Star into a training mission for indigenous tribal groups.[29]

Based on French experience during the Indochina War, the CIA knew the Hmong were natural warriors. The French described the Hmong as a mountain tribe "known for their martial spirit, courage and dedication to the protection of their region."[30] The French began formally training Hmong tribesmen during the French-Indochina War.[31] The Hmong (also called Meo at the time), a culturally remote, politically ostracized, Lao Sung tribal group living on the mountaintops of northern Laos, became an obvious choice. The Hmong clans were a tough, resilient people living in the heart of the communist-controlled areas of northern Laos. Hmong soldiers were familiar with the region and proved particularly adroit at operating within its dense jungles and rough terrain.[32]

The Hmong, a territorial people politically isolated from Vientiane and the lowland Lao, abhorred central authority and the notion of being subjected to the control of the Lao Lum (lowland Lao); the feeling was mutual on both sides. Phouma distrusted the Hmong forces. These animosities, as well as a dearth of leadership, precluded the RLG from controlling Hmong forces. Further, direct contact with U.S. personnel added tremendously to Hmong morale and provided additional encouragement that the cause for which they were fighting would not be subjugated to the desires of the RLG.[33]

Unlike the RLG and RLA, the Hmong would enable the United States to extend its influence in Laos and halt communist advances.[34]

Considering the other available options, especially among a largely pacific, Buddhist population, the Hmong—an animist, warrior culture—were an obvious favorite. Emphasizing the danger communists posed to the Hmong way of life, the CIA persuaded a significant number of the Hmong clans to ally themselves with the United States to defend Laos from the Pathet Lao and the North Vietnamese.[35] The CIA created a Hmong paramilitary program under the rubric of Operation White Star that involved "recruiting, training, and directing a tribal army."[36]

The only resources the Hmong needed to compete with the enemy were weapons, mobility assets, logistical supplies, and close air support. Hmong soldiers were sent to Thailand for training in guerrilla warfare tactics, to learn how to use modern weapons and radios. By 1963, "the CIA had instituted a vigorous, Thailand-based, offense-oriented paramilitary training program for [the Hmong]."[37] The CIA's efforts produced a thirty-thousand-man irregular army, ten thousand of which were organized into Special Guerrilla Units.[38] The Hmong could infiltrate areas behind enemy advances and inflict heavy losses as communist forces executed their seasonal retreats.[39] Although U.S. forces were undoubtedly better trained, equipped, and disciplined, their inability to speak the language and blend into the surroundings would have made it difficult and costly to operate in Laos. Supporting Hmong forces, however, required a significant effort that relied heavily on American air power.

COHERENCE

The initial U.S. policy of pursuing indirect intervention through the method of donating assistance in Laos failed because of the reluctance and corruption of Lao elites entrenched in the RLG and the incoherence of the departments and agencies implementing U.S. policy.[40] Although the stakes did not warrant direct intervention, the desire to prevent Laos from falling to the communist Pathet Lao led the United States to continue its indirect intervention, yet shift its policy to proxy war.

The primary U.S. objective was to tie up communist forces in Laos to protect Thailand. Washington desired to circumvent the restrictions listed in the Geneva Accords to influence the outcome of the intrastate conflict in Laos, yet prevent any damage to the United States' reputation abroad. U.S. policy had to negate the internal pressure from the Pathet Lao and limit the effects of external support from the Soviet Union, China, and North Vietnam. Domestically, decision makers did not believe that the American people had the desire to commit to a direct intervention, and Congress did not see the need to support efforts against communist expansion in Laos.

Because of the circumstances discussed earlier, the United States shifted its strategy from attempting to cooperate and co-opt the RLG to co-opting the Hmong. The Hmong could not match NVA regulars supporting the Pathet Lao, leading the United States to engage in unconventional warfare to harass communist forces.

How Did the United States Ensure Coherence and What Was the Overall Effect?

The delicate situation in Laos and the growing communist presence in Southeast Asia challenged the United States' ability to maintain a consistent, coherent policy. After nearly ten years, senior White House officials in 1964 were still uncertain of what the U.S. policy in Laos aimed to achieve.[41] Ultimately, the United States sought to minimize its commitment to the conflict in Laos, seeking to hold back communist advances without committing U.S. forces or getting the U.S. drawn in so deeply that it could not get out without incurring heavy costs to its prestige and reputation. More specifically, the United States wanted to disrupt Pathet Lao's hold on Lao territory and avoid the appearance of "the American giant dominating and controlling events in neutralized Laos."[42]

North Vietnam refused to comply with the newly established accords. Instead, Washington and Hanoi continued to operate covertly in Laos and engage overtly in a battle of rhetoric about the exploits of the other side's activities.[43] Washington wanted to show that it was not immobilized by Hanoi's political campaign and was determined to use other options that would minimize the neutralizing effects of the Geneva Accords.[44]

INTERNAL COHERENCE   One of the most important ways the United States sustained the internal coherence of its proxy war policy was to keep the objective limited to a holding action. In 1967, Washington rejected requests to expand involvement. Ambassador William H. Sullivan outlined the conditions that warranted an expansion of the war in Laos: when "our war effort in Vietnam would be substantially helped; the security of Thailand and of presently held territory in North Laos would be significantly enhanced, or our relations with the RLG would be significantly enhanced, or that our failure to support expansion in North Laos would result in substantial deterioration in our relations."[45] Later in the conflict, the United States also rejected Hmong requests to expand the war. For example, Sullivan rejected repeated requests by Vang Pao, the Laotian leader of the Hmong irregular forces, to reclaim the Plain of Jars and refused to supply arms and send forces to protect an area south of Sam Neua because he saw "the commitment to support the villagers involved as an excessive burden."[46]

The United States managed to provide the necessary resources without revealing the degree of its involvement and sustained its desire to limit U.S. commitment. The United States avoided having to overtly acknowledge its support of the Hmong until the latter half of 1969 and refused to put itself in a position where it would have to commit an undesirable amount of resources or personnel to protect its proxy. Although rescue assets were instructed to assist Hmong forces when necessary, the number of casualties the Hmong suffered reflects the U.S. desire to avoid getting too committed in Laos.[47] As CIA station chief Douglas Blaufarb suggests in his previously classified study of U.S. involvement, "the unconventional military effort of the U.S. in Laos, although inconclusive, thus achieved a significant part of its goals at a relative low cost."[48] At home, the substantial opposition to the war in Vietnam later overshadowed the war in Laos, but the covert character of operations in Laos prevented the American public from limiting the U.S. president's ability to act in Laos.

Intrastate Coherence   Supporting the Hmong did not engender support for the RLG. The people living in northern Laos did not witness RLA forces fighting to preserve their lives and property. U.S. support for the Hmong and the RLA's unwillingness to fight only served to further isolate the RLG from the people living in the rural areas of northern Laos. As a result, the RLG was unable to inspire the people to passively join in the fight and make it difficult for Pathet Lao and NVA forces to operate there. U.S. support for the Hmong also failed to inspire the RLG to increase its support of U.S. efforts inside Laos, but it did not inhibit the RLG's tacit approval. The RLG was suspicious and dubious about the U.S. decision to support the Hmong—a group that had traditionally been a problem in the domestic sphere—but it was willing to allow the Hmong to fight on its behalf.[49]

International/Domestic Coherence   The Geneva Accords challenged the international coherence of America's proxy war policy because it did not permit direct military involvement from any country other than France. Political maneuvering, however, created the conditions under which the RLG extended a formal request in 1959 for military assistance from the United States. Vientiane's request provided Washington with a way to justify its involvement.[50] The United States also used the language in Article 6 of the new accords signed in 1962 that permitted military support that "the Royal Government of Laos may consider necessary."[51] The language in Article 6 allowed U.S. assistance and helped sustain the policy's international coherence.

To maintain an internationally coherent policy, the United States continually related the conflict in terms of North Vietnamese aggression and Hanoi's failure to honor the 1962 Geneva Accords. McGeorge Bundy related this part of U.S. strategy as a means of showing the "seriousness of US will and the limited character of US objectives."[52] Bundy also suggested that the United States ought to expose communist aggression in Southeast Asia with the intent to "give worldwide publicity to the basic problem" and to "make it perfectly plain if we move to further action that we had done our best at the UN."[53] America's efforts to justify its involvement did not prevent outside states from intervening and escalating the conflict, but it did arguably reduce the degree of escalation. China refused to fight directly and only sent its forces to protect the personnel sent to build roads. Soviet intervention (predominantly in the form of airlift) mostly ended after the conclusion of the Geneva Accords of 1962.[54]

Because of the contentious aspects of U.S. policy, Washington sought to keep its military involvement as secret and deniable as possible. The arguments for keeping U.S. involvement covert were to keep the Soviets out of Laos and avoid a direct confrontation between U.S. and Soviet forces, prevent the Pathet Lao from gaining control of the government, avoid becoming overly committed to the conflict, and avoid losing the propaganda battle with North Vietnam.[55]

Keeping its involvement secret, Washington minimized the international costs of intervening in Laos's affairs. For example, U.S. exports and foreign direct investment increased significantly throughout the 1960s and 1970s.[56] Keeping the conflict covert denied North Vietnam the ability to enlist widespread international support against U.S. transgressions of the Geneva Accords and gave the Soviet Union and China a reason to remain relatively uninvolved.[57] Although North Vietnam complained of U.S. involvement in Laos, the lack of credible evidence and Hanoi's own involvement seems to have eliminated the international community's will to take formal action.

Supporting the Hmong also seems to have allowed Washington the ability to deny giving Hanoi any rhetorical leverage on the Laos issue. An unnamed U.S. official in Vientiane stated, "If we [acknowledged bombing Laos] . . . every dove in the US would hit us over the head with it like they did with Johnson and the bombing of North Viet Nam. The North Vietnamese don't admit the presence of their 47,000 troops. Why should we give them the advantage of admitting the bombing?"[58] The lack of response from the international community suggests that the United States was justified to intervene in Laos's affairs because it was supporting a recognized belligerent.

North Vietnam, however, was undaunted. Hanoi's willingness to increase the number of its forces in Laos denied the United States the ability to maintain relative superiority. The United States was unable to provide the type and amount of assistance necessary to maintain relative superiority in the battlespace. Undoubtedly, the increasing amount of U.S. air power provided a significant advantage to Hmong forces. Characteristic of air power when used in isolation, the duration of relative superiority was fleeting at best. Despite many tactical victories, Hmong soldiers suffered far too many losses for such a limited, irregular force, an issue that ultimately led to the Hmong's demise and the dwindling efficacy of America's proxy war policy.

Despite the operational failures that prevented America's ability to sustain the proxy war in Laos indefinitely, Bundy's recommendations worked from a strategic perspective. Moscow occasionally accused Washington of intervening in Laos, but those charges never escalated to an attempt at sanctioning the United States in an international forum such as the United Nations. Further, the covert character of U.S. operations provided Moscow with the opportunity to look the other way and stay out of Laos after 1962. For example, William Sullivan testified before the hearing of the Senate Foreign Relations Subcommittee, chaired by Senator Stuart Symington, that

> a senior Soviet official has said that insofar as he reads things in newspapers or hears statements and allegations about US operations, he does not have to take any official cognizance of them. But if they are made directly by US officials he does have to take cognizance of them and this will color, to some extent, the Soviet attitude toward Souvanna Phouma's neutrality and toward the retention of the understanding which underlie the agreement between ourselves and the Soviets for the neutrality of Laos.[59]

Although Senator J. William Fulbright argued that the Soviets would not have gotten involved whether they knew or not, the bottom line is that the Soviets significantly limited support to the Pathet Lao after 1962.[60]

Aside from U.S. efforts to maintain coherence with rhetorical maneuvers related to the Geneva Accords and countering communist advances, Washington also relied heavily on secrecy. Keeping its involvement covert provided several advantages in terms of international coherence, but it also came with limitations. Hanoi steadily increased its support to the Pathet Lao as U.S. efforts strengthened Hmong forces. Although the United States diverted significant air power resources from the war in Vietnam, Hmong forces suffered massive attrition when fighting against North Vietnamese regulars. Each time the Hmong made gains on the

Plain of Jars, North Vietnam responded by sending more of its regular forces into Laos to assist the Pathet Lao. The Hmong proxy in Laos offered the United States only a fig leaf to conceal its involvement, but the lack of any response in the UN Security Council or General Assembly to deliver some form of sanction and the lack of international response based on the reports coming from inside Laos suggest that Hanoi's involvement and the RLG's willing acceptance of U.S. intervention sustained the policy's coherence at the international level.

Before concluding this discussion about the benefits of keeping the proxy war in Laos secret, I first want to establish the degree to which U.S. involvement remained secret. Senator Fulbright stated that neither Congress nor the American public knew what the president was doing in Laos.[61] What Senator Fulbright or other members of Congress knew about U.S. activities in Laos remains obscure. On May 28, 1964, under secretary of state George Ball told President Lyndon Johnson that he had discussed U.S. actions in Southeast Asia with Senator Fulbright and explained that "he is not going to do any talking and wants to do everything that keeps the maximum freedom of maneuver for the President—which distinguishes him from some of his colleagues."[62] After the Symington subcommittee hearing in October 1969, Senator Mike Mansfield told the *Washington Post* that he "didn't learn much from the Laos hearings that he didn't already know." In 1965, President Johnson briefed a bipartisan group of congressional leaders on operations in Southeast Asia. After a brief discussion about covert operations, Senator Russell B. Long interjected that he did not want to hear all the details and that he wanted to avoid being told things he should not know. Secretary of defense Robert McNamara continued the briefing and described U.S. activities in Laos, including the training and deploying of proxy forces into North Vietnam and the use of U.S. aircraft to take out a heavily defended bridge at Ban Ken that the Royal Lao Air Force (RLAF) T-28s were incapable of destroying because of the heavily armed defenses surrounding the bridge.[63]

Regardless of what Senator Fulbright or other senators truly knew, none of the administrations were wholly forthcoming about U.S. involvement. Near the end of the subcommittee hearing, Fulbright complained,

We do not know enough to ask those direct questions, and this is what I meant about quibbling about whether the US role in Laos is exclusively advisory. When you take a group of Senators who are primarily concerned with their own states, and only incidentally in this foreign affairs area, the responsibility for which we are given by the Senate, we do not know enough to ask you these questions unless you are willing to volunteer the information. There is no way for us to ask you questions about things we don't know you are doing.[64]

In his book *War and Responsibility*, Professor John Ely argues that there were also two unstated arguments: to allow the executive to conduct foreign policy without concern for domestic interference and to "still domestic criticism" of U.S. operations in Laos.[65] Blaufarb supports Ely's claim, purporting that the U.S. policy in Laos was guided by the belief that Congress would not likely support the amount of aid required, even though the sum necessary was far lower than many of America's other concerns.[66]

Ely concludes that some members of Congress may very well have known the extent of U.S. involvement in Laos and later feigned surprise to avoid being labeled an accomplice, but "to a significant degree the administration succeeded in maintaining secrecy."[67] In 1968, *Time* released a story about U.S. bombing of the Ho Chi Minh Trail but still maintained that the U.S. was upholding the 1962 Geneva Accords. It was not until September 1969 that the *New York Times* began publishing more extensive reports of U.S. involvement that eventually led to the Symington subcommittee hearings in October. That the information was often based on rumor and publicly denied by the U.S. government significantly diminishes any claim that the U.S. public knew what was going on in Laos.[68]

The United States used several different methods to hide its involvement in Laos from the American public. First, few American forces were sent to Laos, allowing Washington to avoid significant pressure from the press. Second, U.S. military personnel who did participate transferred to different organizations such as the United States Agency for International Development (USAID) or the embassy in Vientiane. Third, the United

States kept correspondents out of Laos for reasons of security, though most observers believed it was for political reasons.[69] In 1970, three correspondents walked from Sam Thong to Long Tieng and were detained, threatened with execution by Vang Pao, and shipped back to Vientiane—all this after U.S. operations in Laos had become more open.[70]

The CIA also took careful measures to avoid congressional scrutiny. First, efforts were made to hide the money being spent on operations in Laos.[71] U.S. domestic laws prevented the General Accounting Office from auditing the CIA's books for most of the war.[72] Second, government officials outside the executive branch and war correspondents were given briefings and were shown glimpses of operations in a manner that represented only half-truths. Fred Branfman overheard James Chandler, the deputy chief of USAID, tell Edgar "Pop" Buell that State's briefing to visiting members of Congress had been a "beautiful snow job."[73] It has also been argued that Long Tieng was purposely called "Alternate" to hide the fact that it was the main staging area for military operations against the Pathet Lao.[74]

Government officials involved in the operations in Laos also helped keep details hidden from Congress. For example, William Sullivan testified before the Symington subcommittee in 1969 that there were no Americans flying bombing missions in Laos, and subsequently failed to recall that testimony a year later.[75] Colonel Robert Tyrell told the Symington subcommittee that pilots had their regular United States Air Force (USAF) identification cards and that they did not fly operational training missions in Laos. Based on more recent evidence, it appears that Tyrell was not telling the truth.[76] Tim Castle, an expert on U.S. operations in Laos, wrote, "The [Ravens] wore civilian clothes, carried USAID identification cards, flew RLAF aircraft, and operated under the direction of the American ambassador in Vientiane."[77] Lieutenant Colonel (ret.) Jerry Klingaman, an Air Commando operating off and on in Laos from 1966 to 1969, described his experience: "The conditions of our operations were a little bit extraordinary, it was a covert operation. I crossed the river into Laos wearing jeans and a jean jacket. I had no uniform, no ID and no Geneva Convention card . . . your weapon was willed to you by the guy that you were replacing."[78]

Domestically, four different presidential administrations kept U.S. involvement in Laos quiet enough to avoid any serious scrutiny; there were virtually no demonstrations, petitions, or marches opposing U.S. action in Laos. Even after finding out about U.S. activities in Laos, or at least having to admit to knowing about U.S. involvement, Congress only upheld President Richard Nixon's decision to avoid committing U.S. ground troops.[79]

Proxy Coherence   With U.S. support, the Hmong managed to disrupt and deter the Pathet Lao and the NVA from expanding their influence much beyond northern Laos. The United States established a system of supporting the Hmong that could easily be terminated. William Sullivan made this point during the Symington subcommittee hearing in 1969, stating, "we used to use as a rule of thumb our ability to make [our presence in Laos] reversible and terminate it within eight hours. It would probably take twenty-four hours now, but it still could be done."[80] Because of a lack of proxy coherence, the United States allowed the Hmong forces to engage in conventional-style combat on the Plain of Jars for over half a decade—a choice that eventually led to the near extinction of Hmong soldiers.

The methods used to support the Hmong proxy enabled the United States to hold back communist expansion in Southeast Asia for almost two decades. The Hmong, with relatively minimal support, steadily proved themselves capable of holding communist forces at bay by standing their ground against NVA regulars when RLA soldiers tended to flee. The Hmong were also familiar with the people living in the region and were used extensively for spotting and identifying Pathet Lao and NVA activity.[81] One drawback was that moving Hmong clans to critical areas created such a high level of dependence that the United States had to create programs to deliver supplies to those remote Hmong outposts. The dependence of the Hmong and the U.S. need for their assistance led Washington to invest in an elaborate air support operation capable of delivering the supplies necessary to sustain the Hmong outposts.[82]

CONTROL

The United States maintained all three elements required to control a proxy. First, like Washington, the Hmong wanted to keep Laos free from communist control. Second, the Hmong were a capable force and with only minimal assistance, making them an even match for the Pathet Lao. Third, the remote and isolated location of Hmong villages combined with their dependence on subsistence farming—an activity made impossible during the conflict—meant that the Hmong heavily depended on the United States for their survival. In addition, the United States became the sole provider for Hmong needs. Although the Hmong came very close to the ideal type proxy mentioned in Chapter 4, the United States did not control its Hmong proxy very well.

The Hmong did have liabilities as a proxy. The Hmong were uninvolved and uninterested in Lao politics. As a result, the RLG gained no credibility with the Lao population based on Hmong efforts to protect its citizens from the violence of the Pathet Lao. Because of cultural (and motivational) issues, the Hmong could never and would never lead the people of Laos. The United States cultivated a proxy solely capable of winning the military aspect of the conflict, a violation of one of Carl Clausewitz's main principles of war that states that the use of force and politics are indubitably and inherently connected.[83]

How Did the United States Use and Control Its Proxy and to What End?

THE COMPATIBILITY OF OBJECTIVES   Although U.S. objectives did not match Hmong desires exactly, they were initially compatible. The Hmong wanted to remain free from a communist government that would destroy their way of life. Unfortunately, the Hmong also wanted to remain clear of lowland Lao politics. As the conflict in Vietnam began to influence the conflict in Laos, the United States began to shift its objectives to shutting down the Ho Chi Minh Trail and interdicting support flowing from North Vietnam across the 17th parallel.

Hindering communist advances in northern Laos, however, suited both America and the Hmong well. Early in the conflict, Vang Pao developed a plan to move two hundred Hmong villages in northern Laos to seven mountain sites surrounding the Plain of Jars, each overlooking a potential enemy supply route.[84] U.S. Special Forces personnel encouraged the move because it would allow more of the Hmong men to join in the fight because they would have fewer responsibilities for providing food and security.[85]

Later in the conflict, the United States encouraged the Hmong clans to move to strategic sites such as Long Tieng and Phou Pha Thi to increase the security of the locations and decrease the size of supply routes. The proximity to conflict had mixed effects. The already aggressive Hmong fought even harder because their families were close to the fighting. The presence of Hmong families in the battlespace, however, also imposed a significant cost. Hmong soldiers, often outnumbered, would fight to the bitter end rather than pursuing the irregular warfare tactic of slipping away to fight another day. The Hmong accepted greater risks and held a lower regard for their own safety due to the proximity of their own families. The result of having Hmong families in the battlespace and within striking range of the Pathet Lao and NVA was that the attrition of Hmong forces sped up; the return on the U.S. investment of training and equipping Hmong soldiers was eclipsed prematurely due to proximity.

During the Pathet Lao and NVA dry-season offensives, Hmong villagers living in the newly captured areas were forced to serve as porters and were subjected to harsh disciplinary measures and intense indoctrination, an added incentive to join forces against the Pathet Lao. In addition, Hmong irregulars hiding among the population could provide useful intelligence during their dry-season advances and inflict losses as they retreated during the rainy season. The Pathet Lao and NVA put an end to this in the late 1960s when they began a scorched-earth policy and began cleaning out the inhabitants in local villages.[86]

The ability of the Hmong forces to stall Pathet Lao and NVA advances and the growing importance of the Ho Chi Minh Trail to the Vietnam War led to a shift in focus and a shift in strategy. Looking through President Johnson's letters during this period, the situation in Laos, once a somewhat independent concern, became completely entangled with the situation in Vietnam after 1965.[87] The irregular war in Laos started to transition into a conventional war to gain control of the Plain of Jars and cut off the Ho Chi Minh Trail.[88] For the remainder of the war, the conventional battle to control the Plain of Jars dominated U.S. policy in Laos.[89]

THE CAPABILITY OF A PROXY   Under the direction of the CIA, the United States provided military training to Hmong forces with the intention of using them to conduct a guerrilla-style war against the Pathet Lao. U.S. advisors were included down to the company level to assist in directing Hmong soldiers in battle. By 1961, the CIA had equipped about 7,700 Hmong soldiers and had created a logistical support network independent from the RLA.[90] Lieutenant Colonel Vang Pao, a Hmong officer in the RLA, quickly established himself as the leader of the Hmong irregular forces and worked diligently to establish a cooperative atmosphere among the Hmong clans loyal to him.[91] As U.S. support and training increased, the Hmong predominantly engaged in harassment operations to avoid the appearance of illegal U.S. support in Laos and to deter Hanoi from increasing its support for the Pathet Lao.

In 1963, after extensive guerrilla warfare training in Thailand, the CIA changed its original plan for Hmong forces and directed them to begin an offensive campaign to free and fortify Hmong villages in northern Laos, and to build airstrips nearby for resupply by Air America.[92] The CIA also started sending Hmong units of ten to twelve men deep into northern Laos and North Vietnam to report on enemy activity and to conduct "harassment raids" on enemy forces, such as "ambushing and destroying enemy trucks, ammunition, and fuel supplies."[93]

Throughout the mid-1960s, the employment of Hmong forces gained a steady rhythm, slowly transitioning from an irregular force aimed at stalling and harassing NVA and Pathet Lao operations to a conventional force bent on capturing and holding territory. U.S. policy, however, denied the Hmong the ability to gain relative superiority in the battlespace. Early Hmong successes suggested that they could force the communists out of northern Laos, but the United States miscalculated Hanoi's response. Hanoi, apparently less concerned about international opinion, increased its support to the Pathet Lao to ensure that they could defeat the Hmong and maintain the security of the Ho Chi Minh Trail. Washington, constrained by the desire to uphold the Geneva Accords, could not sufficiently respond. The United States could not send ground troops or provide equipment to make up for the Hmong's inability to compete with both Pathet Lao and NVA forces. Instead, Washington had to rely almost exclusively on air power.[94]

In 1966, the United States began allocating more strike aircraft for missions in Laos to enhance the ability of Hmong forces to counter Pathet Lao and NVA advances. During each rainy season (June to October), Hmong forces went on the offensive and made substantial gains in territory due to their near-exclusive use of air support. The Pathet Lao and the NVA were dependent on roads to move supplies during this time of year and made easy targets for U.S. warplanes. During the dry season, the Hmong forces retreated in the face of communist offensives supported by better environmental conditions.[95] To assist the Hmong in calling in air strikes, the CIA convinced Washington to station USAF forward air controllers (FACs) in Laos. These pilots, known as the Ravens, flew with Hmong pilots to provide effective and valuable assistance to the Hmong irregulars on the ground.[96]

By 1968, the United States substantially stepped up its air campaign in Laos, dropping more than 350,000 tons of bombs.[97] At this point in the war, Hmong forces had almost completely transitioned to conventional operations. To roll back the Pathet Lao and threaten the communist stronghold in the north, Vang Pao led his Hmong forces onto the Plain of Jars and defeated the communists in a conventional battle. Although this was a huge blow to communist forces, Hanoi responded six months later by sending a second NVA battalion equipped with tanks to defeat Hmong forces and reclaim the Plain of Jars and better defend the Ho Chi Minh Trail. To prevent a communist rout, the United States sent B-52s to stop the enemy's pursuit. Despite the enormous casualties suffered by Hmong forces attempting to gain and hold the Plain of Jars, the United States allowed Vang Pao to retake the plain the following May. After a predictable retreat six months later, the Hmong were spent. Vang Pao's forces had sustained heavy attrition and the commander resorted to calling thirteen- and fourteen-year-old boys into service.[98]

THE DEPENDENCE OF A PROXY ON OUTSIDE SUPPORT   America's ability to control its proxy benefited from the proximity of the fighting to Hmong villages. Considering that Hmong families lived in conflict areas, Hmong forces did not need additional performance incentives. Instead, the United States doled out logistical support—both military and non-combat-related items—based on Hmong needs for survival. The Hmong, emboldened and enabled by U.S. air support, shifted America's concept of operations. Harassment tactics that stalled communist efforts were initially so successful that the United States began to support Hmong desires to drive the communists away from their villages and out of northern Laos. Failing to limit Hmong objectives ultimately led to the demise of America's proxy in Laos.

The escalation of U.S. air operations in 1968 and 1969 increased the refugees receiving USAID support from roughly 130,000 to over 250,000.[99] The depleting numbers of Hmong soldiers and the increasing danger of living in and around the battlespace created a breaking point in 1971. The increased pressure from Pathet Lao and NVA forces and the collateral damage inflicted from American air strikes led Vang Pao to consider moving Hmong tribes to safer areas in northwestern Laos. This concerned the United States because Hmong soldiers would move with their families, leaving little hope of continuing to tie down enemy forces north of Vientiane.[100] The United States convinced Vang Pao to remain and fight, despite depleted numbers.

As Hmong forces dwindled, the United States attempted to backfill them with Thai mercenaries paid by the CIA. Thai soldiers resigned from Thailand's armed forces and received Lao identity cards.[101] Without an increase in U.S. involvement, this move only slowed the inevitable fall of the neutral government in Vientiane. U.S. air support decreased substantially after 1973. By 1975, the war in Vietnam had been lost and the United States withdrew from Laos. Vientiane fell to the Pathet Lao shortly thereafter.

SUMMARY

Considering the conditions present in Laos and their effect on utility and efficacy of America's proxy war policy in Laos, Blaufarb presents an interesting conclusion:

Given these difficulties, the US backed resistance effort from 1962–1970 seems to have been at least a qualified success. As of end 1970, it had achieved its overriding aim of preserving the RLG, and leaving the government in control of most of the populated Mekong lowlands. . . . It implies that the North Vietnamese have been forced to settle for a good deal less in Laos than they would have obtained without the US involvement there, and have paid a considerable price for rather little in the way of progress toward their ultimate objective. A second achievement is that, with many compromises and at considerable cost, the fabric of the Geneva Accords has been precariously preserved.[102]

The incompatibility of the Hmong's political isolation and the need to conduct counterinsurgency operations complicated America's effort to hinder communist advances in Laos. The U.S. decision to use the Hmong as its proxy made it nearly impossible to inspire popular support for the RLG. The conspicuous absence of the RLG in northern Laos prevented Vientiane from providing the protection and services necessary to gain the support of the population. Further, the Hmong only enhanced their autonomy from the RLG because of U.S. support. The RLG never felt compelled to fight for its survival and once the Hmong forces had been exhausted, the United States lost its means to indirectly intervene in the Laotian conflict.

Regardless of the moral implications of encouraging the Hmong to move their families into the battlespace so that more Hmong men could participate in the war, the result was that they fought harder. It also caused the Hmong to sustain higher casualty rates. Guerrilla-style operations require mobility, but families living in the battlespace created anchor points that limited mobility and led the Hmong to fight more pitched battles than they should have.

The focus on the Plain of Jars had a similar effect. The conventional mentality of taking and holding a piece of territory was not conducive to the type of fighting the Hmong could do best, given their limited numbers and the limited support on the ground from the United States. The evidence suggests that the Hmong, lacking familiarity with modern technology and its limitations, were overconfident about the capabilities of the United States. It is possible to think how an immense and over-whelming display of air power could create the illusion that American forces could do anything. It appears that the Hmong may have often overcommitted themselves in the expectation that the United States could prevent them from being overrun.

This case adds a different dimension to the idea of how autonomy relates to costs and benefits. Unlike the literature on principal-agent rela-tionships (see Chapter 2), a low level of autonomy did not correspond to an increase in U.S. monitoring costs. The alignment of U.S. and Hmong objectives—to keep the Pathet Lao from gaining control of northern Laos—reduced concerns that the Hmong would expand their sights be-yond what the United States wanted to support.

The Hmong proxy did provide the U.S. with the benefit of giving those that might be inclined to raise the costs of U.S. involvement the ability to look the other way. Internationally, the Soviets avoided get-ting involved after leaving Laos in 1962. Prominent senators (Symington and Fulbright being the most obvious) avoided having to acknowledge that they knew about U.S. operations. Interestingly, even when U.S. in-volvement became public there was little change to U.S. policy in Laos. It is difficult to explain exactly why this occurred, other than that key members of Congress supported the policy. If that is the case, this point suggests that plausible deniability may make it possible for policies that are considered pragmatic to gain the necessary domestic support, despite violating international law.

When it comes to domestic willingness, this case suggests that a proxy matters more in the sense that it will bear most of the casualties. Most of the discussions focused on concerns about American casualties rather than the amount of material resources the United States had been providing to the Hmong. This point is potentially lessened if supporting a proxy causes the intervening state's people to suffer economically. The fact that the United States had the world's largest economy somewhat obscures this point.

The most important conclusion in this case is how the Hmong's de-pendence on the United States emerged as the predominant condition influencing U.S. utility and efficacy. In this sense, Washington overculti-vated Hmong dependence and created a situation that would inevitably increase U.S. resources and commitment. Although Blaufarb's quote is arguably correct, the strategy could never have served as anything more than a delaying action—leaving the United States with limited options had things gone better in South Vietnam.

America's use of the Hmong as a proxy sustained international and domestic coherence for four reasons. First, because the Hmong were an obscure ethnic group living in a small, remote country, many people did not really know or care about the extent of Hmong losses. Second, Hmong deaths were related to a civil war, an event that many people recognize produces high casualty rates. Third, because the United States kept such tight controls on access to northern Laos and because the North Vietnamese had no desire to publicize the human costs on the Lao population, very little information made its way to international or U.S. domestic audiences. Finally, keeping its involvement secret allowed Washington to avoid having to garner public support or from getting entangled in a conflict from which it could not easily and cheaply disengage. Roland Paul notes,

> As far as a commitment through a general American identification with the Laotian cause, by contrast with Vietnam, the way we have "packaged" our position in Laos has been a classic case of low profile. Until recently the operation was an official secret. This secrecy was regrettable from an American constitutional point of view, and after a time should have ceased, but from the point of view of commitments it avoided the Vietnam type of entanglement. If we had ever been faced with the unfortunate choice between a Laotian capitulation and the dispatch of large numbers of American combat troops, we could have chosen the former and walked away from the situation.[103]

Without having to deploy and sustain its own combat forces in Laos, the United States could conserve a considerable amount of its material and political resources. From a material perspective, installing the force protection measures and the logistic centers necessary to support regular American forces would have almost certainly exceeded the amount of support given to the Hmong over the entire period.[104] Overt deployments almost always include the means necessary to secure and support American armed forces sent abroad.

As a final point, Washington's ability to keep its involvement in Laos secret may not so easily transfer into today's environment. In the 1950s and 1960s it was possible to keep operations secret because of the U.S. ability to restrict access to the theater and the remoteness of northern Laos. In addition, the lack of knowledge of Laos and its people also logically contributed to the ease of keeping operations secret. Advances in communication have likely changed the ability of any government to keep its support for a proxy in another country secret for a significant length of time.[105]

Although policy makers in Washington never overtly admitted their concern that the U.S. public would not support an interventionist policy in Laos,[106] all three presidential administrations took steps to obscure U.S. involvement. Regardless of how much members of Congress knew about the war in Laos, the secrecy of U.S. operations allowed four different presidents to maintain greater latitude and flexibility in their policy because members of Congress could plausibly deny knowledge of U.S. involvement.

When the United States officially acknowledged its involvement in Laos in 1969, Congress did not limit operations in Laos, though it did formally ban the introduction of American forces. The author of the legislation, Senator Frank Church, stated, "We are not undertaking to make any changes in the status quo. The limiting language is precise. And it does not undertake to repeal the past or roll back the present. It looks to the future."[107] The high priority Washington placed on keeping its involvement secret, the restricted access of the press in the battlespace, and the relatively little focus on events within Laos avoided issues related to international support and toleration. The United States did not use its proxy to justify its involvement, and the secrecy of the operation avoided international condemnation. Secrecy, restricted access, and limited emphasis on Laos also prevented actors in the international sphere from pressuring the United States to expand its involvement.

The secrecy of the war in Laos precluded the U.S. government's need to publicly justify its involvement. Although the U.S. government did not overtly justify its involvement based on the Hmong's acceptance of the majority of the burden in terms of personnel and suffering, supporting Hmong forces enabled Washington to forestall public scrutiny because of the relatively low number of American casualties incurred during the conflict.

Once it was revealed that the United States had intervened in Laos, those involved in making and executing policy often justified U.S. involvement based on its small costs in terms of American casualties and resources.[108] The continuation of U.S. involvement for several years after Washington publicly acknowledged its involvement in 1969 suggests that supporting a proxy that shoulders most of the burden, especially in terms of casualties, can help garner and sustain public support for an otherwise unpopular, interventionist policy. Further, this case suggests that the lack of affiliation between the American people and the Hmong fighting in Laos and Washington's justification for its involvement lowered U.S. commitment costs.

How Do My Proposed Maxims Apply to the Intervening State's Use of a Proxy?

KNOW YOUR ENEMY, BUT KNOW YOUR PROXY EVEN BETTER   The United States and the Hmong had overlapping goals. The United States wanted to prevent the spread of communism, especially into the countries of Thailand and South Vietnam. The Hmong were fighting a territorial war, aimed at preserving their freedom, land, and culture.[109] The intersection of American and Hmong goals was keeping the Pathet Lao and the NVA from forcefully taking control of northern Laos. The United States would have liked a proxy that could unite Laos against the communist threat. The Hmong had no interest in politics. This made the Hmong a convenient, but not optimal proxy. Although the United States had access to the elements needed to control its proxy, the limited aims of the Hmong made it a useful but not efficacious proxy. Had Washington understood its proxy and the cultural aspects of the Lao population better, it is possible that some errors could have been avoided.

The people of Laos were both diverse and disconnected. The Lao Lum, the lowland dwellers, made up roughly 30 to 50 percent of the population. Representing the most educated portion of the population, the Lao Lum dominated commerce and politics. Their position in Lao society gave them an elitist perspective and led them to look upon Laos's other ethnic groups as either subordinates or servants. The Lao Tai, the higher-valley dwellers, were a tribal people made up of approximately twelve subgroups. Living in relative isolation in the upland river valleys and plateaus, the Lao Tai managed to exist in relative autonomy, allowing them to mostly avoid urban areas. Unsurprisingly, the geographical separation of the Lao Tai from Laos's urban areas gave them little influence in the country's politics. Even further down the social ladder, the Lao Theung represented the weakest social group in Laos. Characterized as mountainside dwellers, the Lao Theung lacked the ability to exist independently from the other social groups, leading to their domination and exploitation by the Lao Lum and, to a lesser extent, the Lao Tai. The last major Lao ethnic group, the Lao Sung, belonged to a larger ethnic group dispersed throughout Southeast Asia. Within the country, the Lao Sung predominantly lived in the mountains of northern Laos and survived as subsistence farmers and ranchers who raised opium poppies as a cash crop. The Lao Sung were a tribal people who maintained strong regional ties and lived completely outside the influence of the lowland Lao due to poor transportation networks and the nearly impenetrable geography of their homeland.[110] One of the Lao Sung tribes, the Hmong, displayed a strong predilection toward violent behavior and tended to fight with other ethnic groups as well as among themselves.[111] The ideological character of the conflict, however, overwhelmed these divides, but the Hmong were an aggressive people that needed restraint.

The Hmong did not share America's desire to conduct a holding action in Laos. The Hmong wanted their land back, to be free from the Pathet Lao and the RLG. When Hmong irregular forces made gains, it emboldened both the Hmong and the United States. The United States began to overreach, shifting from an unconventional campaign to more force-on-force combat aimed at liberating the Plain of Jars. Loosening the reins on Hmong forces and keeping families in close proximity to the fighting created a problem for controlling Hmong operations to preserve combat capability. The high number of Hmong losses, due to their exuberance and desire to protect their territory and families, undermined America's ability to continue its holding action in Laos.

Interestingly, the Washington's use of incentives worked. Although agency theory suggests that the United States should have offered the Hmong outcome-based incentives to reduce agency costs, the use of behavior-based incentives still managed to produce a high degree of control with no loss in coherence. The United States made no promise to deliver an outcome in exchange for its support.[112] Services were provided to families in the form of food, health care, and education to encourage more Hmong men to join the fight. These services enabled the Hmong to resist NVA and Pathet Lao forces and provided some hope to the Hmong for a better standard of living.[113] In addition, the use of behavior-based incentives allowed the United States to avoid the extra costs that would have been required to guarantee an outcome that would have inspired the Hmong to fight for U.S. interests. In this case, it appears that the convergence of U.S. and Hmong objectives—the aim of keeping NVA and Pathet Lao forces at bay—was enough for the Hmong.

LET THE PROXY LEAD, BUT ONLY SO FAR   The low level of Hmong autonomy on and off the battlefield provided an effective means of control. With relatively few personnel, especially compared with U.S. efforts in South Vietnam, Washington maintained tight control of Hmong operations in northern Laos and ensured that the resources apportioned served US interests.[114] The Hmong lacked the technical capability necessary to allow the United States to provide them with a high degree of autonomy and still compete adequately with opposing forces. For example, the Hmong could not operate highly complicated and expensive weapons systems that might have leveled the playing field. The resources necessary to make up for Hmong shortfalls in capability would have been too costly and too visible to allow the United States to maintain its covert involvement.

Counter to the proposition, the increase in U.S. costs associated with the low degree of Hmong autonomy stemmed from the need to provide increasing amounts of support and how that conflicted with the U.S. desire to keep its involvement in Laos secret, or at least plausibly deniable. The transition from a guerrilla-style strategy to a conventional strategy further complicated this problem. When the emphasis of Hmong operations was intended to harass and disrupt Pathet Lao and NVA efforts to control northern Laos, Washington managed to keep the degree of its involvement relatively quiet providing limited air support under the auspices of "armed reconnaissance." When the focus of operations shifted to capturing and holding the Plain of Jars, the United States could not match North Vietnam's response. As Hmong forces became progressively more overwhelmed, the air power necessary to balance the increase in NVA forces made it difficult to keep a lid on US operations.

The extreme dependence of the Hmong and the limited nature of U.S. involvement created a situation where the Hmong did not have the resources to make it necessary for the United States to increase its monitoring of Hmong operations. As U.S. involvement increased to bolster Hmong forces against the increasing capabilities of Pathet Lao and NVA forces, the Hmong's inability to act autonomously put the United States in a position where it had to reveal its involvement. In this sense, the lack of Hmong autonomy created a condition where the United States had to increase its support to a level where it could no longer expect to keep its involvement secret. This level of support exposed the United States to the potential of increasing international and domestic costs based on the revelation that it had been secretly supporting Hmong forces in violation of the 1962 Geneva Accords. The United States, however, arguably avoided those costs for the same reasons it avoided international costs as discussed in Proposition 3. The United States also incurred negligible domestic costs related to Hmong autonomy—the limited information about the conflict and the apparent willingness of the U.S. public to accept the limited amount of U.S. involvement prevented effect.

CULTIVATE RESOURCE DEPENDENCE   Although the convergence of U.S. and Hmong objectives, as well as the limited autonomy of Hmong forces, significantly increases America's ability to control its proxy, the high level of dependence of Hmong forces on the United States made it even easier to control the Hmong. The U.S. decision to move Hmong families and provide support to allow the men to join the war guaranteed that the Hmong would have a significant need for food and other supplies. Hmong villagers lacked the manpower to put in crops and harvest them. The extreme dependence of the Hmong and Washington's commitment to limit its involvement on the ground made it easier for the U.S. embassy in Vientiane to control Hmong operations and avoid supporting actions that were not in accordance with U.S. interests.

The increasing need for U.S. support, however, eventually forced the United States to acknowledge its presence in Laos. The combination of high proxy dependence and low autonomy did not match well with the U.S. desire to keep its involvement hidden. High dependence ensured that the Hmong did not use U.S. resources in a way that proved counterproductive. Low autonomy, however, required the United States to increase the level of its involvement to the point where it was no longer possible to keep it secret. Although the United States avoided sending in its own ground forces, its commitment increased because the Hmong continually faced a scenario of military inferiority in the battlespace. Pathet Lao augmented with NVA regulars far exceeded the capabilities of the Hmong militias. To counter this lack of relative superiority in the battlespace, the United States augmented Hmong forces with air power, a move that significantly increased U.S. visibility. Initially, Washington used close-air support, aerial resupply, air mobility, and airborne strike assets to support the Hmong irregulars in conducting hit-and-run attacks against Pathet Lao and North Vietnamese forces.[115] As the war transformed into a conventional battle to control the Plain of Jars and the Ho Chi Minh Trail, the United States made increasing amounts of air power available. Although this allowed Hmong forces to make gains during the rainy seasons, Hanoi often responded by sending more and better-equipped forces to recapture the territory it had lost. This back-and-forth only increased Hmong dependence on the United States.

The seasonal exchange of territory created a tremendous number of refugees in northern Laos. The United States had to increase the amount of supplies accordingly to provide for the influx of people fleeing from the Pathet Lao and NVA advances. Douglas Blaufarb notes:

> Estimates place the refugee population as of April 1970 at 246,000. But over the years many more—possibly as many as 700,000 people out of the roughly 1.9 million under RLG control—have left their homes to resettle permanently or temporarily in safer areas. . . . For the [Hmong], it has been particularly painful; various [casualty] estimates place it somewhere between 40,000 and 100,000.[116]

The high level of Hmong dependence had disastrous consequences. Rather than abandoning the gains that had been made previously, the Hmong would stand their ground too long and needlessly suffer enormous casualties in anticipation of U.S. air support. It is fathomable that the Hmong simply believed they were invincible with U.S. air support—an understandable conclusion when considering how a primitive people exposed to the awesome display of hundreds of U.S. fighter and bomber aircraft decimating Pathet Lao and NVA forces bogged down during the rainy season. Without understanding the limits of air power, the Hmong likely believed they could hold their ground against a conventionally and numerically superior enemy and often got caught overextended.

The Hmong's utterly complete dependence on the United States for its survival put them in a position of near-total commitment to U.S. objectives in Laos. Although this high level of dependence supports the idea that cultivating proxy dependence increases an intervening state's ability to control its proxy, it also demonstrates that too high a level of dependence can raise costs in terms of resources, visibility, and commitment. Fortunately for the United States, in this case, the extreme dependence of the Hmong did not really undermine international or domestic support for the United States' indirect intervention in Laos. It did, however, damage the United States' ability to preserve the capability of its Hmong proxy. In a proxy war designed to provide a holding action, an intervening state must consider how to keep its proxy in the field for as long as needed.

CHAPTER 6

SOUTH AFRICA'S PROXY WAR IN ANGOLA

THE PATH TO PROXY WAR

In 1974, a coup occurred in Lisbon that changed the course of Portugal's role in Angola. The new regime in Lisbon set the date for Angola's independence for November 11, 1975, and helped create the Alvor Agreement, a move intended to unite three competing liberation movements into a single unity government in Luanda. The three factions—the Popular Movement for the Liberation of Angola (MPLA), the National Liberation Front of Angola (FNLA), and the National Union for the Total Independence of Angola (UNITA)—were divided ethnically, geographically, and to a lesser extent, ideologically.[1] The MPLA combined the Mbundu ethnic group living in central Angola and the Portuguese-African mestizo population living in the urban areas in and around Luanda. The MPLA faction accounted for approximately 26 percent of the population and had ideological tendencies toward socialism, a fact that some argue has often been overblown. The FNLA represented roughly 17 percent of Angola's population and belonged mostly to the Bakongo ethnic group living in the border region between Zaire and Angola. UNITA, the newest of the three, was predominantly Ovimbundu, the largest ethnic group in Angola, and made up approximately 38 percent of the population.[2] The Ovimbundu were relatively spread out living in southern Angola, the more remote regions of eastern Angola, and the state's central highlands.[3]

The Alvor Agreement lasted for only a short period before the three factions returned to the use of armed force. Making matters worse, the politics of the Cold War infused Angola with an abundance of arms and created a new region of superpower rivalry. Although the FNLA was initially militarily superior to the MPLA because of support from Zaire and the United States, the Soviet Union made a decisive move to support the MPLA with a rapid infusion of military hardware and leadership. Cuba also moved decisively, sending highly capable troops into theater. Communist support from the Soviet Union and Cuba gave the MPLA a military edge and forced UNITA and FNLA into an alliance. UNITA, however, had very little military capability. This allowed MPLA to focus its efforts against FNLA and ultimately contributed to the elimination of FNLA as a serious competitor in Angola by the end of 1975.

The conflict in Angola was an ethnic war set in the context of a global, ideological competition. Although the local struggle stemmed largely from ethnic divides, it was also a battle for power and control among the prominent players.[4] The communist thrust into southern Africa provided a significant threat to South Africa. The introduction of Cuban forces into Angola and MPLA's significant backing from Moscow intensified South Africa's concerns for four reasons.[5] First, Angola enabled the Soviet Union and Cuba to expand their influence in the region, and Pretoria worried that Moscow might later set its sights on South Africa. Second, the MPLA enabled a Soviet proxy in neighboring Namibia, the South West African People's Organization (SWAPO), to expand operations inside Angola's borders. Third, South Africa feared that it could lose electrical power from the Cunene River hydroelectric project in Angola that powered its uranium mines and other South African industries in Namibia. Fourth, Pretoria worried about its ability to maintain control of its own territory if the Cubans joined forces with the African National Congress (ANC).[6] Pretoria believed that a transition in Angola by force would create a dysfunctional, Marxist government that would destroy the economic and industrial advances the apartheid government had made during the previous two decades.[7]

What Were the Barriers to Direct Intervention and Nonintervention?
If elections had been held when Portugal left in 1975, UNITA would likely have fared better than either the MPLA or the FNLA because of its popularity among rural Angolans and its affiliation with the Ovimbundu ethnic group.[8] Soviet and American influence on events surrounding the transition to independence from Portuguese rule, however, overlaid the façade of an ideological struggle. The conflict in Angola was largely a battle for territory, and the underlying tension between competing factions was predominantly ethnic. Ideology had some part in the conflict, but it was something to be manipulated along ethnic lines. South Africa, France, the United States, Cuba, and the Soviet Union all put ideological overtones on the war in Angola, but this was mostly just posturing and justification.[9] Jonas Savimbi, the leader and founder of UNITA, was especially skilled at manipulating ideology to serve his own purposes but admitted "there was no fundamental ideological conflict between the two movements."[10]

In the mid- to late 1970s, South Africa's economy was threaded into both U.S. and European economies, with Europe's stake being significantly higher.[11] Geo-strategically, South Africa was of considerable importance based on the naval choke point at the Cape of Good Hope. According to Richard Bissell, "the military perspective on the Cape sea-lanes has thus involved two elements. On the one hand, the growth of Western imports of energy has made the Cape route far more important: over 2,300 ships transit the Cape each moth, including 600 tankers. In terms of NATO planning, 57 percent of Western Europe's oil needs and 20 percent of American oil needs pass by the Cape."[12]

South Africa's apartheid government had already been subjected to intense political isolation both inside and outside the African continent. In addition to the international scrutiny of maintaining apartheid and denying political rights to black South Africans, Pretoria also refused to release its control of Namibia (formerly South West Africa), even though in 1966 the UN General Assembly declared that South Africa had no right to administer the territory and in 1971 the International Court of Justice found that South Africa's presence in Namibia was illegal.

South Africa's involvement in Angola helped legitimize Cuban and Soviet efforts to support the MPLA and damaged UNITA's credibility.[13]

For example, UK prime minister James Callaghan stated at the NATO Foreign Ministers' meeting in Brussels that he "was plainly anxious to avoid any suggestion that any NATO member become involved in support for UNITA/FNLA" and that "neither Britain nor NATO can afford to be seen by Africans to be making common cause with Mr. Vorster."[14] Further, China terminated its eight-year support of UNITA, embarrassed by South African involvement.[15]

In the face of rising domestic unrest over the government policy of apartheid and the subsequent attacks against "white" targets, South Africa's population was hesitant to support operations on the Angola/Namibia border. SWAPO's attempts to take Namibia by force, however, appear to have fostered some support. A public opinion poll conducted by Market Research Africa in May 1976 showed that most white South Africans supported the government's policy of conducting cross-border raids to engage SWAPO forces operating from inside Angola. That same poll, however, also revealed that the people surveyed did not feel that the government was keeping the public well informed about its involvement in Angola.[16]

Why Did South Africa Choose a Proxy War Policy?
Pretoria recognized that it lacked sufficient justification for its direct involvement in Angola. South Africa had to find a way to keep the Cubans from getting across the border into Namibia and wipe out SWAPO's base in Angola. Based on that, South Africa elected to secretly back UNITA in 1975.[17] South Africa did not want to enable UNITA to defeat the MPLA and gain sole control of Angola. Rather, Pretoria wanted to prevent Luanda and the Soviets from gaining control of Angola by force.

In addition, South Africa wanted to push SWAPO out of the border region and curtail its operations in Namibia; the fact that UNITA was pro-SWAPO and pro-ANC did not deter Pretoria.[18] South Africa wanted to work through UNITA because it offered a level of legitimacy and provided a force that would prevent South Africa from having to send a significant amount of its force to the region. Ultimately, Pretoria's policy aimed to allow South Africa to bargain from a position of strength on Namibia and to do it in a way that prevented a rapid escalation of violence and dissent along and within South Africa's own borders.

After the defeat of the FNLA, UNITA became South Africa's only real option for a proxy. UNITA's opposition to the MPLA and its significant rural support in southern Angola added to the organization's potential. The reality, however, was that UNITA forces were poorly trained and equipped. UNITA's first patron, China, believed in the concept that a revolutionary movement must rely on its own abilities and accordingly provided very little in the way of training and equipment.[19]

UNITA initially sought the assistance of South Africa with help from President Kenneth Kaunda of Zambia and President Félix Houphouët-Boigny of the Ivory Coast.[20] South Africa contributed training, arms, air support, and artillery assets to bolster UNITA's efforts. South Africa's involvement in Angola also included the deployment of a limited number of regular forces into Angola to secure the Namibian border and protect the Cunene River hydroelectric project inside Angola's border.

Supporting UNITA allowed Pretoria to field a much larger and stronger opposition in Angola than would have been possible if just using SADF units. Although estimates on the number of UNITA soldiers vary, Savimbi claimed in 1980 to have twenty thousand men under arms.[21] This number is probably overstated, but it is undeniable that South Africa's support of UNITA put considerable pressure on the MPLA government in Luanda and significantly curtailed SWAPO incursions into Namibia.

For Pretoria, the conditions that would protect South Africa's security—both domestically and regionally—required a peaceful transition to an independent state in Namibia and the removal of Cuban forces in Angola.[22] Although FAPLA was somewhat of a concern, UNITA was more than capable of holding those forces well north of the Namibian border. The Cuban forces with Soviet support, however, outmatched UNITA. UNITA provided the buffer necessary to allow a rather modestly deployed SADF to keep SWAPO forces from massing on the Angolan border and securing a military victory in Namibia.[23]

COHERENCE

Considering that the conflict inside Angola fell mainly along ethnic lines, South Africa benefited greatly from its affiliation with UNITA. Working through UNITA enabled South Africa to operate in a relatively permissive environment and subjected FAPLA and Cuban forces to the opposite.[24] This, in turn, put a great deal of pressure on opposing forces with a rather limited amount of South Africa's personnel and resources. Pretoria worried, however, that its domestic policy would jeopardize UNITA's legitimacy both in Angola and on the continent. Apartheid and the Namibian issue meant that South Africa had to proceed carefully in Angola; Western and African states were already somewhat reluctant to support Pretoria's policies in southern Africa.[25]

The situation in southern Africa created an opportunity for South Africa to break down some of its isolation.[26] Pretoria sold UNITA as a strong, anti-Marxist movement to the West, and it helped alleviate some of the problems caused by the apartheid government and recast the conflict in terms of stopping the spread of communism in Africa.[27] In 1978, Robin Hallett described this phenomenon:

> The United States was not the only "free world" power likely to welcome a move to check the MPLA. France, too, had recently developed an interest in the area, particularly in Cabinda, and there is evidence of the dispatch of arms and even of mercenaries to help FNLA and UNITA. Put all these associations together and it becomes clear that Pretoria, which for so long had suffered a position of diplomatic isolation, found itself in September 1975 in the gratifying and unusual position of pursuing the same objective as at least two—and possibly three, if the Ivory Coast is included—African states, the United States and France.[28]

How Did South Africa Attempt to Ensure Coherence?
Domestically, Pretoria felt that the South African public would reject an intervention into Angola designed to support "terrorists." The white population of South Africa saw UNITA much the same as it saw SWAPO: as a terrorist organization. The feeling in South Africa was that the West had abandoned southern Africa and that South Africa had to fend for itself. The people were reluctant to support operations on the Namibian border that would result in large numbers of white casualties, but they also recognized and supported a policy that protected South Africa's interests. Pretoria sold UNITA as an anti-Marxist movement that would

do most of the fighting in Angola and would prevent South Africa from having to send more of its own white soldiers to protect Namibia's northern border.[29]

The war was kept secret in its early stages to avoid domestic and international costs. Internationally, Pretoria worried that a connection with its apartheid regime would ruin UNITA's credibility in Angola and would threaten its support among other African states and in the international community at large.[30]

South Africa's involvement in Angola, however, soon became an open secret. The predominant view of the international community was that South Africa was attempting to prolong the war in Angola in hopes that it could hold on to Namibia.[31] Despite this view, certain conditions enabled South Africa to violate international norms of nonintervention without really suffering for it. First, the political isolation of South Africa created the impetus for self-reliance that took away many of the instruments other states could use to coerce Pretoria to adhere to nonintervention norms. For example, in 1977, 55 percent of South Africa's military procurement was imported. The 45 percent that was produced indigenously, however, revealed competence, depth, and sophistication. In 1979, Chester Crocker (an American expert on southern Africa) suggested that Pretoria's isolation due to a UN embargo would only "accelerate further the development and diversification of South African arms production, both for local consumption and export." Second, South Africa was such a lucrative economic market that it deterred many states from enacting economic sanctions that could have inflicted significant costs on Pretoria.[32] Third, the desire of the United States to stem Soviet expansion in southern Africa curbed concerns about Pretoria's involvement in Angola.[33]

How Was Coherence Sustained or Lost and What Was the Overall Effect?

INTERNAL COHERENCE   As the war progressed into the late 1970s and early 1980s, SADF commanders realized that the real value of UNITA was not in its conventional capability but in its ability to move and operate in southern Angola.[34] Over time, UNITA's SADF advisors began emphasizing the importance of focusing operational efforts against Cuban forces and bypassing FAPLA units when operationally or tactically feasible. The intent of focusing on the Cubans was to raise Havana's costs and weaken Cuba's resolve.[35] In many cases, the SADF was used only to prevent UNITA forces from suffering significant losses based on operational or tactical mistakes.[36] If UNITA could maintain a fielded force capable of keeping FAPLA and Cuban forces from gaining control of southern Angola, then South Africa's strategic goals would be fulfilled.[37]

The involvement of the SADF remained hidden from the public only for a short time. The need for higher levels of intervention to curb Cuban/FAPLA moves in southern Angola and to provide UNITA with additional equipment and training soon overrode the desire to keep South Africa's involvement secret. The limited means with which SADF units carried out their mission, however, helped keep the level of South Africa's involvement somewhat obscure until 1985, when General Magnus Malan, the minister of defense, publicly acknowledged that South Africa had been supporting UNITA.

The accomplishments of South Africa during the period of the Angolan Civil War reveal the utility and efficacy of using UNITA to conserve resources. Between 1975 and 1990, South Africa sustained its involvement in Angola, developed a nuclear program, and fostered a robust arms industry. More surprisingly, the percentage of South Africa's gross domestic product allotted to the armed forces remained at or below 5 percent—an amazing feat considering the level of operations and Soviet competition in Angola.[38]

INTRASTATE COHERENCE   Jonas Savimbi was somewhat of an opportunist. In 1964, he joined up with Holden Roberto's FNLA. He left the movement because of Roberto's ethnic favoritism and then courted the MPLA. Failing to gain his desired level of influence, Savimbi formed UNITA in 1966.[39] Shortly after UNITA's inception, Savimbi and eleven other members went to China to receive military training and instruction in the Maoist philosophy of revolutionary war. Savimbi cultivated close relationships with both SWAPO and the ANC and managed to gain the support of key ethnic groups, such as the Ovambu and Ovimbundu, in the rural areas of southern Angola. Savimbi's opportunism may have even extended to involving UNITA in a secret alliance with Portugal against MPLA forces in the early 1970s.[40] Savimbi worried about affiliating with South Africa because of the unpopular apartheid regime, but he had no other good options. When the MPLA failed to solidify enough support to gain recognition from the Organization of African Unity (OAU), UNITA seized on the opportunity to work with South Africa to make sure the MPLA did not get control of Angola.[41]

South Africa's proxy war in Angola benefited from UNITA's ethnic ties in the region. Although SWAPO and UNITA maintained amicable relations, Pretoria's support for UNITA's operations in the border region did not sour the organization's ability to garner support from locals. Providing support for programs other than those focused on military operations helped UNITA's standing and improved the intrastate coherence of South Africa's policy. The people in the border region did not see South Africa as trying to take control of the territory. Instead, SADF forces provided the necessary support to keep UNITA from suffering too many losses without overreaching.

The combination of South African and UNITA forces proved so effective against FAPLA (the militant faction of the MPLA) that Cuba rushed additional forces to stop UNITA/South African advances. Through Cuban and Soviet efforts, the MPLA managed to hold on to Luanda and declared itself as the legitimate government of Angola on November 11, 1975. The Soviet Union, along with many of its satellites, quickly recognized the MPLA government while the United States and most other Western states refused to do the same. The local people did receive the presence of Cuban soldiers in their territory well, contributing to South Africa's intrastate coherence.

INTERNATIONAL/DOMESTIC COHERENCE   Between 1976 and 1981, Pretoria engaged in rather limited operations designed to enable and sustain UNITA's ability to hold southern Angola. Plagued internationally by its apartheid regime and its refusal to vacate Namibia, South Africa failed to put much pressure on the MPLA government and only managed to minimize SWAPO advances in Namibia. As the war progressed in 1981, many Western states began to either tacitly or actively support South Africa's support of UNITA, but those same states continued to oppose direct intervention and criticize Pretoria for its apartheid government (Barber and Barrat 1990).[42] Washington's support, however, became more evident and more consistent after Ronald Reagan took office and was most visibly demonstrated when the United States promptly vetoed a proposal by members of the UN Security Council (the United Kingdom, France, and Germany) to condemn South Africa for the incursion of SADF units into Angola during an operation (Protea) in 1981.

Directing and supporting UNITA, South Africa found a way to bridge many of the barriers it had with Western states who opposed Soviet/communist expansion in Africa. Savimbi's success in selling UNITA to the United States and many of its allies as an anti-Marxist movement afforded Pretoria the opportunity it needed to pursue its interests and intervene in Angolan affairs without the fear of significant international costs. Although direct incursions into Angola by SADF personnel often caused international scrutiny among Western European countries, the effects were often inconsequential. Most importantly, South Africa's support of UNITA allowed the United States to take a more active and protective political stance toward those operations.[43] For example, in 1981 the United States vetoed a proposed UN Security Council Resolution calling for the immediate withdrawal of South African forces from Angola.[44]

Although Soviet involvement arguably influenced the United States and other Western European states to accept South Africa's policy in Angola, Cuba's involvement had a subtler effect on the international community. Havana's involvement did not justify Pretoria's operations in Angola, but it did lead many Western states to work toward a Cuban withdrawal in conjunction with South Africa's withdrawal of Namibia. For example, during the decade-long process of negotiating an end to the Angolan Civil War, European states closely aligned with the United States would not openly support "linkage"—the idea that Cuban forces in Angola and South African forces in Namibia would withdraw simultaneously—but they privately put pressure on negotiators from Cuba and the MPLA to settle along the lines of what linkage was trying to accomplish.[45]

South Africa's support of UNITA did not really hide or obscure the state's involvement. In the early stages, Pretoria's direct involvement to protect a critical hydroelectric plant in southern Angola and its overt use of SADF units to engage SWAPO forces operating north of the Namibian border was scrutinized by several states. South Africa's strong economy and its political isolation, however, protected the state from damaging costs linked to its international relations. Further, Pretoria's relatively quiet support of UNITA avoided an increase in commitment to maintain South Africa's reputation or prestige. From an international perspective, Pretoria had very little invested in UNITA—it only needed UNITA to provide a buffer on the Angola-Namibia border.

South Africa's support of UNITA did not avoid unwanted escalation. As the opposition to MPLA forces in Angola gained strength, Moscow and Havana responded with increases in equipment, funding, and personnel. Based on the responses of these two states, it appears Soviet and Cuban interest in Angola had reached such a point that the two states remained determined to ensure that the MPLA government in Luanda survived, regardless of South Africa's or any other state's support. At the peak, different estimates show that approximately forty thousand to fifty thousand Cubans were operating in Angola while only five thousand to six thousand South Africans were there opposing them.[46]

After 1981, the election of conservative governments in the United Kingdom and the United States enabled Pretoria to operate in Angola and Namibia with a freer hand.[47] When President Reagan came into office, Washington renewed its commitment to the strategy of containment and once again began supporting South Africa and UNITA. At this point, the idea of linkage was born and the United States and South Africa submitted that the issues in Namibia and Angola would have to be resolved simultaneously—South African forces would leave Namibia at the same time Cuban forces left Angola.[48] Although the change in sentiment among prominent Western states caused negotiations to become more structured and focused through the 1980s, the shift also contributed to a steady increase in the level of violence. As the Soviets and Cubans struggled to consolidate the MPLA's hold on Angola, the United

States and South Africa used violence to increase the pressure and force a settlement.[49]

In 1987, multiple factors at international and domestic levels pushed the main players in Angola to move toward a settlement. The United States was pressuring South Africa to settle because of the upcoming election.[50] The Soviet Union faced a rapidly declining economic situation at home. Cuba had convinced Moscow to allow it to take over operations in Angola.[51] South Africa had been forced to deploy SADF units within its own borders to control domestic unrest. Most importantly, however, South Africa and Cuba finally reached an agreement about how to get out of Angola; Pretoria could say that it had managed to get the Cubans out of Angola and Havana could say that it had freed Namibia.[52]

In 1988, a series of agreements were signed that created the conditions necessary for an election in Angola: South Africa agreed to comply with UN Security Council Resolution 435 and vacate Namibia, Cuba agreed to a staged withdrawal of its forces from Angola, the MPLA agreed not to support SWAPO, and the MPLA agreed to open elections in Angola. In 1990, SWAPO won the election in Namibia and South Africa relinquished its hold on the territory. In 1992, Angola's open election granted the MPLA's candidate, Eduardo José dos Santos, the presidency and a majority in the parliament. In 1994, South Africa's last white president, F. W. de Klerk, conceded defeat in an open election to Nelson Mandela and the ANC.

International isolation helped maintain domestic support for the border war. The people of South Africa felt that the world had turned its back on them and that South Africa must fend for itself.[53] Although many South Africans acknowledged the threat of Cuban and Soviet influence in southern Africa and the lack of international support for South Africa to protect the region from communism, they still reacted negatively to white casualties in the border region. Based on those negative reactions, South Africa had to be careful of how it employed SADF units and had to bolster those forces to minimize casualties when they were operating in Angola. This caused an increase in commitment from SADF units engaged in supporting or rescuing UNITA forces.

Finally, on September 20, 1985, Malan admitted publicly that South Africa had been supporting UNITA with aid "of a material, humanitarian, and moral nature."[54] Generally, white South Africans supported Pretoria's continued involvement because it cost very little, caused very few casualties, and helped jump-start relations with the West. The public and the government, however, remained highly sensitive to any casualties. In one example, an air attack on an SADF position near Calueque Dam on June 27, 1988, that resulted in ten white casualties created significant pushback and concern from the cabinet and started questions about border war operations.[55]

Although many South African newspapers suggested that the people were shocked and angered by the SADF's involvement in Angola, it was an inaccurate representation of the country's position. General Johannes Geldenhuys argues that the confusion stemmed from the fact that Pretoria had kept its initial involvement secret and that the far right and far left both hated the P. W. Botha administration and therefore showed resentment toward his policy in the border region. According to Geldenhuys, "Prime Minister Botha was a polarizing figure in South African politics. The conservatives considered him a sellout and the liberals considered him a racist. Yet there were no demonstrations or protests of considerable or significant size during the nearly fifteen-year conflict. It was P. W. Botha's prior affiliation with the SADF that tainted these groups' attitudes toward the SADF."[56]

PROXY COHERENCE   South Africa's strategy mainly entailed supporting UNITA to blunt advances by both FAPLA and Cuban forces. UNITA's control of the southern region of Angola forced FAPLA and Cuban forces to maintain long, vulnerable supply lines. When needed, UNITA and SADF cooperated to defend key areas and raise the costs of gaining ground in southern Angola so high that Cuban and FAPLA forces were often forced to pull back to the north.

In creating UNITA, Savimbi specifically set out to create a peasant-based, rural movement in southern Angola.[57] The relationship between UNITA forces and the people living in the region strongly influenced the beneficial effects of having civilians live in close proximity to the fighting in southern Angola.[58] Both the Ovimbundu and Ovambo people were supportive of UNITA.[59] The lack of professionalism and training, at least by modern standards, did not give way to retaliatory attacks on civilians because UNITA forces were never threatened by the population. UNITA's relationship with the civilian population in the region and its ability to blend in to local villages provided excellent opportunities to collect good intelligence about FAPLA/Cuban forces and to harass enemy movements.

The proximity of civilians in the battlespace enhanced UNITA operations. While it is true that civilians were occasionally caught in the crossfire or were killed because of tactical or operational mistakes, UNITA actively cultivated and sustained the population's support. South Africa encouraged this behavior, teaching Maoist principles of revolutionary war to UNITA forces and providing resources to create services that would further garner civilian support.[60]

South Africa also made an investment to enlarge UNITA's following among southern Angola's rural population. Although the resources necessary to provide services to the people did not contribute directly to the war, Pretoria recognized that giving UNITA the ability to provide resources to these people solidified its control of the region.[61]

South Africa's support of UNITA had negative international effects as well. Within Africa, the OAU voted to recognize the MPLA government in Luanda when it became evident that Pretoria had been assisting UNITA operations in Angola. Outside Africa, Pretoria's support of UNITA did not prevent Moscow and Havana from condemning South Africa's involvement in Angola and increasing their support of the MPLA.[62] International scrutiny of South Africa's actions also went beyond the communist bloc. The UN Security Council passed five resolutions (387, 428, 447, 454, and 475) between 1976 and 1980 condemning South Africa for its direct involvement in Angola. In 1981, France and the United Kingdom proposed that the UN Security Council condemn South Africa for SADF incursions into Angola (though the proposal was vetoed by the United States).

Throughout the conflict, South Africa maintained a relatively low degree of involvement in Angola. UNITA forces, in most cases, managed to defeat FAPLA forces and proved competent at harassing Cuban forces when they attempted to gain ground in southern Angola. South Africa remained confident that its forces deployed to the border region were quite capable of holding their own, despite being outnumbered in terms of both personnel and equipment. Even more importantly, SADF units continued to put pressure on Luanda, Moscow, and Havana. This was especially evident when Cuba's lead negotiator in Cairo in 1988 became incensed after threatening to deploy fifteen thousand more troops to Angola in response to the recent escalation in violence and R. F. "Pik" Botha (South Africa's minister of foreign affairs) coolly responded that deploying an additional thousand SADF personnel would effectively negate such a move. On that day, Cuba and South Africa agreed to the terms put forth by Chester Crocker's Contact Group.[63]

South Africa consolidated its support in southern Angola through its affiliation with UNITA and by providing resources to the people living in the region. Although the resources were given to UNITA rather than to the people directly, the connection still enabled South Africa to operate more freely and effectively in southern Angola.

In September 1975, Lieutenant Colonel Willem van der Waals, an officer in the SADF, and his team of SADF volunteers were sent to establish contact and advise UNITA. His objectives were to train two UNITA brigades, provide strategic and operational guidance, stop MPLA and Cuban forces from taking Huambo, avoid casualties, and ensure that South Africa's assistance remained plausibly deniable. Originally, Pretoria intended that van der Waals and his team would be out before independence on November 11, 1975. The events leading up to independence, especially the rapid escalation of Soviet and Cuban involvement, persuaded South Africa to continue its efforts after that date.[64]

To keep Pretoria's involvement secret, South African volunteers sent to Angola were told they would be disavowed if they were caught or exposed. In addition, UNITA had to accept weapons and armament that were plausibly deniable.[65] This left UNITA and supporting SADF units with a more limited ability to engage FAPLA and Cuban forces. For example, UNITA and SADF units would not be allowed to use modern antitank weapons and would instead have to rely on outdated and rather ineffective bazookas.[66] It also, however, kept the costs of supporting UNITA to a minimum.

Pretoria, however, was relatively overt with its support of UNITA among the strongly anticommunist governments of the United States and Western Europe before 1985.[67] Even after Pretoria admitted its support of UNITA in 1985, the costs of supporting UNITA remained relatively low. The South African public (the whites) were outraged when they found out that the government had been supporting and fighting alongside what they considered terrorists. The public, however, was also concerned about Cuban and communist involvement in the region and how they might affect the efforts of the ANC inside South Africa. This allowed Pretoria to continue its current course in Angola without significant domestic interference.[68]

UNITA and SADF were not terribly constrained by the secrecy/obscurity of the relationship early on because of Pretoria's limited strategy. Staying with a predominantly guerrilla strategy and operating in an unconventional manner, South Africa steadily moved toward its objectives. Had the war shifted to a more conventional style, then the constraints of secrecy would logically have played a larger role. UNITA had to accept this limitation, even if Savimbi wanted more, because it was the only way UNITA could create the conditions necessary to gain a significant amount of influence in Angola.

Although Pretoria's support of UNITA contributed to Soviet and Cuban retaliation, it appears that the limited and obscure way in which it was done allowed South Africa to keep its involvement limited without generating a large enough reaction that would have caused South Africa to commit its forces directly. Havana might have had some difficulty, even considering the authoritative nature of it government, justifying the need to send more troops in addition to the forty thousand to fifty thousand Cuban soldiers that were already in country to counter an indigenous threat and a modest South African contingent of four thousand to five thousand soldiers.

Politically, South Africa's support of UNITA did not have the proposed effect of diminishing the organization's credibility with the population for two reasons. First, the ethnic ties between UNITA and the population likely minimized the issue. Second, and probably even more important, UNITA's commitment to providing services and its efforts to offer an inclusive organization to all the rural people of southern Angola, not just the Ovimbundu, stemmed any criticism that UNITA was doing Pretoria's bidding. From its inception, UNITA's political competence remained a significant strength, largely due to the presence of Jonas Savimbi as its leader.[69]

CONTROL

How Did South Africa Use and Control Its Proxy and to What End?

THE COMPATIBILITY OF OBJECTIVES   Among others, Jonas Savimbi was an ambitious leader with flexible loyalties as indicated by his willingness to cooperate with whoever could provide him with power, status, and influence. His reliance on South Africa—a point I will develop further shortly—kept his pursuits in Angola relatively in check. Once South Africa achieved its goals in Angola and Namibia, it no longer had the influence over Savimbi it once had. Savimbi's desire for power became even more evident after he lost the elections in 1992, denounced the elections as a fraud, and returned to the bush to plunge Angola back into civil war for another two years.[70]

South Africa did incur a small increase in its commitment costs and its costs to gain support in Angola. According to Chaim Kaufmann, the ethnic character of the conflict should have made it nearly impossible for the people of southern Angola to join the MPLA because of the ethnic divide.[71] Pretoria, however, still invested resources that deepened its commitment to UNITA in an effort to expand the movement's popularity and influence. Although this may have been unnecessary, it did deny the MPLA government the ability to gain access to southern Angola by extending services to the people there.

South Africa did suffer one unexpected cost related to the ethnic dimension of the war in Angola. The Ovimbundu were closely aligned and supportive of the Ovambu people living in the transborder region between Namibia and Angola. The Ovambu were a prominent ethnic group in SWAPO, and UNITA refused to provide information or assistance to SADF units pursuing SWAPO forces. South Africa had to tread carefully in its operations with UNITA and against SWAPO to ensure that it did not jeopardize its ability to operate in the border area.[72]

The relationship between South Africa and UNITA supports the idea developed in Chapter 2 that ethnic lines are often well established and durable. In spite of the ideological differences between the apartheid government in Pretoria and the rural people living Angola, South Africa supported UNITA for fifteen years without jeopardizing the population's support.

This case does, however, challenge the notion that an ethnic conflict negates the need of a proxy to gain legitimacy. It is impossible to say if the people of southern Angola would have supported UNITA if they had not received social services in the form of education and health care. It is possible to say, however, that it did not hurt. The people of southern Angola endured over fifteen years of bitter conflict and stayed loyal to UNITA, as evidenced by the 40.7 percent of the vote share Savimbi received in the presidential elections in 1992 and the 70 seats (out of 223) that UNITA won in the parliamentary election.[73] Further, the election results provide evidence of the durability of ethnic ties; UNITA's affiliation with Pretoria did not damage its legitimacy among the people of southern Angola.

THE CAPABILITY OF A PROXY   UNITA originated in the rural areas of southern Angola and managed to gain the support of most of the population living in that area. Because of this, UNITA forces moved easily without being detected by the enemy. In addition, UNITA collected useful intelligence on FAPLA or Cuban forces operating in the region and harassed them, making it difficult to move or operate without losing supplies, equipment, or personnel.[74] For this reason, SADF personnel assigned to train UNITA were told to focus on providing weapons training; the tactics of operating in the bush were largely left to UNITA because senior SADF officers believed UNITA was better at conducting guerrilla operations than the SADF.[75]

The conditions in the battlespace meant that South Africa had the luxury of supporting a proxy that required essentially no restraint. UNITA was fighting on its home turf, and the rural population living in the battlespace supported them. Because UNITA was popular in the rural areas of southern Angola where much of the fighting took place, Pretoria did not have to worry about UNITA subjecting the population to atrocities—a point that also spared South Africa domestic and international costs stemming from an affiliation with a proxy terrorizing innocent civilians.[76] As an added benefit, the MPLA and Cuban forces were forced to fight in hostile territory; the necessary rearguard actions and UNITA's ability to blend into the surrounding environment made UNITA an effective guerrilla force.

South Africa provided UNITA with considerable resources not only to prosecute the war against FAPLA and Cuban regulars but also to establish basic services such as health care and education. UNITA's ability to deny prolonged access to FAPLA forces and provide resources to the people living in the region made it difficult for the MPLA to provide an alternative source for the services necessary to gain popular support and overcome ethnic divides. SADF operations without UNITA would have been far more demanding in terms of both money and personnel. The force protection measures that would have been necessary to continue operations without UNITA would have been considerable, even without considering the corresponding effects it would have caused in terms of escalation with the Cubans and the Soviets.

THE DEPENDENCE OF A PROXY ON OUTSIDE SUPPORT   UNITA's efforts to gain control of Angola's government in Luanda fulfilled Pretoria's desire to protect Namibia's northern border and pressure Cuban and Soviet efforts to consolidate the MPLA regime in Angola. Although the objectives were significantly different, the means by which the two sides went about achieving those objectives were complementary. Insurgency experts tend to agree that the population is the key to an insurgent group gaining influence in a state.[77] The resources and operational support South Africa provided UNITA to gain and sustain the population's support in southern

Angola also created the necessary barrier to protect Pretoria's interests in Namibia.

UNITA's lack of operational and tactical prowess occasionally required SADF units to rescue UNITA forces that had been overcommitted. Although South Africa incurred significant operational costs in terms of equipment, supplies, and personnel due to UNITA's autonomy and its operational and tactical mistakes, Pretoria benefited more from the relatively few SADF units required to protect the Namibian border because of UNITA's efforts.

SUMMARY

In terms of both utility and efficacy, UNITA served as an effective proxy for Pretoria's indirect intervention in Angola. South Africa adapted the mutable aspects of its policy to promote coherence and control. There were also two important immutable conditions that helped: first, UNITA's need for support combined with the reluctance of outside states to refrain from opening a secondary supply of resources, and second, South Africa's political isolation due to its apartheid government, which made South Africa highly sanction-resistant. South Africa's robust economy with influential links to U.S. and Western European economies reduced the desire to deliver sanctions that could produce the coercive effects associated with issue linkage and international sanctions. Giving states that were important to South Africa's economy or its policy in Angola the means to look the other way made it easier for South Africa to support its proxy in a controversial and widely scrutinized manner. When an intervening state has something that other states want and could potentially withhold if states attempted to initiate or leverage sanctions to change that behavior, then a proxy appears to provide a useful means for would-be sanctioners to look the other way.

South Africa's isolation also provided an important source of domestic support, or at the very least, toleration for supporting UNITA and staying involved in Angola. Because the white public perceived that the international community would not help South Africa because of apartheid, it justified the need to pursue a solution without international support. Pretoria avoided any serious challenges to its policy because

UNITA provided the largest share of the fighting forces and provided the connections necessary with the population of southern Angola to allow SADF units to engage in limited operations with a relatively low threat of casualties.

Because UNITA was ethnically tied to a majority of the people living in the battlespace, it remained relatively invulnerable to enemy infiltration and did not suffer attacks from an enemy that could hide among the population and cause an overreaction. South Africa also made it possible for UNITA to provide services that further garnered support for the movement. A third contributing factor was that the people of southern Angola did not care for the fact that Cuban forces were fighting on their soil.[78]

An important point that this case demonstrates was that secrecy did not necessarily contribute as much to lowering costs and maximizing benefits as did the appropriate strategy. South Africa remained committed to its limited aims of protecting the border region between Angola and Namibia and getting Cuban forces out of southern Africa. Further, South Africa kept its focus on the political aspects rather than getting sidetracked on military aspects.

A second point is that the costs of blowback are blunted when the government can justify its policy in terms of security; the communist threat was a serious consideration to the white population of South Africa. Although this is somewhat obvious, it does provide some guidance for when a secret policy may not create significant blowback costs.

How Do My Proposed Maxims Apply to the Intervening State's Use of a Proxy?

KNOW YOUR ENEMY, BUT KNOW YOUR PROXY EVEN BETTER   South Africa wanted to keep the territory in southern Angola free from communist control to protect its interests in Namibia and prevent an influx of communist influence in its own country. UNITA, and more specifically Savimbi, wanted control of the government in Luanda. Pretoria never promised Savimbi that he would get control of Angola, but it did support efforts to put UNITA in a position to win, or at least share, control of the government.[79] Although South Africa's objectives were significantly different from UNITA's, the support given and the tactics employed supported both sides. Holding to a guerrilla-style operation with the objective of denying Cuban and FAPLA forces from establishing a presence in the region worked well in the predominantly rural area. Having strong support of the region's people also enhanced UNITA's security. The MPLA government in Luanda could not get access to the people long enough to establish the types of services necessary to gain their support. Further, FAPLA's affiliation with Cuban forces and the MPLA's predominantly mestizo population identified them as enemies rather than Angolan forces with the legitimate right to use force. Guerrilla warfare, however, would not get Jonas Savimbi what he really wanted.

This is not to say that Savimbi did not want peace. Savimbi, in discussions with Chester Crocker, stated that he did not want the war to endure. The problem was that Savimbi was ambitious and egoistic. He admitted that there were people in the MPLA that he respected and could work with, such as Agostinho Neto (the leader of the MPLA), but Savimbi considered dos Santos a lackey of the Soviet Union and would not agree to work with him. At the end, Savimbi got greedy and refused to join the unity government in Luanda after he lost the election. Savimbi also refused the position of vice president. South Africa's foreign minister, Pik Botha, brokered a deal with the Angolan government for Savimbi to take a position as the commissar for the reconstruction of Angola. Savimbi initially agreed but then quickly changed his mind and went back to the bush and plunged Angola back into civil war for two more years.[80]

LET THE PROXY LEAD, BUT ONLY SO FAR   Pretoria gave UNITA a high degree of autonomy and did not pressure Savimbi to alter or change UNITA's operations.[81] South Africa did not fear political backlash from the behavior of UNITA because they were fighting among their own people and because UNITA's own objectives complemented South Africa's desire to protect the northern border of Namibia and gain a more moderate government in Angola. South Africa did not even feel the need to curb

UNITA's practice of taking hostages as a means of gaining recognition and publicity, so long as the hostages were always returned unharmed.[82]

Although UNITA was quite capable at operating in the bush, its operations often lacked the vision and planning necessary at the operational level—coordinating tactical events over time to accomplish larger objectives—to conduct a more conventional-style campaign. UNITA operations were most useful when SADF commanders avoided conventional operations and played to UNITA's strength as a guerrilla force. According to Geldenhuys, UNITA managed to keep FAPLA and Cuban forces from making lasting incursions into southern Angola because its forces were disciplined, had been given excellent weapons training (but not tactics or operations—the SADF thought it was unnecessary because UNITA was from the area and understood it better), had the support of the people, and were fighting in territory that had very few enemies and many friends and supporters. Based on these factors, the SADF did not feel the need to strictly control UNITA's operations.[83]

Despite the overall view of South Africa's senior leaders, mistakes were sometimes made on the battlefield because of a lack of internal or proxy coherence. SADF advisors had a more active role at the operational level. SADF advisors occasionally directed UNITA forces during large battles to make up for UNITA's lack of training and skill in operational planning. In some cases, SADF commanders had too high an expectation of UNITA's capabilities and pushed them in ways that contributed to higher losses.[84] Other times, Savimbi's ambition and impatience pushed UNITA into force-on-force skirmishes.[85] When UNITA forces got into a bind, Pretoria often had to send SADF units to their aid, further exposing South Africa's involvement in Angola.[86]

CULTIVATE RESOURCE DEPENDENCE   Throughout the conflict, UNITA depended on SADF for training, for strategic and operational advice, and as a backstop in cases when UNITA forces were overcommitted against superior numbers of FAPLA/Cuban forces.[87] UNITA gained momentum and strength throughout the conflict, but Savimbi and UNITA remained highly dependent on South Africa militarily, politically, and financially.

Militarily, UNITA needed the support of the population to pressure Luanda and to avoid being isolated and destroyed by superiorly equipped and trained Cuban forces—FAPLA was never proficient enough to challenge UNITA.[88] Ensuring that UNITA forces were only minimally capable in conventional warfare and needed rescuing from time to time exposed South Africa's involvement in Angola, but it also provided a significant check on UNITA's operations and ambitions. UNITA was so closely tied to the population and its dependence so severe that it could not really use its resources in a way that would have been detrimental to South Africa's interests. The only way UNITA could really use the resources it had been given to promote its cause was to stick with a guerrilla-style campaign and provide support to the population—anything else would have been counterproductive.

Politically, South Africa's position was already contentious; supporting a proxy that further aggravated the international community could have soured the relationship and terminated Pretoria's support. UNITA worried that South Africa would lose interest in supporting the movement's operations. To help ensure that Pretoria would remain interested, UNITA often provided false reports of its progress.[89] Savimbi also worried that South Africa was going to sell him out during the negotiations led by Crocker and the "Contact Group." In his private discussions with Crocker, Savimbi continually asked to be included in a settlement, and Crocker told him repeatedly that provisions could be made that would increase the likelihood of him getting what he wanted, but no settlement could be arranged that specifically guaranteed his desires to get UNITA a share of the power in Angola.[90] Savimbi accepted the arrangement to keep Pretoria's support.

Financially, UNITA needed to show Pretoria that it was worth supporting, and the most obvious means of demonstrating that support was UNITA's use of the resources it received to gain the support of the population in southern Angola. Pretoria also served as the main financier for many of the commodities UNITA could sell on its own such as diamonds, ivory, or hardwoods.[91] UNITA's dependence, however, ensured that the resources provided were used to further South Africa's interests, causing UNITA to forgo any self-interested behavior that might jeopardize future allotments.

UNITA's dependence coupled with its ethnic connections to the people living within the battlespace provided significant boundaries to the kind of conduct that could harm South Africa's pursuit of its objectives. Although Savimbi suffered some degree of international scrutiny later in the conflict, due to allegations of harsh treatment of civilians and executions of UNITA leaders that were a potential threat to his position, UNITA's efforts at keeping FAPLA and Cuban forces at bay remained stalwart.[92] Savimbi himself admitted that he did not want the war to go on longer than necessary and that he was willing to compromise and work with leaders of the MPLA who had earned the right to lead Angola.[93]

UNITA's dependence on South Africa protected Pretoria from Savimbi's ambition; he could not force South Africa into supporting his own objectives and had to settle for making the most of what support South Africa was willing to provide. Although more than one principal was involved, UNITA could not get the United States involved in a way that would alleviate its dependence on South Africa. Further, Washington's and Pretoria's objectives overlapped sufficiently to prevent UNITA from leveraging its position into greater support and a guarantee that negotiations among the principals would yield the inclusion of UNITA in the settlement.

CHAPTER 7

INDIA'S PROXY WAR IN SRI LANKA

THE PATH TO PROXY WAR

When the British controlled Sri Lanka (formerly known as Ceylon), they promoted Tamil interests and provided opportunities well beyond the Tamils' ethnic representation to weaken the more numerous Sinhalese.[1] Because ethnic conflicts were not allowed under British rule, the Tamils and Sinhalese lived under a forced peace.[2] After independence in 1948, the Sinhalese began exploiting their majority to undermine the Tamil position. The Sinhalese, under the auspices of Sri Lanka's constitution, started passing legislation to restrict the rights of Tamils. Attempts to make Sinhala the official and only language of Sri Lanka polarized the two ethnic groups and clearly signaled a Sinhalese effort·to use the democratic process to marginalize and discriminate against the Tamils. For example, the Sinhalese majority made it legally possible to erode dominant Tamil businesses, reduce Tamil appointments to bureaucratic offices, and restrict Tamil access to universities. Small-scale race riots began as early as 1956. By 1972, Sri Lanka's constitution provided superior status to both the Sinhala language and the Buddhist religion and put an end to what was once a secular democracy.[3]

Lacking protection from Sri Lanka's constitution, Tamils formed the Tamil United Liberation Front (TULF) in 1972 and began to clamor for an independent state. Around the same time, Tamils frustrated with

TULF's failure to enact changes diplomatically formed militant organizations bent on using violence to coerce the government into allowing Tamil areas to secede.[4]

In the 1970s, Sri Lanka's domestic squabbles posed no threat to India. Prior to the election of President J. R. Jayewardene in 1976, Sri Lanka and India both stood firmly in the nonalignment movement.[5] Shortly after Jayewardene took office, however, Sri Lanka began courting the West.[6] Sri Lanka's deep-water port at Trincomalee—often considered the best on the Indian Ocean—and its proximity to both India and the main sea lanes between the Middle East and East Asia made the island a desirable location for distant global powers such as the United States and the United Kingdom.

As the ethnic crisis in Sri Lanka worsened, New Delhi started to perceive the situation in Sri Lanka as a growing threat to India's security.[7] India wanted to prevent outside intervention in South Asia. A humanitarian crisis blended with strategic access to deep-water ports could draw American or Soviet interest and weaken India's influence in the region.[8]

In 1979, Sri Lanka's government passed the Prevention of Terrorism Act, which "allowed the security forces to arrest, imprison, and leave incommunicado for eighteen months without trial anyone suspected of unlawful activity. Applied retroactively, the Act led to widespread torture and human rights abuse of many young Tamils. That such abuse occurred at a time when the military was viewed as an occupation force in the north only exacerbated the Tamils' sense of alienation."[9] The government in Colombo had even begun—tacitly and actively—to support widespread violence against Tamil citizens. For example, government vehicles were used to transport Sinhalese rioters to destroy Tamil stores and businesses; the rioters were also given electoral registration forms to identify Tamil targets.[10]

In 1983, a group of Tamil students attacked a detachment of Sri Lankan soldiers, killing thirteen of them. The Sinhalese people responded by killing hundreds of Tamils and forcing thousands more out of their homes. Because of the violence, many Tamils fled to Tamil Nadu—a nearby state in southern India—where a predominantly Tamil population provided sanctuary and support. Outraged Tamils in Tamil Nadu pressured the local government in Madras (later named Chennai in 1996) to support Tamil militant groups and demanded that New Delhi take action in Sri Lanka.[11]

What Were the Barriers to Direct Intervention and Nonintervention?
Despite international concerns, India could not sit on the sidelines. India's domestic affairs pushed New Delhi toward intervention in Sri Lanka. Since Indira Gandhi's election in 1980, her Congress Party had been suffering an erosion of its support throughout India. Supporting the Tamils in Sri Lanka provided a means of shoring up much needed support in southern India.[12] Gandhi faced a difficult dilemma: she did not want an independent Tamil state in Sri Lanka, but she needed the support of Tamil Nadu's politicians to sustain her political position. This led Gandhi to accommodate Tamil concerns regarding Sri Lanka in hopes of gaining the support of the dominant political party in Tamil Nadu. Making nonintervention even more difficult, many Indian Tamils even pushed for the creation of an independent Tamil state—a sentiment known as Tamil Eelam.[13] India's government, however, was opposed to a separate state for the Tamils in Sri Lanka. New Delhi worried that the ethnic conflict and the influx of Tamil refugees might incite a secessionist movement in Tamil Nadu as well.[14]

Fearing India's meddling, Sri Lanka solicited support from the United States and the United Kingdom. Acknowledging India's rising global influence and its dominance in South Asia, the United States and the United Kingdom denied Sri Lanka's request that they intervene directly and instead encouraged Colombo to enlist the assistance of Israel's Mossad and retired Special Air Service (SAS) commandos to train its forces in counterinsurgency tactics.[15] India's regional rival, Pakistan, also agreed to help Sri Lanka and provided both equipment and training. Outside assistance improved Sri Lanka's ability to counter LTTE's efforts, confounding India's efforts to please both ethnic Tamils in Tamil Nadu and the government in Colombo.

Colombo hindered India's ability to shepherd negotiations. From 1984 to 1986, the Sri Lankan government would agree to concessions as long as it preserved some way of reversing them in the future. During that time, Sri Lanka continually stepped up military operations to counter LTTE's efforts. Frustrated, Rajiv Gandhi, Indira Gandhi's son, returned to his mother's policy of simultaneously engaging Colombo diplomatically and militarily.[16] In 1985 and 1986, negotiations made little headway because of the efforts of LTTE and the mutual distrust between India and Sri Lanka. Colombo's representatives engaged in negotiations to provide its military with more time to train and acquire better equipment. India continued to covertly support Tamil militant groups while pushing overtly for a diplomatic solution.

LTTE used the population to hide from Sri Lankan forces and used its frustration and low regard for Tamil citizens to provoke Sinhalese violence against Tamil civilians. The atrocities committed by the Sri Lankan armed forces generated a great deal of scrutiny from India and other states in the international system; it also put more pressure on India to take action.

LTTE specifically planned its operations to derail negotiation efforts by making it difficult for Colombo to offer up the concessions for which India was pushing. To strengthen its bargaining position and maximize concessions from the Sri Lankan government, LTTE steadily worked toward expanding its influence in the north and east. LTTE also began to establish a parallel government in the Jaffna region providing social services to Tamils.[17]

Frustrated by LTTE's unwillingness to accept its concessions and outraged at the movement's attempts to establish a parallel government, Colombo launched a major offensive—Operation Liberation—against LTTE in January 1987. Sri Lanka's armed forces, having received support from Pakistan and Israel, had become more adept at counterinsurgency and counterterrorism operations, allowing them to push LTTE back into the Jaffna Peninsula and threaten the organization's extinction.

Despite having the upper hand, Sri Lanka made a critical operational error in stiffening its efforts to roll back LTTE's influence. Focusing on the effort to eliminate LTTE and neglecting the importance of gaining the support of the civilians in the battlespace, Sri Lanka's tactics caused widespread civilian casualties and sent a new wave of Tamil refugees to India.[18] Operation Liberation renewed the sympathy of Indian Tamils who once again demanded that New Delhi intervene. As a result, India warned Colombo to stop the siege of the Jaffna Peninsula and restore

Tamil access to vital resources. When President Jayewardene refused to stop the blockade, Rajiv Gandhi authorized Indian ships to carry supplies across the Palk Strait; the Sri Lankan Navy, however, promptly turned those ships back. Unwilling to be denied, New Delhi then sent cargo aircraft, under fighter escort, to provide aerial deliveries of critical supplies.

Lacking outside support and unable to counter India's actions without inviting a military invasion, Colombo capitulated.[19] Three months later, India and Sri Lanka signed an accord to end the crisis. This move, unlike the others, did not involve LTTE in the negotiations. Sri Lanka agreed to Tamil autonomy in the northern and eastern provinces as long as India agreed to offer military assistance should Colombo have difficulty disarming LTTE and reasserting its control over the island. India acquiesced.

Why Did India Choose a Proxy War Policy?
To ensure that Sri Lanka's domestic unrest did not attract unwanted intervention from the West and interfere with India's regional interests, New Delhi used the eruption of the ethnic crisis in 1983 to exert greater influence in Colombo.[20] India argued that the ethnic character of the violence made the conflict an exclusively regional affair.[21] India aimed to reverse Sri Lanka's efforts to involve extraregional states and keep the situation in Sri Lanka a local affair.[22] To preserve its image as a leader of the nonalignment movement and avoid giving outside states a reason to intervene, India's policy had to provide a means to influence the Sinhalese government in Sri Lanka without resorting to an overt military intervention.[23] Most importantly, India wanted to avoid destroying or weakening Sri Lanka's democratic government, despite its evolution to a sectarian, control-democracy.[24] By the mid-1980s, Rajiv Gandhi's administration clearly committed to a settlement that would keep Sri Lanka intact.[25]

COHERENCE

*How Did India Attempt to Ensure Coherence
and What Was the Overall Effect?*

INTERNAL COHERENCE   To balance regional security objectives with domestic imperatives, India formulated a two-pronged policy. Overtly, India strong-armed its way into serving as an intermediary between the Tamils and the Sri Lankan government and used diplomacy to prevent outside states from supporting Sri Lanka's government and gaining a foothold in south Asia.[26] Covertly, India used its Research and Analysis Wing (RAW) to infiltrate and manipulate numerous Tamil militant groups— LTTE being the most capable and influential—to increase the pressure against the Sri Lankan government to grant concessions to ethnic Tamils.[27] India also began providing covert support to LTTE and other Tamil militant groups to quiet concerns in Tamil Nadu and counter increasing support for Sri Lanka's government from Pakistan and Israel.[28]

INTRASTATE COHERENCE   India's decision to fuel ethnic divides to accomplish its foreign policy reflected a lack of sensitivity to one of the most intractable problems in the region—ethnic fragmentation. New Delhi's decision to use LTTE and other Tamil militant groups to influence Sri Lanka's foreign and domestic policy did not adequately consider the effect it might have on the ethnic divides within its own borders.[29] India overplayed the ethnic divide to gain favor with its domestic public, a move that played into the hands of LTTE and significantly raised the costs of India's policy.

The high level of enmity between Tamil and Sinhalese ethnic groups led to widespread violence, and the ruthless treatment of ethnic Tamils did not erode the Sri Lankan government's support among the Sinhalese people. The ethnic hatred between Sinhalese and Tamils created two problems for India's proxy intervention. First, animosity led the Sinhalese majority and the Tamil minority to seek a solution through violence rather than negotiation.[30] Second, the Sinhalese people resented India's support of Tamil militants, causing domestic pressure to distrust India's efforts to broker a settlement to the conflict. As the conflict swung in Colombo's favor in 1987, India pushed even harder for a settlement. To prevent LTTE from losing its foothold in Sri Lanka, India conducted an aerial resupply under armed escort to protect LTTE on the Jaffna Peninsula. India's airdrops angered most Sinhalese citizens and further undermined support for the proposed Indo-Lanka Accord in Sri Lanka.[31]

India's policy of backing LTTE interfered with its ultimate goal of shaping Sri Lanka's foreign policy. The problem was that India was negotiating with Jayewardene, but the president did not have the support of his cabinet, nor did he have the power to push his policies through without some degree of support.[32] India's pressure had the unintended effect of undermining Jayewardene's position and pushing public support into the hands of Sinhalese conservatives. When India threatened Jayewardene with intervention after the spike in violence in January 1987, his decision to sign the Indo-Lanka Accord was viewed by the Sinhalese public as a sign of weakness. LTTE's behavior had already cast a sense of enmity into the Sinhalese population—granting LTTE and the Tamils autonomy resulted in Jayewardene losing control of the government and nullified the Indo-Lanka Accord.

Given LTTE's previous efforts to derail negotiations short of a two-state solution, India purposefully excluded the Tamil militants from this round of negotiations. India's decision widened the divide between its interests and its proxy's.[33] Sri Lanka's government, however, had doubts about the willingness of ethnic Tamils to support the proposed accord. To get Colombo to sign the agreement, India offered security assistance to Sri Lanka's government to guarantee LTTE's compliance.

INTERNATIONAL/DOMESTIC COHERENCE   The unrestrained violence perpetrated against Sri Lanka's Tamils—especially the civilians—reinvigorated sympathy among Tamils in Tamil Nadu. When Sri Lanka began a concentrated assault against LTTE in January 1987 and later blockaded the Jaffna Peninsula, India was pressured domestically to intervene.[34] India still wanted to avoid direct military intervention, but it could not afford to allow the Tamils to be slaughtered either. India's support for Sri Lanka's Tamils played to the immense empathy of the Tamil population living in Tamil Nadu.

Outside Tamil Nadu, India succeeded in hiding its support to LTTE and other Tamil militants.[35] Judging from the articles written in 1988, India's support of Tamil militant groups appears suspect until the *Jain Commission Interim Report* was released in 1997. For example, Robert Oberst comments that India's role had been that of an intermediary and that India had been further drawn in because of the presence of LTTE bases in Tamil Nadu and the concern of Indian Tamils about the plight of Sri Lankan Tamils.[36] Kumar Rupesinghe only mentions that Indian intelligence had been suspected of supplying arms to LTTE.[37]

Sri Lanka repeatedly accused India of intervening through its support of Tamil militants—providing safe havens and training in weapons and tactics. Sri Lanka, however, was unable to provide actual proof, leaving India with the ability to plausibly deny any involvement. India's policy precluded direct involvement from the United States, United Kingdom, and China. Without clear evidence of India's violation of Sri Lankan sovereignty, states interested in taking action were denied an obvious justification for doing so. It did not, however, stop the United States and the United Kingdom from providing support to Colombo through unofficial channels. For example, the United States encouraged Israel to assist the Sri Lankan government with counterinsurgency training; the United Kingdom did the same, sending former SAS commandos.[38] Further, the United States cut its support to Colombo because of its reluctance to make concessions regarding its mistreatment of the Tamil people. Finally, India's veiling of its support to LTTE allowed relations—though strained—to remain open between India and Sri Lanka.[39]

PROXY COHERENCE   The proximity and relationship between Indian and Sri Lankan Tamils precluded India from hiding its support of LTTE from the Tamils living in Tamil Nadu. LTTE's illicit activities and its wanton use of violence in Tamil Nadu wore out the group's welcome in Tamil Nadu after a few years. Support among Indian Tamils waned until early 1987, when Sri Lanka's armed forces renewed their efforts and pursued the eradication of LTTE.[40] LTTE's behavior was overt enough that it created resentment among the people living in Tamil Nadu and allowed India to put pressure on LTTE. LTTE's existence as the sole Tamil group capable of standing up to Sri Lankan forces and the sympathetic reactions of Indian Tamils toward the plight of Sri Lanka's Tamils, however, prohibited India from undermining LTTE's ability to operate independently and effectively.

India's desire to slow LTTE operations met with resistance because the Tamil militant group wanted to push even harder to bargain from the strongest position possible.[41] The divergence created a rift and fostered a sense of growing animosity among LTTE members toward India. Although LTTE understood the importance of India's support and participation and India's interest in the region, LTTE began to see that India was motivated by its own interests and not by any humanitarian or human rights considerations.[42] Not only did LTTE block efforts to resolve the conflict diplomatically (raising India's costs), it also created a situation where India could not broker an agreement without providing its own military forces as leverage to police LTTE forces in Sri Lanka.

Despite India's efforts to keep all Tamil militant groups relatively equal in capability and influence, LTTE emerged—through its efforts to eradicate rival Tamil militant groups—as the dominant and most widely recognized symbol of Tamil interests in Sri Lanka. India's desire for secrecy made it difficult to enable LTTE to compete with Sri Lanka's improved counterinsurgency tactics. When Sri Lanka's armed forces threatened LTTE's survival in 1987, India had to abandon its covert support and provide overt support to prevent the group's extermination. Although Indian Tamils had grown disillusioned and weary of LTTE's presence in Tamil Nadu, the extreme pressure put on Tamils during the blockade of the Jaffna Peninsula forced India's hand. India could not cut off LTTE for fear of appearing to have abandoned the Tamil cause in Sri Lanka, a perception that could have created unwanted civil unrest within India's borders.[43]

As the conflict progressed, India began to pressure both sides to negotiate and reach a settlement that involved a one-state solution. Considering LTTE's dominant position among the Tamil militant groups, India made efforts to include the leaders of the organization in the negotiations.[44] LTTE, however, did not desire a one-state outcome and sought to disrupt negotiations using flagrant violence and taking an unwavering stance on secession. LTTE succeeded in derailing efforts on two different occasions.[45] Frustrated, India excluded LTTE from the negotiations in 1987 that resulted in the Indo-Lanka Accord.

CONTROL

How Did India Use and Control Its Proxy and to What End?

THE COMPATIBILITY OF OBJECTIVES   India and LTTE had convergent objectives in only one way, to reduce Sinhalese discrimination and violence against ethnic Tamils in Sri Lanka. Beyond that, India's and LTTE's objectives diverged widely. India desired a one-state solution that provided for the safety, security, and equality of Tamils. LTTE, however, wanted a two-state solution. Tamil militants knew they could not regain Tamil security without assistance. As is often the case with groups in need of support, LTTE stated they wanted a separate Tamil state but rhetorically conceded to the creation of autonomous, Tamil-dominated regional governments that would remain within the Sri Lankan state.[46]

To increase its leverage against the undesirable one-state solution, LTTE wanted to merge the northern and eastern provinces of Sri Lanka where most ethnic Tamils lived, but Colombo demanded that the two remain separate; this became a major sticking point that stalled negotiations.[47] LTTE wanted the two provinces fused together because Tamils from the northern province were of a higher caste, Vellala, and held the most political clout. Although the Vellala Tamils had embraced the LTTE out of necessity, they had not embraced them politically. Because of this, the TULF had an upper hand in political elections on the Jaffna Peninsula. The members of LTTE varied widely in their castes, and they therefore wanted a merger between the two provinces to combine the economic potential of the East province and its largely mixed-caste population to offset the TULF's dominance in Jaffna.[48]

India wanted to broker a peace settlement. Although New Delhi had some success in getting Colombo to agree to Tamil autonomy within a single state, LTTE refused to accept Colombo's concessions and instead engaged in terror operations to derail negotiations. LTTE leaders rejected any proposal that did not allow the northern and eastern Tamil provinces to merge into a single region.[49] Unable to secure LTTE support for the settlement, India initiated an operation with the Tamil Nadu government to crackdown on Sri Lankan Tamil militants living in India on November 8, 1986. The act, however, was intended to influence an upcoming meeting between Prime Minister Rajiv Gandhi and President Jayewardene in Bangalore; those arrested were released within a day and the weapons that had been confiscated were later returned.[50] The action suggests India's desire to control LTTE without cutting it off its ability to augment the diplomatic pressure on Sri Lanka's government.

As negotiations progressed, Tamil militants lost confidence in India's commitment. India stopped pushing for guarantees that the Sri Lankan government would uphold its promise of Tamil autonomy. Believing that New Delhi had only its own interests at heart, LTTE shifted its efforts toward improving its ability to negotiate with Colombo, regardless of the effects on India's policy.[51] Because India focused on its own desire to negotiate a settlement and demonstrate its influence in south Asia, it failed to address one of the core issues of the conflict—the deep ethnic bias that precluded either side from committing to a negotiated settlement. India had to offer the Indian Peace Keeping Force (IPKF) as a guarantee to Sri Lanka's government that the Tamils would honor the accord. India did not, however, offer a similar guarantee to the Tamils. Although the policy addressed many Tamil concerns, LTTE felt that New Delhi had sold them out and chose to ignore the accord.[52]

THE CAPABILITY OF A PROXY   Although India supported several Tamil militant groups, LTTE quickly became India's most dominant proxy. India's policy failed to keep all Tamil militant groups relatively equal in their capabilities and influence. With the help of India's training and resources, LTTE steadily eradicated rival Tamil militant groups. Inside India, LTTE engaged in widespread illicit activities such as drug running, smuggling, and terrorism that likely provided some degree of independence.[53] In addition, the state of Tamil Nadu provided support independent of India's central government.[54]

Even with India's covert support, LTTE could not compete with Sri Lanka's armed forces by the late 1980s. The inability of LTTE and other Tamil militant groups to withstand Sri Lanka's assault in 1987 caused India to intervene directly.[55] India not only had to air-drop supplies to circumvent Sri Lanka's blockade of the Jaffna Peninsula and provide relief to the Tamils, it also had to prevent LTTE from losing its appearance as an effective counter to Sri Lanka's armed forces. LTTE was the predominant hope of the Tamil people against Sinhalese domination; keeping LTTE viable allowed India to preserve the possibility that Colombo would make concessions to the Tamil people.[56]

Sustained by contributions from outside sources, LTTE did not feel compelled to adhere to India's demand to disarm. LTTE delivered only a token number of weapons to Indian authorities and later began engaging the IPKF directly. India's first experience policing LTTE proved shocking. When IPKF captured the first seventeen LTTE soldiers, each took the cyanide capsule they wore around their neck. Twelve of them died. In retaliation, LTTE executed eight IPKF soldiers it had captured.[57] What was believed to be a simple operation for Indian forces turned out to be a difficult and costly task in terms of resources and reputation. India's forces face the difficult task of fighting an insurgency as a third party caused numerous civilian casualties and employed many of the same tactics they had criticized Sri Lankan forces of in previous years. New Delhi quickly found out that its forces were grossly underprepared and that it was now engaged in a conflict among an unfriendly population—a surprise considering that the same population had previously considered India as its protector.[58]

LTTE's ability to operate effectively among civilians presented as significant a challenge for the IPKF as it had for Sri Lanka's armed forces. After only a short time, Indian forces began committing similar atrocities and inflicting casualties on Tamil civilians.[59] LTTE continued to use civilians to shield their operations and incite violent responses from Sri Lanka and IPKF. LTTE's tactics did not engender greater support for Sri Lanka or IPKF—instead they had the opposite effect and discredited efforts to disband LTTE.

THE DEPENDENCE OF A PROXY ON OUTSIDE SUPPORT   To provide India with enough leverage to control LTTE and other Tamil militant groups, RAW distributed its support in a way that would preclude a single Tamil militant group from emerging as a dominant force—stronger groups received less support while weaker groups received more.[60] India controlled

Tamil sources for weapons and other necessary supplies to keep Tamil militants from looking for support from outsiders. India also kept the Tamils from looking elsewhere by providing adequate levels of support and training and keeping alive the possibility that India might intervene directly on the Tamils' behalf.[61]

The only overlap between India's and LTTE's objectives was to stop the violence being waged against Sri Lankan Tamils; it stopped promptly thereafter. India did not want a separate Tamil state—something LTTE adamantly demanded. The point to be made here is that India did not push to include LTTE in negotiations to settle the Tamil issue. Instead, New Delhi purposely excluded LTTE from the final negotiations. India also lacked the leverage to force LTTE to accept the terms of the accord—LTTE was too independent and too autonomous. India's offer to make LTTE's leader, Velupillai Prabhakaran, the chief minister of the Tamil regions and the ability to select the majority of the members of the administrative council failed to make amends.[62]

SUMMARY

The ongoing Cold War and the accompanying bipolar order had only a minimal effect on India's indirect intervention in Sri Lanka. India effectively used norms such as the right to intervene when human rights had been violated and the right to intervene when the conflict spills over into another state's borders to cover its support of LTTE and other Tamil militant groups. The former was used when LTTE was on the brink of destruction during Operation Liberation; the latter provided India with the means to establish training camps and create safe havens for Tamil militant groups on Indian soil. Further, India's political intervention as an active mediator in the conflict was justified by the fact that the conflict spilled over into Tamil Nadu.

The connection between Indian and Sri Lankan Tamils created a situation where India faced significant domestic pressure to assist Tamil militant groups. The perception that supporting the Tamils in Sri Lanka could provide a means of pressuring the government in Colombo to stop courting the United States and United Kingdom blinded India to the possibility that it could lose control of LTTE. India also underestimated the LTTE. India's inability to control the militant group, especially when it was operating within India's borders, provided LTTE with the means to pursue its own objectives, independent of India's desires. When the Sri Lankan armed forces increased the pressure beyond LTTE's capabilities and drove the militant group to the brink of destruction, the sympathy of the Tamil population in India and the delicate political atmosphere inside India forced New Delhi to support the LTTE regardless of the group's aims.

From a utility perspective, LTTE looked like a good policy option. From an efficacy perspective, the divergence between India's and LTTE's objectives, the inability of New Delhi to cultivate LTTE's dependence, and the primacy of keeping its involvement secret all combined to cause India's policy to fail. The only overlap between India's and LTTE's objectives was to stop the violence being waged against Sri Lankan Tamils; it stopped promptly thereafter. India did not want a separate Tamil state—something LTTE adamantly demanded. The point to be made here is that India did not push to include LTTE in negotiations to settle the Tamil issue. Instead, New Delhi purposely excluded LTTE from the final negotiations. India also lacked the leverage to force LTTE to accept the terms of the accord—LTTE was too independent and too autonomous. India's offer to make Prabhakaran the chief minister of the Tamil regions and giving him the ability to select most members of the administrative council failed to make amends.[63]

The sympathy of Indian Tamils and the vulnerability of India's central government to domestic politics created a scenario where New Delhi could not effectively use incentives to control LTTE. The secrecy of India's support to LTTE and the decision to offer sanctuary to Tamil militant groups in Tamil Nadu provided LTTE with alternative sources of resources needed to conduct operations independent of India's support. India's failure to monitor LTTE's operations, specifically those involving the elimination of rival Tamil militant groups, undermined New Delhi's plan to keep LTTE and other Tamil groups responsive to India's direction. When Sri Lanka stood on the verge of defeating the Tamil insurgency, India felt it had to support LTTE to complement its diplomatic efforts to secure Tamil autonomy from the Sri Lankan government and to mollify the Indian Tamils' desire for direct intervention.

India's policy of backing LTTE interfered with its goal of shaping Sri Lanka's foreign policy. The problem was that India was negotiating with Jayewardene, but the president did not have the support of his cabinet, nor did he have the power to push his policies through without some degree of support.[64] India's pressure had the unintended effect of undermining Jayewardene's position and pushing public support into the hands of Sinhalese conservatives. When India threatened Jayewardene with intervention after the spike in violence in January 1987, his decision to sign the Indo-Lanka Accord was viewed by the Sinhalese public as a sign of weakness. LTTE's behavior had already cast a sense of enmity into the Sinhalese population—granting LTTE and the Tamils autonomy resulted in Jayewardene losing control of the government and nullified the Indo-Lanka Accord.

*How Do My Proposed Maxims Apply to the
Intervening State's Use of a Proxy?*

KNOW YOUR ENEMY, BUT KNOW YOUR PROXY EVEN BETTER   Because LTTE was fighting for secession/autonomy and India wanted the prestige of settling the conflict and to keep Sri Lanka's government intact, India had no ability to offer LTTE an attractive, outcome-based incentive. India's only card to play was keeping the possibility of direct intervention open to prevent LTTE from seeking outside help.[65] Saddled with the enormous domestic pressure to support LTTE, India should have more carefully considered the disparity of its objectives compared to LTTE's and blended some outcome-based incentives into its support. This case suggests that when an intervening state's ability to control its proxy is questionable, outcome-based incentives of some sort should be used to ensure that the proxy remains sufficiently committed to the intervening state's objectives.

Giving LTTE a place to train, weapons with which to fight, and supplies to sustain its operations mollified Indian Tamils, but it failed to structure India's support in a way that would promote more control. India prioritized keeping the LTTE as a viable means of leverage rather than recognizing the problems with exerting control. Any action that was taken to check LTTE operations was usually just a warning with no consequences. Although troublesome LTTE leaders were deported to Sri Lanka, weapons and equipment confiscated in retribution for undesirable behavior were usually returned within a very short period. Worse, India continued to support LTTE despite its willingness to derail negotiations, its efforts to destroy other Tamil militant groups, its illicit activities inside India, and its decision to use violence against civilians as leverage against Sri Lanka (and later India).

India's primary failure in its indirect intervention was underestimating the LTTE. Following the signing of the accord, LTTE only partially complied and then later began to use terror and violence to reassert its dominance in Tamil areas. India had to deploy over fifty thousand soldiers in the IPKF to disarm the LTTE and help Sri Lanka reestablish peace and stability in Tamil regions. Because Sri Lanka also had a Sinhalese insurgency operating in the south, this provision of the accord allowed Sri Lanka to focus its efforts in the South while putting India on the spot to deal with the Tamil militants in the north and east.[66]

Unexpectedly, India found that its forces were grossly underprepared for conducting counterinsurgency operations against the LTTE. The strain of operating in Sri Lanka led IPKF soldiers to commit the same strategic error as Sri Lanka's forces: tactics that resulted in weakening LTTE's forces caused widespread civilian casualties, discrediting IPKF's actions and bruising India's prestige on the world stage. The failure of the IPKF to disarm LTTE and reports of IPKF soldiers killing innocent civilians and raping innocent women turned India's public against the policy. The IPKF failed to bring LTTE under control, contributing to Rajiv Gandhi's loss of the election in 1988 and India's government pulling its forces out of Sri Lanka in 1989.

LET THE PROXY LEAD, BUT ONLY SO FAR   Initially, LTTE's ability to operate autonomously provided a boon because it prevented India from having to intervene directly and could keep India's involvement covert.

Giving LTTE such a high degree of autonomy, however, also meant that India could not monitor LTTE's operations or limit the group's self-interested behavior. LTTE's duplicitous use of India's support eventually undermined New Delhi's policy. While LTTE used India's assistance to help pressure Colombo to grant the desired concessions to ethnic Tamils, it also used those resources to eliminate other Tamil militant groups. RAW failed to provide other Tamil militant groups with enough assistance to compete with LTTE, an error that allowed LTTE to emerge as the primary symbol of Tamil resistance.

India could not control LTTE because it had eliminated other Tamil militant groups. The Tamils in Sri Lanka saw LTTE as their best hope for getting the autonomy they desired from Colombo. India could not allow LTTE to be destroyed by either the Sri Lankan armed forces or the IPKF because of the sympathy of the Tamils living in India. Operating independently, LTTE derailed negotiations and prolonged the conflict. Making matters worse for India, LTTE also revolted against the Indo-Lanka Accord that had been brokered in its absence, drawing India deeper into the conflict and visibly demonstrating India's impotency in solving the crisis.

India's need for secrecy worked against its ability to control its proxy. If sustaining multiple insurgent groups was the plan, much like it was for Pakistan during the Soviet occupation of Afghanistan, India failed to put the resources into monitoring each of its proxies to protect them from each other. Putting more advisors on the ground would have increased India's ability to monitor LTTE's operations and curbed its ability to eliminate competing Tamil militant groups, but it would have exposed India's support for LTTE's operations against the Sri Lankan government. The effort required to limit LTTE's ability to lead operations in Sri Lanka would not have supported India's greater objectives of demonstrating its ability to influence affairs in south Asia and sustaining its leadership in the nonalignment movement.

CULTIVATE RESOURCE DEPENDENCE   Although LTTE proved a capable, motivated, and independent proxy, LTTE needed India. Without assistance from New Delhi and Tamil Nadu, LTTE would not have become such a potent force. The problem, however, was that India was unable to cultivate LTTE's dependence in a way that would provide adequate control. India used RAW to increase LTTE's dependence using behavior-based incentives, playing the different Tamil militant groups off one another and offering support based on each group's performance.[67] India did not monitor LTTE's operations closely enough, however, to cultivate the group's dependence. LTTE used its training and weapons to eliminate rival militant groups, undermining RAW's plan to control India's proxies. The secrecy of the affair also complicated using resources to promote control. India had to use third parties to provide items such as weapons that were difficult to veil or deny. As an unintended consequence, using third parties introduced additional ways for the militants to acquire weapons and other resources.[68]

Sympathy for the plight of Sri Lankan Tamils also made it difficult to police the actions of Tamil militants in Tamil Nadu. The delicate political environment turned any action to control Tamil activities into a weapon for opposition parties to claim that the policy was insensitive to the current situation in Sri Lanka. When LTTE resistance to negotiations led New Delhi to attempt to curb both its support and that from the local government in Tamil Nadu, Sri Lanka's renewed efforts to destroy LTTE led to a resurgence of support among Indian Tamils.[69] LTTE and other Tamil groups continued to receive support, despite their efforts to spoil India's attempts to foster negotiations and their illicit use of Indian territory to further their own agenda. Only after the talks in Bangalore did India and, more importantly, the state of Tamil Nadu begin restricting LTTE's support.[70] By this time, however, enough time, space, and resources had been given to allow LTTE to set up its own organization independent of India's assistance.

The widespread support LTTE and other Tamil militant groups received from sources other than India's central government suggests that a significant consideration in a conflict with strong ethnic overtones is the size, location, commitment, and resources of the proxy's diaspora. India's decision to give LTTE access to Tamil Nadu provided an additional means of gaining resources—mostly through smuggling and gun running. The political situation in India and the sympathy of Indian Tamils allowed LTTE to exploit decision makers at the local (Tamil Nadu) and national level and play them off each other. LTTE managed to secure support despite its disregard for India's interests because of the political vulnerability of elected officials.[71] Operating safely from inside Tamil Nadu, LTTE succeeded in expanding its international contacts. Not only did LTTE manage to gain equipment and supplies from foreign governments interested in profiting from arms sales, it also gained the support of a sympathetic Tamil diaspora that lobbied governments to provide additional resources. Fourth, India's insistence that LTTE's leader—Velupillai Prabhakaran—participate in negotiations with Sri Lanka at Thimphu in 1986 forced both India and Sri Lanka to publicly recognize LTTE as a legitimate party with whom a settlement should be worked out.[72] As a result, LTTE gained a formal role in the negotiations and could voice its own opinions with some legitimacy. LTTE's participation marginalized TULF's moderate position and shifted the focus to secession.[73]

CHAPTER 8

CONCLUSION

PROXY WAR, despite its ugliness and exorbitant human costs, is here to stay. As the world becomes more interconnected, the affairs in one state or region will affect others. Governments, regardless of regime type, will continue to find a need to indirectly intervene elsewhere. In this book, I argue that understanding the means of conducting foreign policy between direct intervention and nonintervention, be it donating assistance to a third party or via proxy, matters. When the situation in another state influences a state's interests and demands some response but does not cross the threshold for direct intervention, policy gets very complicated. Add to that, financial restrictions and increasing pressure from peer or near-peer competitors continue to lead states to look for opportunities to manage commitments abroad.

For states with the means, one of the main ways to solve resource issues and overstretch has been to engage and/or develop partners with common interests. Further, opportunities to hamstring a competing state may lead to engaging in an indirect intervention without adequately considering secondary or unintended effects. As I have demonstrated in this book, however, those partners are self-interested. Threats to national interest or security can alter perceptions about the prospective value of helping a group that appears to want the same thing as policy makers in Washington, D.C. Partners do not always lower risks or offer cheap ways of positively influencing events in another state. Unfortunately, political pressure has a way of altering the utility and efficacy of indirect intervention. Short-term desires can quickly overwhelm good choices based on long-term objectives. Worse, the pressure only increases as events in the target state heighten demands for a response. These conditions lead to choosing the *least bad option* available.

Indirect intervention finds its place in the realm of policy options that falls between applying a state's instruments of power directly and doing nothing. Providing support of any kind to influence events in another state requires delineation. Indirect intervention, whether through donating assistance or proxy war, is about exerting influence in a way that either obscures or hides an intervening state's level of involvement. It does not have to be about controlling the outcome of an intrastate conflict, per se. It does, however, require a willing or, at the very least, coercible participant to act in the intervening state's best interests.

My concern is that both policy makers and academics have skewed the definition of proxy war, making it an ambiguous and misunderstood method of indirect intervention. The participation of a third party does not automatically indicate a proxy war. Regardless of how the policy has been articulated, the difference between the two is important. Donating assistance provides resources and grants the local actor full autonomy to influence political affairs in the target state. Proxy war, on the other hand, demands a hierarchical relationship between the intervening state and its proxy. Assistance comes with the requirement that the local actor subjugate its own interests to the those of the intervening state. The intervening state directs the use of force in a way that usefully and efficaciously influences political affairs in the target state. The local actor's (the proxy's) interests and desires remain relevant, but only in the way that it impacts the intervening state's ability to achieve its objectives.

PROXY WAR AS A TOOL OF FOREIGN POLICY

Proxy war, or, put in contemporary policy terms, "operating by, with, and through partners," is not a panacea. Such a policy deserves a healthy dose of trepidation, and it does not improve just because the other options look worse. Equally important, as events in the target state increasingly demand a response, proxy war does not get more attractive just because a decision has to be made. A good place to start when exploring policy options is articulating why an indirect intervention, and more specifically, a proxy war is necessary. As stated previously, states choose such a policy when the risk of escalation increases if a state directly intervenes, a lack of domestic support may risk the sustainability of the intervention, a lack of international support negatively affects the cost/benefit ratio of the intervention, or a lack of capacity makes direct intervention untenable. Each reason for indirect intervention inherently bears some incentives, but each equally brings some concerns. Under any of the four cases, proxy war offers the perceivable opportunity to balance the costs and benefits of indirect intervention while reducing risk.

Proxy war, and more broadly indirect intervention, is about influencing events in another state. Sometimes that means winning, but more often it means accomplishing other objectives. Parsing out the objective of an indirect intervention or proxy war into four categories (*in it to win it*, *holding action*, *meddling*, and *feeding the chaos*) provides a much better perspective. Each category has its advantages and disadvantages. What is important, however, is that an intervening state recognizes which type of intervention matches its desired objectives with the conditions that will ultimately affect the outcome of the policy. To facilitate analysis, I broke conditions into four categories: time, the proxy, domestic influences, and international influences. As I explained in Chapter 4, some conditions are immutable—those the intervening state must accept as permanent and work around. Some are mutable—those the intervening state can influence. Taken together, an intervening state should assess both sets of conditions and tailor the policy accordingly. Further, assessments should follow a prescribed process, also explained in Chapter 4, that mitigates the negative effects of bias and misperception.

As the world drifts further away from a unipolar order, proxy wars will increase in both frequency and scope. Proxy wars aimed at securing a victory for one side in a civil war (in it to win it) or to prevent the spread of violence into a particular state or region (holding action), which were absent after the end of the Cold War, will most certainly return. Global powers armed with nuclear weapons and competing on the margins of their spheres of influence will employ proxies at a higher rate and will prolong the duration of civil wars, similar to the bipolar order of the Cold War. Rhetorical battles fought between the United States, China, and Russia will manifest into arguments for indirect interventions in strategic locations around the world. Global powers, however, will likely resist proxy wars aimed at solely prolonging violence (feeding the chaos) to sustain or cultivate their image as a world leader, but such an option will remain for regional powers with a smaller sphere of influence and unhindered by democracy, such as Iran in Yemen.

Acknowledging that proxy war is not a desirable action, coherence and control will improve the utility and efficacy of its use. In the case of Laos, the United States' use of the Hmong as a holding action worked, but it wasn't sustainable because of the way it conducted the proxy war. The Hmong had too much autonomy at times and had such overwhelming dependency that they couldn't adapt to changing conditions in a way that would have allowed them to survive. The Hmong proxy provided a convenient means of masking involvement so that the Soviet Union remained clear of the conflict, and it ultimately protected Thailand from an unencumbered communist wave. America's proxy war in Laos also highlights that high costs of support are bearable at home and abroad, as long as the intervening state's casualty rates remain extremely low. The Laos case may not be repeatable in the twenty-first century, because of the inability to restrict the flow of information from the battlespace. I am not so sure, however, that social media will significantly hinder proxy war's utility and efficacy in the future. The international community remains fickle when it comes to intrastate conflicts. The world is well aware of the ethnic cleansing that took place in Myanmar, a country with tight controls on social media and information, allowing the tragedies that have befallen the Rohingya to receive global attention, yet little has been done. Perhaps it only demonstrates a growing reluctance for states to become directly involved in states or regions in a global power's sphere of influence (China in this case).

The Laos case also highlights how coherence exists in more than one aspect of a proxy war. The United States maintained a coherent policy regarding its overall commitment to the conflict. From beginning to end, Washington did not intend for the Hmong to win but only to prevent the

Pathet Lao from taking Vientiane. The coherence of U.S. policy, however, suffered in regard to managing the longevity of its Hmong proxy. Allowing the fight to transition at times to conventional battles to hold or gain territory led to undesired attrition and the need to increase America's visible commitment to the conflict. The United States had to acknowledge its activities in Laos later in the conflict to avoid the extermination of its proxy. Fortunately, U.S. efforts did not completely undermine the efficacy of its Hmong proxy to give the Soviet Union a reason to remain uninvolved.

The Angola case reveals both how the structured isolation of a proxy improves control and that providing a proxy with support that engenders local support improves its ability to accomplish an intervening state's objectives. Providing resources that allow the proxy to engender support with local communities provided an advantage—it prevented outside influences from gaining a foothold to interrupt the proxy's isolation and ensured that the population living in the region within which the proxy operates would support the proxy.

The Angola case supports the idea that a proxy provides other states a means of looking the other way, rather than concealing an indirect intervention. Further, South Africa's ability to maintain its strategic perspective and not overreach in Angola ensured that its proxy war policy remained coherent for over two decades. Pretoria correctly understood that it was time to abandon Jonas Savimbi and UNITA and support a peace deal in Angola.

In almost every way, the Sri Lanka case provides an ideal example of how not to conduct a proxy war. Allowing LTTE to cultivate such strong support within the Indian state of Tamil Nadu created alternative means of support and applied political pressure that unhinged the coherence of New Delhi's proxy war policy. Failing to establish control over LTTE and then later committing to policing its proxy in support of peace negotiations, India's indirect intervention turned direct intervention devolved into a political nightmare. Although the use of LTTE did keep the United States out of Sri Lanka and helped sustain India's hold on the region, it dealt a blow to India's desire to influence events in the region. Most of all, India serves as a note of caution of what can happen when a state fails to consider how to gain and maintain coherence and control in a proxy war.

WHERE DO WE GO FROM HERE?

Proxy war remains chiefly about relying on another to provide the instrument of force to achieve political goals. Different stakes and different perceptions about risks and rewards enter into the equation. Therefore, studying proxy war fills an important gap in the study of why states go to war. More specifically, proxy wars provide insights about the threshold for when a state wants to act forcefully to protect its interest without sufficient provocation or justification to participate directly.

The twenty-first century and its associated advances in information sharing, communication, and social media will not likely create a revolutionary change in the utility and efficacy of proxy war. If anything, social media will push states to consider proxy war more often. Social media could exacerbate the control problem because it will make it harder to embed (the intervener's forces can get caught on video) with proxy forces, but the plausible deniability that comes along with supporting a proxy in its own political struggle will remain, despite Twitter or YouTube. Obscurity applies to those that want to hide their involvement from others and to those that want others to hide their involvement from them (i.e., how the Soviet Union knew that the United States was in Laos but confirmed that Moscow would stay out so long as the United States kept it quiet). Even today, Russia's involvement in the Donbass region of Ukraine remains an obscure but open secret. Proxies facing abandonment, much like how Savimbi felt South Africa and the United States sold him out at the conclusion of the Angolan civil war, could use social media to blackmail interveners into supporting additional operations. Experience, however, has not shown that previously embarrassing connections with proxies have deterred the use of proxy war over time.

Discussions regarding the use of proxy war should range far beyond comparing the relative military capability of the proxy versus the adversary or the types and means of support to enable the proxy to achieve the intervening state's objectives. Further, discussions about the utility of using a proxy should occur separately from discussions about how to specifically use and employ the proxy. The discussion should not hinge on how to do it rather than if it makes sense. Something that may appear easy to accomplish could cloud the decision about whether it is a good decision in the first place; this is how operational-level influences can lead strategic-level decisions astray. For example, supporting Kurdish forces against the Islamic State of Iraq and Syria (ISIS) could hamper U.S. relations with governments in both Iraq and Turkey; this is not to say that it is or is not the best course of action to support American interests, but it should at least be considered in addition to the potential for a Kurdish proxy to defeat ISIS.

Proxy war is highly uncertain. Whether they know it or not, decision makers will have to make choices based on many different assumptions and unknowns. There will be limits to the information available about the conditions on the ground, the motivations of the proxy and the adversary, the reactions of domestic and international audiences, and the reality of successfully providing the proxy with the support needed to win, hold, meddle, or indefinitely extend the violence. Uncertainty is a concern because it tends to drive decision makers (often unknowingly) to desire more specific information as a means to make better decisions.[1] In the absence of more specifics and better information, decision makers often use analogies to frame the context.[2] This is problematic during the policy formulation phase because efforts to overcome feelings of uncertainty can lead to the use of familiar analogies that are literally shoehorned to fit the situation. For example, in 1954 the United States perceived that the left-leaning regime of Jacobo Árbenz in Guatemala might provide the Soviet Union with a potential foothold in the Western Hemisphere; Moscow had yet to act, making it impractical to overtly send in U.S. troops to depose Árbenz. Instead, the United States helped a small group bring down the Árbenz government. The operation cost very little and provided enough secrecy to allow the United States to deny its involvement; as a result, it was viewed in Washington as a tremendous success. Seven years later, the United States decided to attempt to remove Fidel Castro from power in Cuba. Based on the previous success in Guatemala, the United States decided to support a small group of Cuban exiles to bring down the Castro government. Despite the perceived similarity to the Guatemalan operation, Washington overestimated the capabilities of its proxy and grossly underestimated the ability of Castro's forces. In what has come to be known as the "Bay of Pigs" incident, Cuban forces easily deposed the U.S. proxy, and the affair drove Fidel Castro even deeper into Moscow's sphere of influence.

The overall policy should reflect the larger picture of what the intervening state must do, acting through its proxy, to achieve its desires. In the absence of specific information, decision makers should rely on a more general explanation—a theory—of how a proxy war policy can best contribute to the desired outcome. Considering how the policy will support the state's security interests from a holistic perspective helps. Acting through a proxy expands the scope of considerations; second- and third-order effects, as well as unintended effects, become more difficult to predict and invite greater risk. Understanding how the proxy fits into the fabric of the target state's political landscape matters, but knowing what the proxy intends to gain from cooperating with the intervening state is vital. For example, the Northern Alliance in Afghanistan were good fighters and wanted the Taliban government out of power, making them an attractive proxy for the United States in 2001. The tribal and ethnolinguistic affiliations of Northern Alliance members created enmity with any Pashtun-dominated government. Afghanistan, however, has rarely been ruled by any tribe or ethnic group outside the Pashtun. If U.S. objectives had sought only to unseat the Taliban regime, the Northern Alliance fit the policy well. As soon as the objectives began to include state-building and attempting to reduce the amount of ungoverned space available to Al Qaeda or other terrorist organizations, the second-order effect of giving greater prominence to non-Pashtun ethnic groups in the Afghan government would complicate the expansion of the central government in Kabul. This, in turn, led to a prolonged engagement in Afghanistan and the shift in policy to a direct intervention. The question that remains is whether U.S. objectives could have been met sooner and more efficiently though direct intervention from the beginning. A more careful deliberation of the use of a proxy in Afghanistan could have potentially produced a better outcome.

The temporal aspect of policy selection must also factor in the potential for a decision maker to feel compelled to make a quick decision. The closer the would-be intervener gets to a perceived deadline for a decision, the more pressure there will likely be on taking some sort of action; as a result, the basis for a decision can become distorted and cause an unjustified increase in optimism about the proposed policy's ability to achieve the desired objectives.[3] Under such conditions, deliberations turn from questions like "Is this a good idea?" to "How do we make this work?" Objectivity falls to the wayside and the potential for getting bogged down in a poorly chosen proxy war increases dramatically.

An intervening state should first understand the immutable conditions—those it cannot influence or change—that contextualize the entire affair and then tailor the policy specifically to account for local (target state), global, and domestic conditions. Tailoring the policy means an intervening state should manipulate the mutable conditions—those it can influence or change—to help it work around the immutable conditions so that it stands the best chance of achieving its objectives in the target state. For example, a state cannot change the physical aspects of a country to be less remote and make it easier to monitor the proxy's actions, but it can change the ways in which it uses its own personnel to watch the proxy. Using embedded personnel (mutable) can help the problems posed by difficult terrain (immutable).

Finally, the intervening state should determine how immutable a proxy's isolation is under the conditions found in the target state. Initially, isolation should be treated as an immutable condition that represents a proxy's access to people and resources. A geographically and socially isolated proxy will likely fail, or at the very best struggle, to establish and/or capitalize on outside sources of support; a lack of external support helps guarantee the proxy's dependence and makes the proxy far easier to control (I discuss this concept in depth in Chapter 4). If a proxy has unfettered access to the larger population that remains unengaged in the conflict, then strategists and policy analysts should consider whether that helps or hinders the intervening state's objectives. In either case, discussions should include the costs associated with controlling a proxy's access.

If an intervening state can take steps to isolate effectively its proxy, then it is reasonable to predict that control costs will remain relatively low. Caution should be taken, however, to incorporate the careful management of a proxy's isolation.

Understanding the elements that constitute the phenomenon of proxy war and indirect intervention should lead to better policy. Knowing how those constitutive elements interact and influence the conduct of a proxy war should lead to either a productive policy or avoiding a proxy intervention altogether. When conditions force some form of indirect intervention and proxy war becomes an imperative, policy makers require a model for knowing when and how to use proxy war under suboptimal conditions. This is important because the optimal condition for a proxy war does not exist. The parties involved in a proxy war will have their separate interests and they will conflict more than they overlap. In addition, the structural conditions under which states enable a third party to use force to influence events in another state affects the utility and efficacy of the policy. Just because a third party is available and willing does not mean that proxy war becomes the least bad option. If the intervening state does not construct a coherent policy—a task that requires synthesis across five different areas—and maintain adequate control over its proxy, then the likelihood of achieving the intended objectives quickly fades.

The way globalization has increased the speed and availability of information complicates policy deliberation. Domestic and international audiences are now permanently and indelibly linked—articulating policy to one audience has the potential to bleed over into any interested party. Those involved in the making and execution of policy would do well to recognize the pitfalls of supporting a third party when it appears that neither direct intervention nor nonintervention is possible.

During the Cold War, proxy war provided an attractive option that reduced the risk of nuclear escalation and pushed the costs of fighting a war, in terms of lives lost, to indigenous actors. Today, numerous states see proxy war as an attractive policy for similar reasons. As a resurgent Russia and an expanding China (both equipped with a capable nuclear force) push outward from their existing spheres of influence, willing proxies offer opportunities to increase their influence and undermine the current world order. Iran, hemmed in by international sanctions and America's concerns about its nuclear program, has found proxy war a convenient way to counter Israeli and Saudi influence.

As the world moves further away from a unipolar order, more states will find proxy war an appealing and accessible way to influence global events. Especially if the world drifts more toward a multipolar order, intrastate conflicts will likely increase in frequency and duration as states engage in proxy wars less from an "in it to win it" perspective, and more from the other three—holding action, meddling, and feeding the chaos. For states with limited ability, these three methods of proxy war permit intervening states that are unconcerned about increasing prestige to throw support into an intrastate conflict with the hope of some gain but little concern about the outcome. Unlike the Cold War, supporting a proxy will become less about creating the conditions to improve negotiation and protecting the state's reputation. Instead, proxy war will be about adventuristic foreign policy—long shots that could provide some perceivable improvement in security. For more powerful states, proxy war will follow a similar pattern, allowing them to sustain their prestige and gain rhetorical advantages over peer or near-peer competitors. In a similar vein, supporting proxies will enable more powerful states to be more adventurous, hoping to drain the resources of their adversaries without risking direct confrontation. Iran's current support of Houthi rebels in Yemen reflects a current example.

In the cases of Russia, China, and the United States, intrastate conflicts on the periphery will once again become proxy war hotbeds. Similar to the Cold War, indirect intervention will most likely follow a policy of donating assistance, meddling, or feeding the chaos in states near their competitors. Further, proxy wars will be covert and deniable. For example, the United States will not indirectly intervene in western China to support Uighur dissidents in Xingjian because of the proximity to Beijing's sphere of influence. Countering a China-friendly regime in Myanmar (Burma), however, would not be out of the question. Russia will likely continue its presence in Ukraine, even resorting to proxy war, should the regime in Kiev become capable of resisting Moscow's advances in the East. Indirectly intervening in the Baltic States, however, would be unlikely because of the risk of confrontation with NATO and the United States.

One caveat, however, is that proxy war will become more secretive in less contentious regions. Undoubtedly, the information age complicates covert operations. Current and past cases used in this book, however, have shown that secrecy under the right conditions helps. Keeping the policy quiet allows states to probe the limits of a powerful state's interests. Although a multipolar world order means that there are more states with global interests, the heightened competition in key regions mean that gains can be made in areas that are less strategic. Unfortunately, this probably means that Africa will experience an increase in civil wars.

Even if a state gets caught indirectly intervening via proxy war, its involvement may be overlooked. Open secrets are still quiet and they offer a degree of plausible deniability that serves two different interests. On the one hand, supporting a proxy in a way that does not allow potentially interested parties to definitively demonstrate violations of the target state's sovereignty may escape sanction or unwanted involvement. On the other hand, plausible deniability allows other states that do not wish to get involved to look the other way.

To maximize the benefits of proxy war, the policy has to maintain coherence among those directing and executing the policy (internal coherence), the use of force has to support the conditions existing in the target state to ensure that the population doesn't reject the proxy's efforts (intrastate coherence), international and domestic audiences have to see a policy that appears to match the situation in the target state (international/domestic coherence), and the intentions and actions of the proxy have to support the policy's objectives (proxy coherence). Flaws in any of these areas can undermine the efficacy of the policy. Secrecy complicates the internal coherence of the policy and requires significant oversight. Intelligence assets must continually collect information about the situation in the target state to determine the continuing utility and efficacy of the policy. Secrecy may alleviate some of the need for international/domestic coherence, but sacrificing this part of the policy can cause significant blowback.

The conditions that lead states to choose proxy war may vary over time, but the necessity of controlling the proxy does not. Proxy war is messy. Done well, proxy war requires the ruthless application of measures that subjugate the proxy's actions to the pursuit of the intervening state's interests. Among policy makers, proxy war should not ever be viewed as a policy that helps both sides. Any benefit the proxy receives should only come as a by-product of the intervening state getting what it wants. Ultimately, an intervening state must ensure that its support follows three maxims to guarantee its proxy's obedience: know your enemy, but know your proxy even better; let the proxy lead, but only so far; and cultivate proxy dependence. Proxy war should immediately be dismissed as an option if the proxy's motives and objectives diverge significantly from the intervening states. If some overlap exists, at least enough to allow behavior-based incentives to provide some degree of control, an intervening state must consider the proxy's need for support and ensure that it remains exclusively dependent on that support. If the proxy proves highly capable in the use of force, then the intervening state must eliminate alternative means of support and become the proxy's only means of survival.

I admit that proxy war, done this way, may not garner domestic or international approval. It may also create tension with the proxy. The consequences of neglecting this method of proxy war, however, can cause the policy to backfire. Proxy war should never be considered a good option. If the safeguards needed to ensure that the policy remains coherent are unattainable, then some aspect of the policy should change. If no other option exists, then the intervening state must start with limiting its objectives in the target state. Another option is to change the method of proxy war to something that requires less commitment. For example, if pro-Hadi forces in Yemen begin to fracture and Riyadh can no longer control how its proxy uses its resources, then Saudi could alter its policy to meddling, backing a smaller faction, reducing its support only to ensure that a Shi'a-dominated government remains unable to assert its authority throughout the state.

In the meantime, the logical course of action is to continue to cultivate relationships with potential partners in regions that are likely to be contested as the world order drifts away from unipolarity. The United States continues to make this a priority in its national security strategy. What needs to change, however, is the perception that such actions are mostly beneficial. The advantages of operating "by, with, and through" partners must be counterbalanced with a rigorous consideration of the policies' negative aspects. Policy deliberations demand effective intelligence about adversaries and would-be partners or proxies. Weighing bad but necessary options should not lose objectivity simply because a situation demands a timely response. Decision makers must consider the negative aspects of proxy war and the associated challenges of maintaining the coherence of the policy and control of the proxy. Under the right conditions, proxy war is useful and efficacious, but it is never pretty.

NOTES

CHAPTER 1

1. Quoted in Eugene Scott, "McCain Rips Trump Administration over Syria Policy," *CNN Politics* (April 5, 2017), http://www.cnn.com/2017/04/04/politics/john-mccain -syria-trump-cnntv/index.html.

2. United States and Barack Obama, *National Security Strategy of the United States: The White House* (2010): 26, http://nssarchive.us/NSSR/2010.pdf; Stephen Daggett, *Congressional Research Service Report R41250,* "Quadrennial Defense Review 2010: Overview and Implications for National Security Planning" (May 17, 2010), https://fas.org/sgp/crs /natsec/R41250.pdf.

3. Philip Towle, "The Strategy of War by Proxy: Faculty Working Paper 20," Research School of Pacific Studies, Australian University at Canberra (1980); Bertil Duner, "Proxy Intervention in Civil Wars," *Journal of Peace Research* 18, no. 4 (1981): 353–361; Chris Loveman, "Assessing the Phenomenon of Proxy Intervention," *Journal of Conflict, Security, and Development* 2, no. 3 (2002): 30–48; Jeffrey Record, "Collapsed Countries, Casualty Dread, and the New American Way of War," *Parameters* 2 (2002): 4–23; Richard Andres, Craig Wills, and Thomas E. Griffiths, "Winning with Allies: The Strategic Value of the Afghan Model," *International Security* 30, no. 3 (2005–2006): 124–160.

4. Alexander George, *Bridging the Gap: Theory and Practice in Foreign Policy* (Washington, DC: United States Institute of Peace Press, 1993): xix, xxiv.

5. Michael Innes, ed., *Making Sense of Proxy Wars: States, Surrogates and the Use of Force* (Washington, DC: Potomac Books, 2012).

6. Ibid., 10.

7. Geraint Hughes, *My Enemy's Enemy: Proxy Warfare in International Politics* (Portland, OR: Sussex Academic Press, 2012).

8. Andrew Mumford, *Proxy Warfare: War and Conflict in the Modern World* (Malden, MA: Polity Press, 2013).

9. Robert J. Art, "The Strategy of Selective Engagement," in *The Use of Force: Military Power and International Politics*, eds. Robert J. Art and Kenneth N. Waltz, 6th ed. (Lanham, MD: Rowman and Littlefield, 2004): 302.

10. Kristian Skrede Gleditsch, David Cunningham, and Idean Salehyan, "Transnational Linkages and Civil War Interactions," paper presented at the annual meeting of the International Studies Association, Town & Country Resort and Convention Center, San Diego, California, March 22, 2006, http://citation.allacademic.com/meta/p99114_index .html.

11. Scott Gates, Haavard Mokleiv Nygaard, Haavard Strand, and Henrik Urdal, "Trends in Armed Conflict, 1946–2014," *Conflict Trends* (January 2016), http://file .prio.no/publication_files/prio/Gates,%20Nyg%C3%A5rd,%20Strand,%20Urdal%20- %20Trends%20in%20Armed%20Conflict,%20Conflict%20Trends%201-2016.pdf.

12. This concept comes from Carl von Clausewitz's distinction between the nature and character of warfare. In this sense, the term *character* refers to the underlying impetus behind an intrastate conflict. See Carl von Clausewitz, Michael Howard, Peter Paret, and Bernard Brodie, *On War*, Book 1 (Princeton, NJ: Princeton University Press, 1984).

13. Kichiro Fukusaku and Akira Hirata, "The OECD and ASEAN: Changing Economic Linkages and the Challenge of Policy Coherence," in *OECD and ASEAN Economies, The Challenge of Policy Coherence. OECD,* eds. Kichiro Fukasaku, Michael Plummer, and J.L.H. Tan (Paris: OECD, 1995): 312.

14. War crimes are actions taken against an adversary's armed forces that go against international laws of war during periods of hostility. Crimes against humanity are attacks that generally violate international laws of human rights "directed against any civilian population" and require that the actions were centrally orchestrated and executed. For a more detailed explanation of both definitions, see UN General Assembly, *Rome Statute of the International Criminal Court*, Articles 7 and 8 (July 17, 1998), https://www.icc-cpi.int /nr/rdonlyres/ea9aeff7-5752-4f84-be94-0a655eb30e16/0/rome_statute_english.pdf (last amended 2010).

15. Gary King, Robert O. Keohane, and Sidney Verba, *Designing Social Inquiry: Scientific Inference in Qualitative Research* (Princeton, NJ: Princeton University Press, 1994); Alexander L. George and Andrew Bennett, *Case Studies and Theory Development in the Social Science* (Cambridge, MA: MIT Press, 2005).

16. Douglas S. Blaufarb, *Organizing and Managing Unconventional War in Laos, 1962– 1970* (Santa Monica, CA: Rand, 1972): 33.

17. Johannes Geldenhuys, interview with author, Pretoria, South Africa, August 18, 2009; Willem van der Waals, interview with author, Pretoria, 30 Aug 09. General Johannes "Jannie" Geldenhuys served as Chief of the Army from 1980 to 1985 and Chief of the South African Defense Force from 1985 to 1990. Brigadier Willem "Kaas" van der Waals (ret.) was the SADF officer who made initial contact with UNITA in 1975 and later served as the senior SADF liaison to UNITA in 1978–1979.

18. Wayne S. Smith, "A Trap in Angola," *Foreign Policy*, no. 62 (1986): 61–74; Jeremy Grest, "The South African Defense Force in Angola," in *War and Society: The Militarisation of South Africa*, eds. Jacklyn Cock and Laurie Nathan (New York: St. Martin's Press, 1989): 116–132.

19. Frederick R. A. Botha, interview with author, Pretoria, South Africa, August 20, 2009. Frederick "Pik" Botha was South Africa's ambassador to the United States and the United Nations from 1975 to 1977 and held the office of the Minister of Foreign Affairs from 1977 to 1994.

20. Kingsley Muthumuni de Silva, "Indo–Sri Lankan Relations 1975–1989: A Study of Internationalization of Ethnic Conflict," in *Internationalization of Ethnic Conflict*, eds. Kingsley Muthumuni de Silva and R. J. May (New York: St. Martin's Press, 1991): 77–78.

21. Urmila Phadnis and Nancy Jetly, "Indo–Sri Lankan Relations: The Indira Gandhi Years," in *Indian Foreign Policy: The Indira Gandhi Years*, eds. A. K. Damodaran and U. S. Bajpai (New Delhi: Radiant, 1990): 159.

22. *Interim Report of the Jain Commission of Inquiry, Headed by Justice M. C. Jain, Former Chief Justice, Delhi High Court, on the Assassination of Shri Rajiv Gandhi, Former Prime Minister of India, on 21st May, 1991 at Sriperumbudur* (August 1997), https://web.archive .org/web/20030322101159/http://www.india-today.com:80/jain/vol3/chap13.html.

23. Steven R. David, "The Use of Proxy Forces by Major Powers in the Third World," in *The Lessons of Recent Wars in the Third World*, Volume II, eds. Stephanie G. Neuman and Robert E. Harkavy (Washington, DC: Lexington Books, 1985): 199–226; Loveman, "Assessing the Phenomenon of Proxy Intervention"; Andres, Wills, and Griffiths, "Winning with Allies"; Stephen D. Biddle, "Allies, Airpower, and Modern Warfare: The Afghan Model in Afghanistan and Iraq," *International Security* 30, no. 3 (2005): 161–176; Duner, "Proxy Intervention in Civil Wars."

24. Jorge I. Domínguez, "Cuban Foreign Policy," *Foreign Affairs* 57, no. 1 (Fall 1978): 83–108; Piero Gleijeses, "Moscow's Proxy? Cuba and Africa 1975–1988," *Journal of Cold War Studies* 8, no. 4 (2006): 98–146.

25. Alexander Thompson, "Coercion Through IOs: The Security Council and the Logic of Information Transmission," *International Organization* 60, no. 1 (2006): 1–34.

CHAPTER 2

1. Geraint Hughes, *My Enemy's Enemy: Proxy Warfare in International Politics* (Portland, OR: Sussex Academic Press, 2012): 11n1.

2. Michael Innes, ed., *Making Sense of Proxy Wars: States, Surrogates and the Use of Force* (Washington, DC: Potomac Books, 2012): xiii.

3. Ibid., chaps. 2 and 5.

4. Amin Saikal, *Modern Afghanistan: A History of Struggle and Survival* (New York: Palgrave Macmillan, 2004): 204.

5. Stanley Hoffman, "The Problem of Intervention," in *Intervention in World Politics*, ed. Hedley Bull (Oxford, UK: Clarendon Press, 1984); Andrew Bennett, *Condemned to Repetition? The Rise, Fall, and Reprise of Soviet-Russian Military Interventionism, 1973–1996* (Cambridge, MA: MIT Press, 1999); Martha Finnemore, *The Purpose of Intervention: Changing Beliefs About the Use of Force* (Ithaca, NY: Cornell University Press, 2003).

6. Bertil Duner, "Proxy Intervention in Civil Wars," *Journal of Peace Research* 18, no. 4 (1981): 353–361; Steven R. David, "The Use of Proxy Forces by Major Powers in the Third World," in *The Lessons of Recent Wars in the Third World*, Volume II, eds. Stephanie G. Neuman and Robert E. Harkavy (Washington, DC: Lexington Books, 1985): 199–226.

7. Duner, "Proxy Intervention in Civil Wars"; David, "The Use of Proxy Forces."

8. David, "The Use of Proxy Forces," 199-200.

9. Innes, *Making Sense of Proxy Wars*, chap. 5.

10. Kenneth Waltz, *Theory of International Politics* (Boston: McGraw-Hill, 1979); Glenn Snyder, *Alliance Politics* (Ithaca, NY: Cornell University Press, 1997); Thomas J. Christensen and Jack Snyder, "Progressive Research on Degenerate Alliances," *American Political Science Review* 91, no. 4 (1997): 919–922; Brett Ashley Leeds, "Do Alliances Deter Aggression? The Influence of Military Alliances on the Initiation of Militarized Interstate Disputes," *American Journal of Political Science* 47, no. 3 (July 2003): 427–439.

11. Glenn Snyder, *Alliance Politics* (Ithaca, NY: Cornell University Press, 1997).

12. Ibid., 9–10, 44.

13. Kenneth Waltz and John Mearsheimer principally argue that alliances are not binding. See Waltz, *Theory of International Politics*, and John Mearsheimer, *The Tragedy of Great Power Politics* (New York: Norton, 2001). For more on how alliances contribute to binding states, see Alastair Smith, "International Crises and Domestic Politics," *American Political Science Review* 92, no. 3 (1998): 623–638; Brett A. Leeds, Jeffrey Ritter, Sara Mitchell, and Andrew Long, "Alliance Treaty Obligations and Provisions, 1815–1944," *International Interactions* 28, no. 3 (2002): 237–260; and Leeds, "Do Alliances Deter Aggression?"

14. David A. Lake, "Anarchy, Hierarchy, and the Variety of International Relations," *International Organization* 50, no. 1 (1996): 1–34, 15; Snyder, *Alliance Politics*, 44.

15. Snyder, *Alliance Politics*, 9–10.

16. Kathleen M. Eisenhardt, "Agency Theory: An Assessment and Review," *Academy of Management Review* 14, no. 1 (1989): 57–74.

17. Ibid., 71.

18. Barry M. Mitnick, "Agency Theory," in *The Blackwell Encyclopedic Dictionary of Business Ethics*, eds. R. E. Freeman and P. H. Werhane (Malden, MA: Blackwell, 1998): 12–15.

19. Morris Fiorina, "Group Concentration and the Delegation of Legislative Authority," paper presented at the Conference on Social Science and Regulatory Policy, Reston, Virginia, January 22–23, 1982.

20. Robert J. Art, "The Strategy of Selective Engagement," in *The Use of Force: Military Power and International Politics*, eds. Robert J. Art and Kenneth N. Waltz, 6th ed. (Lanham, MD: Rowman and Littlefield, 2004): 302.

21. The evolution of international relations theory in the last sixty years best describes this idea.

22. Art, "The Strategy of Selective Engagement," 302–303.

23. James Fearon argues that states weigh the costs and benefits of engaging in armed conflict. I extrapolate Fearon's concept and suggest here that any form of intervention, including proxy intervention or untethered offers of support, also enter into a state's calculus. See James D. Fearon, "Rationalist Explanations for War," *International Organization* 49, no. 3 (Summer 1995): 379–414. Further, I extrapolate Fearon's argument to include both material and immaterial calculations when measuring costs and benefits.

24. The concept of using multiple theoretical lenses to improve analysis and explanation comes from Peter J. Katzenstein and Nobuo Okawara, "Japan, Asian-Pacific Security, and the Case for Analytical Eclecticism," *International Security* 26, no. 3 (2006): 153–185.

25. David E. Kaiser, *American Tragedy: Kennedy, Johnson, and the Origins of the Vietnam War* (Boston: Harvard University Press, 2000).

26. *Foreign Relations of the United States, 1964–1968, Volume III, Vietnam, June–December 1965*, https://history.state.gov/historicaldocuments/frus1964-68v03/d55, accessed June 2, 2017.

27. Wayne Bert, *The Reluctant Superpower: United States' Policy in Bosnia 1991–1995* (New York: St. Martin's Press, 1997).

28. Central Intelligence Agency, "Soviet Policy Toward Nicaragua" (SOV 86-10061X, November 1986).

CHAPTER 3

1. Patrick Regan, "Third Party Interventions and the Duration of Intrastate Conflicts," *Journal of Conflict Resolution* 46, no. 1 (2002).

2. Richard Haass, *Intervention: The Use of American Military Force in the Post–Cold War World* (Washington, DC: Brookings Institution Press, 1999): 2.

3. Data on the decrease of armed conflict since the end of the Cold War can be found in Scott Gates, Haavard Mokleiv Nygaard, Haavard Strand, and Henrik Urdal, "Trends in Armed Conflict: 1946–2014," *Conflict Trends* (January 2016), https://files.prio.org/publication_files/prio/Gates,%20Nyg%C3%A5rd,%20Strand,%20Urdal%20-%20Trends%20in%20Armed%20Conflict,%20Conflict%20Trends%201-2016.pdf. Explanations for the decrease in civil wars can be found in Stathis Kalyvas and Laia Balcells, "International System and Technologies of Rebellion: How the End of the Cold War Shaped Internal Conflict," *American Political Science Review* 104, no. 3 (August 2010): 417.

4. Gates et al., "Trends in Armed Conflict."

5. Kristian Skrede Gleditsch, "Transnational Dimensions of Civil War," *Journal of Peace Research* 44, no. 3 (2007): 293–309.

6. Herbert K. Tillema and John R. Van Wingen, "Law and Power in Military Intervention: Major States After World War II," *International Studies Quarterly* 26, no. 2 (June 1982): 220–250.

7. Hans J. Morgenthau, *Politics Among Nations: The Struggle for Power and Peace*, 7th ed. (New York: McGraw-Hill, 1978): 4–15.

8. Bruce Bueno de Mesquita, Alastair Smith, Randolph M. Siverson, and James D. Morrow, *The Logic of Political Survival* (Cambridge, MA: MIT Press, 2003): 75.

9. Kenneth Waltz, *Man, the State, and War: A Theoretical Analysis* (New York: Columbia University Press, 1959): chap. 2.

10. Sebastian Rosato, "The Flawed Logic of Democratic Peace Theory," *American Political Science Review* 97, no. 4 (November 2003).

11. The United States has had several instances of when covert action led to public blowback. See Jules Lobel, "Covert War and Congressional Authority: Hidden War and Forgotten Power," *University of Pennsylvania Law Review* 134, no. 5 (June 1986).

12. In the United States, covert action typically falls under the rubric of intelligence operations and is subject to Title 50 of the United States Code. Personnel operating under Title 50 have fewer protections than those operating under Title 10 of the United States Code—the laws that pertain to members of the armed forces. See Andru E. Wall, "Demystifying the Title 10–Title 50 Debate: Distinguishing Military Operations, Intelligence Activities & Covert Action," *Harvard National Security Journal* 3 (2011): 85–142.

13. This concept is explored in detail in my current book project, titled *The Least Worst Option: The of Use Proxy War as a Means of Intervention.*

14. Kenneth Waltz, *Theory of International Politics* (Boston: McGraw-Hill, 1979).

15. John Mearsheimer, *The Tragedy of Great Power Politics* (New York: Norton, 2001).

16. This logic falls under the rubric of instrumental rationality—the idea that the ends justify the means when weighing options. For more on instrumental rationality, see "Instrumental Rationality," in *Stanford Encyclopedia of Philosophy* (February 12, 2013), https:// plato.stanford.edu/entries/rationality-instrumental/. James Fearon also describes the idea that states should make a rational calculation to use force when it provides the greatest opportunity to maximize gains. See James D. Fearon, "Rationalist Explanations for War," *International Organization* 49, no. 3 (Summer 1995): 379–414.

17. Robert Jervis, "Cooperation Under the Security Dilemma," *World Politics* 30, no. 2 (January 1978): 167–214.

18. Robert Keohane, *After Hegemony: Cooperation and Discord in the World Political Economy*, 2nd ed. (Princeton, NJ: Princeton University Press, 2005).

19. Robert O. Keohane and Joseph S. Nye Jr., "Power and Interdependence in the Information Age," *Foreign Affairs* 77, no. 5 (September–October 1998): 81–94.

20. Martha Finnemore, *The Purpose of Intervention: Changing Beliefs About the Use of Force* (Ithaca, NY: Cornell University Press, 2003): chap. 3.

21. The idea of acting outside the boundaries of instrumental rationality falls under the rubric of value rationality. See "Instrumental Rationality," *Stanford Encyclopedia of Philosophy.*

22. Kenneth Waltz argues that nuclear weapons are a stabilizing force in the international system because of the destructive capability and the perceived responsibility that accompanies their possession. See Kenneth Waltz, "Why Iran Should Get the Bomb: Nuclear Balancing Would Mean Stability," *Foreign Affairs* (July–August 2012): 2–5.

23. In structural realism, systemic factors such as anarchy and relative capability are the main drivers of international politics. See Waltz, *Theory of International Politics.*

24. I acknowledge that some nonaligned states remained somewhat outside this bipolar structure, with India being the most significant state to engage in the use of proxy war during the Cold War.

25. As used here, the term *great power* describes states that have relative capabilities allowing them to influence events well beyond their borders.

26. Peter Hopkirk, *The Great Game: On Secret Service in High Asia* (London: Oxford University Press, 2001).

27. The term *regional power* refers to states with relative capabilities that only allow influence closer to home.

28. Great Britain experienced this particular wrath from the United States early in the Cold War for intervening in Egypt. See Paul Hahn, *The United States, Great Britain, and Egypt, 1945–1956: Strategy and Diplomacy in the Early Cold War* (Chapel Hill: University of North Carolina Press, 1991).

29. Kenneth Waltz, "The Stability of a Bipolar World," *Daedalus* 93, no. 3 (Summer 1964): 881–887.

30. Randall Schweller, "Bandwagoning for Profit: Bringing the Revisionist State Back In," *International Security* 19, no. 1 (Summer 1994): 72–107.

31. Robert Gilpin, *War and Change in World Politics* (Cambridge, NY: Cambridge University Press, 1981).

32. Ibid., 31.

33. Stephen M. Walt, *The Origins of Alliances* (Ithaca, NY: Cornell University Press, 1987).

34. Mearsheimer, *Tragedy of Great Power Politics.*

35. Colin Kahl and Kenneth Waltz, "Iran and the Bomb: Would a Nuclear Iran Make the Middle East More Secure?" *Foreign Affairs* (July/August 2012): 157–162.

36. I acknowledge that the number of states also dramatically increased following World War II, allowing for a greater number of states falling into civil wars. For detailed studies on the frequency of civil conflicts, see Kalyvas and Balcells, "International System and Technologies of Rebellion," and Regan, "Third Party Interventions and the Duration of Intrastate Conflicts."

37. Superpowers are states with global reach and global influence, but they also endure restrictions to reach and influence due to the presence of another superpower state.

38. Waltz, "The Stability of a Bipolar World."

39. See Tyrone Groh, "War on the Cheap: Assessing the Costs and Benefits of Proxy War," PhD diss., Georgetown University, 2010.

40. David Lewis Feldman, "The United States Role in the Malvinas Crisis, 1982: Misguidance and Misperception in Argentina's Decision to Go to War," *Journal of Interamerican Studies and World Affairs* 27, No. 2 (Summer 1985): 1–22.

41. For more information on Israel's proxy war in Lebanon, see Shai Feldman, "Israel's Involvement in Lebanon: 1975–1985," in *Foreign Military Intervention: The Dynamics of Protracted Conflict*, ed. A. E. Levite, B. W. Jentleson, and L. Berman (New York: Columbia University Press, 1992): 129–162; and Matthew Hughes, "Lebanon," in *The Oxford Companion to Military History*, ed. Richard Holmes (New York: Oxford University Press, 2001): 498–499. For more information on Syria's proxy war in Lebanon, see Yossi Olmert, "Syria in Lebanon," in *Foreign Military Intervention: The Dynamics of Protracted Conflict*, ed. A. E. Levite, B. W. Jentleson, and L. Berman (New York: Columbia University Press, 1992): 95–128; and Naomi Weinberger, *Syrian Intervention in Lebanon* (New York: Oxford University Press, 1986).

42. Gebri Tareke, The Ethiopia-Somalia War of 1977 Revisited," *International Journal of African Historical Studies* 33, no. 3 (2000): 635–667.

43. The Sri Lankan intervention is covered later in this section. For more information on India's support of Mukti Bahini, see Richard Sisson and Leo E. Rose, *War and*

Secession: Pakistan, India, and the Creation of Bangladesh (Berkeley: University of California Press, 1990); Satish Kumar, "The Evolution of India's Policy Towards Bangladesh in 1971," *Asian Survey* 15, no. 6 (1975): 488–498; and Sucheta Ghosh, *The Role of India in the Emergence of Bangladesh* (Calcutta: Minerva Associates, 1983). South Africa's proxy intervention in Rhodesia is discussed in Guy Arnold, *Wars in the Third World*, 2nd ed. (London: Cassell, 1995); and Leonard Thompson, *A History of South Africa* (New Haven, CT: Yale University Press, 2001).

44. The Vietnam War had widespread effects on numerous organizations involved in policy making and execution. See Morton Halperin and Priscilla Clapp, *Bureaucratic Politics and Foreign Policy*, 2nd ed. (Washington, DC: Brookings Institution Press, 2006).

45. Robert Parry and Peter Kornbluh, "Iran-Contra's Untold Story," *Foreign Policy*, no. 72 (1988): 4.

46. Central Intelligence Agency, "Soviet Policy Toward Nicaragua" (SOV 86-10061X, November 1986).

47. National Security Council Memorandum for W. Robert Pearson, "The 1984 Boland Amendment" (August 23, 1985).

48. Central Intelligence Agency, Office of Inspector General Investigations Staff, *Report of Investigation Concerning Allegations of Connections Between CIA and the Contras in Cocaine Trafficking to the United States* (1998, 96-0143-IG).

49. U.S. Department of State, Office of the Historian, "Central America 1981–1993," https://history.state.gov/milestones/1981-1988/central-america, accessed May 23, 2017.

50. Fried, Amy, *Muffled Echoes: Oliver North and the Politics of Public Opinion* (New York: Columbia University Press, 1997): 82.

51. Frank Newport, Jeffrey M. Jones, and Lydia Saad, "Ronald Reagan from the People's Perspective: A Gallup Poll Review" (June 7, 2004), https://news.gallup.com/poll/11887/ronald-reagan-from-peoples-perspective-gallup-poll-review.aspx.

52. International Court of Justice, "Military and Paramilitary Activities in and against Nicaragua (Nicaragua v. The United States of America)," http://www.icj-cij.org/docket/?sum=367&p1=3&p2=3&case=70&p3=5, accessed May 23, 2017.

53. Thomas Carothers, *In the Name of Democracy: U.S. Policy Toward Latin America in the Reagan Years* (Berkeley: University of California Press, 1991): chap. 3.

54. Marvin G. Weinbaum, *Pakistan and Afghanistan: Resistance and Reconstruction* (Boulder, CO: Westview Press, 1994): 28–32.

55. Ibid, 32–33.

56. Rashid Ahmad Khan, "Political Developments in FATA: A Critical Perspective," in *Tribal Areas of Pakistan: Challenges and Responses*, ed. Pervaiz Iqbal Cheema and Maqsudul Hasan Nuri (Islamabad: Islamabad Policy Research Institute, 2005): 38–39.

57. Kalyvas and Balcells, "International System and Technologies of Rebellion."

58. "How to Stop the Fighting, Sometimes," *The Economist* (November 10, 2013), http://www.economist.com/news/briefing/21589431-bringing-end-conflicts-within-states-vexatious-history-provides-guide.

59. United Nations Security Council Resolution 794 (1992), Item 10.

60. United Nations Security Council Resolution 820 (1993), Item 8.

61. Finnemore, *Purpose of Intervention*.

62. Schweller, "Bandwagoning for Profit," 84; Stephen Van Evera, "American Intervention in the Third World: Less Would Be Better," *Security Studies* 1, no. 1 (Autumn 1991): 12–14.

63. Jon Western, "Sources of Humanitarian Intervention: Beliefs, Information, and Advocacy in the U.S. Decisions on Somalia and Bosnia," *International Security* 26, no. 4 (Spring 2002): 112–142.

64. Charles A. Kupchan and Peter L. Trubowitz, "Dead Center: The Demise of Liberal Internationalism in the United States," *International Security* 32, no. 2 (Fall 2007): 24–35.

65. I acknowledge that Iran's support of Hezbollah could potentially fit into one of these two categories, but my research indicated that Iran's efforts reflect more of a meddling approach. Moscow's efforts to sustain the Najibullah regime in Afghanistan after Soviet forces withdrew in 1989 could be considered a holding action—this case requires more research.

66. For an explanation about Africa's relevance to US policy, see Stephen Van Evera, "Why Europe Matters, Why the Third World Doesn't: America's Grand Strategy After the Cold War," *Journal of Strategic Studies* 13, no. 2 (1990): 1–51.

67. John F. Clark, 2001. "Explaining Ugandan Intervention in Congo: Evidence and Interpretations," *Journal of Modern African Studies* 39, no. 2 (2001): 261–287.

68. Ibid.

69. Ibid.

70. Ibid.

71. Ibid.

72. UN Security Council, "Security Council Condemns Illegal Exploitation of Democratic Republic of Congo's Natural Resources," http://www.un.org/press/en/2001/sc7057 .doc.htm, accessed June 3, 2017.

73. Clark, "Explaining Ugandan Intervention in Congo."

74. UN Security Council, "Security Council Condemns Illegal Exploitation."

75. Ibid.

76. Ibid.

77. Ibrahim Abdullah, "Bush Path to Destruction: The Origin and Character of the Revolutionary United Front/Sierra Leone," *Journal of Modern African Studies* 36, no. 2 (1998): 203–235.

78. Osman Glba, "Post–Cold War U.S. Foreign Policy Toward Liberia and Sierra Leone," in *The United States in West Africa: Interactions and Relations*, ed. Alusine Jalloh and Toyin Falola (Rochester, NY: University of Rochester Press, 2008): 360; William S. Reno, "Liberia: The LURDs of the New Church," in *African Guerillas: Raging Against the Machine*, ed. Morten Bøaas and Kevin C. Dunn (Boulder, CO: Lynne Rienner, 2007): 76.

79. Reno, "Liberia," 75.

80. Abdullah, "Bush Path to Destruction," 225–228.

81. Stanley Hoffman, "The Problem of Intervention," in *Intervention in World Politics*, ed. Hedley Bull (Oxford, UK: Clarendon Press, 1984): 218; Reno, "Liberia," 75.

82. Chantal de Jonge Oudraat, "The United Nations in Internal Conflict," in *The International Dimensions of Internal Conflict*, ed. Michael E. Brown (Cambridge, MA: MIT Press, 1996): 334.

83. Reno, "Liberia," 75.

84. Hoffman, "The Problem of Intervention," 218.

85. Oudraat, "The United Nations in Internal Conflict," 335.

86. Reno, "Liberia," 79.

87. Gilpin, *War and Change in World Politics*.

88. Simon Chesterman, "Leading from Behind: The Responsibility to Protect, the Obama Doctrine, and Humanitarian Intervention after Libya," New York University Public Law and Legal Theory Working Papers, Paper 282 (2001).

89. Ivo Daalder and James Stavridis, "NATO's Victory in Libya: The Right War to Run an Intervention," *Foreign Affairs* (March–April 2012): 2–3.

90. Although Uzbekistan allowed the United States to use an air base at Karshi Khanabad as a staging area, the location was still too far away to be useful for conducting ground operations.

91. For an explanation of why Afghanistan is such a difficult place to conduct military operations, see Milton Bearden, "Afghanistan, Graveyard of Empires," *Foreign Affairs* (2001): 17–30.

92. In 2002, 93 percent of Americans felt the military operation in Afghanistan was the correct choice. See "Afghanistan," Gallup, http://www.gallup.com/poll/116233/afghanistan.aspx, accessed June 3, 2017.

93. *Report to the Committee on Foreign Relations, United States Senate*, "Tora Bora Revisited: How We Failed to Get Bin Laden and Why It Matters Today," November 30, 2009, https://www.foreign.senate.gov/imo/media/doc/Tora_Bora_Report.pdf, accessed July 29, 2018.

94. Seth Jones argues that the lack of governing capacity in Afghanistan, especially the absence of a capable and effective police force, opened the door for nonstate actors to frustrate the process of state-building. See Seth G. Jones, "The Rise of Afghanistan's Insurgency: State Failure and Jihad," *International Security* 32, no. 4 (Spring 2008): 15–19.

95. Zachary Laub, "Yemen in Crisis," *Council on Foreign Relations Backgrounder*, https://www.cfr.org/backgrounder/yemen-crisis, accessed May 24, 2017.

96. Peter Salisbury, "Yemen and the Saudi-Iranian 'Cold War,'" *Chatham House Middle East and North Africa Programme* (February 2015), https://www.chathamhouse.org/sites/default/files/field/field_document/20150218YemenIranSaudi.pdf.

97. "Yemen in Crisis: Who Is Fighting Whom?," BBC News (March 28, 2017), http://www.bbc.com/news/world-middle-east-29319423.

98. According to the UN, half of Yemen's population (25 million people) are considered "food insecure," meaning they have to rely on outside assistance for their survival. Under such harsh conditions, it is reasonable to conclude that people often will often choose tyranny over starvation. See Jeremy Sharp, "Yemen: Civil War and Regional Intervention," Congressional Research Service, Report 43960 (October 2, 2015): 2.

99. "Over 100 Civilians Killed in a Month, Including Fishermen, Refugees, as Yemen Conflict Reaches Two-Year Mark," United Nations Human Rights Office of the

High Commissioner, March 24, 2017, http://www.ohchr.org/EN/NewsEvents/Pages/DisplayNews.aspx?NewsID=21444&LangID=E.

100. "Crisis Overview," United Nations Office for the Coordination of Humanitarian Affairs, http://www.unocha.org/yemen/about-ocha-yemen, accessed May 24, 2017.

101. Edward Schumacher, "The United States and Libya," *Foreign Affairs* 65, no. 2 (Winter 1986): 329–348.

102. United Nations Security Council Resolution 748 (March 31, 1992), Items 4–6.

103. Caitlin Buckley, "Learning from Libya, Acting in Syria," *Journal of Strategic Security* 5, no. 2 (Summer 2012): 82–84.

104. United Nations Security Council Resolution 1973 (2011), Item 3.

105. Daalder and Stavridis, "NATO's Victory in Libya.

106. Ibid., 3.

107. Karen DeYoung, "Western Nations Step Up Efforts to Aid Libyan Rebels," *New York Times* (April 20, 2011).

108. Sharp, "Yemen: Civil War and Regional Intervention," 3; Thomas Juneau, "Iran's Policy Towards the Houthis in Yemen: A Limited Return on a Modest Investment," *International Affairs* 92, no. 3 (2016): 656–658.

109. Salisbury, "Yemen and the Saudi-Iranian 'Cold War,'" 9.

110. Juneau, "Iran's Policy Towards the Houthis in Yemen," 661. Juneau cites the fact that Iran advised the Houthis not to take Sana'a in 2014 and that President Obama's National Security Council staff argued that Tehran was not in command of the Houthi effort.

111. Kenneth Katzman, "Iran's Foreign Policy," Congressional Research Service, Report 44017 (June 27, 2016): 2–3.

112. This behavior highlights Iran as a revisionist state as mentioned earlier in this section.

113. Sharp, "Yemen: Civil War and Regional Intervention," 13–14.

114. Salisbury, "Yemen and the Saudi-Iranian Cold War," 8.

115. Kupchan and Trubowitz suggest that the Bush administration demurred at NATO's offer of military support. See Kupchan and Trubowitz, "Dead Center," 25. This sentiment is also reflected in Ellen Hallams, "The Transatlantic Alliance Renewed: The United States and NATO Since 9/11," *Journal of Transatlantic Studies* 7, no. 1 (2009): 38–60.

116. Compare Stephen Biddle, "Afghanistan and the Future of Warfare," *Foreign Affairs* 82, no. 2 (March-April 2003): 31–46; and H. R. McMaster, "On War: Lessons to Be Learned," *Survival* 50, no. 1 (2008): 19–30.

CHAPTER 4

1. J. Edward Russo and Paul Schoemaker, *Decision Traps: Ten Barriers to Brilliant Decision-Making and How to Overcome Them* (New York: Doubleday/Currency, 1989).

2. Alexander George, "The Two Cultures of Academia and Policy Making: Bridging the Gap," *Political Psychology* 15, no. 1 (1994): 149.

3. Ibid.

4. Joel S. Migdal, *Strong Societies and Weak States: State-Society Relations and State Capabilities in the Third World* (Princeton, NJ: Princeton University Press, 1988).

5. Peter Gourevitch, "The Second Image Reversed: The International Sources of Domestic Politics," *International Organization* 32, no. 4 (1978): 902.

6. Patrick James and John R. Oneal, "The Influence of Domestic and International Politics on the President's Use of Force," *Journal of Conflict Resolution* 35, no. 2 (1991): 308.

7. Allison and Zelikow, *Essence of Decision: Explaining the Cuban Missile Crisis*, Second Edition (Boston, MA: Little, Brown, 1999); Helen V. Milner, *Interests, Institutions, and Information: Domestic Politics and International Relations* (Princeton, NJ: Princeton University Press, 1997); David Clark, "Trading Butter for Guns: Domestic Imperatives for Foreign Policy Substitution," *Journal of Conflict Resolution* 45, no. 5 (2001): 636–660.

8. Alexander George, "Domestic Constraints on Regime Change in U.S. Foreign Policy: The Need for Policy Legitimacy," 233–262, in *Change in the International System*, eds. O. R. Holsti, R. M. Siverson, and A. L. George (Boulder, CO: Westview Press, 1980); Richard Smoke, "On the Importance of Policy Legitimacy," *Political Psychology* 15, no. 1 (1994): 97–110; Branislav L. Slantchev, "Politicians, the Media, and Domestic Audience Costs," *International Studies Quarterly* 50, no. 2 (2006): 445–477.

9. George, "Domestic Constraints"; Martha Finnemore, *National Interests in International Society* (Ithaca, NY: Cornell University Press, 1996); James G. March and Johan P. Olsen, "The Institutional Dynamics of International Political Orders," *International Organization* 52, no. 4 (1998): 943–969.

10. Bruce Bueno de Mesquita, Alastair Smith, Randolph M. Siverson, and James D. Morrow, *The Logic of Political Survival* (Cambridge, MA: MIT Press, 2003).

11. Amos A. Jordan, William J. Taylor, Jr., Michael J. Meese, and Suzanne C. Nielsen, *American National Security*, 6th ed. (Baltimore: Johns Hopkins University Press, 2009): 24.

12. Clark, "Trading Butter for Guns," 641.

13. Sebastian Rosato, "The Flawed Logic of Democratic Peace Theory," *American Political Science Review* 97, no. 4 (November 2003): 585–602.

14. James N. Rosenau, "Foreign Intervention as Adaptive Behavior," *Law and Civil War in the Modern World*, ed. John Norton Moore (Baltimore: Johns Hopkins University Press, 1975); Milner, *Interests, Institutions, and Information*.

15. John E. Mueller, *War, Presidents, and Public Opinion* (New York: Wiley, 1973).

16. Tyrone Groh, "War on the Cheap: Assessing the Costs and Benefits of Proxy War," PhD diss., Georgetown University, 2010.

17. Glenn Snyder, *Alliance Politics* (Ithaca, NY: Cornell University Press, 1997); Alastair Smith, "International Crises and Domestic Politics," *American Political Science Review* 92, no. 3 (1998): 623–638; Bueno de Mesquita et al., *Logic of Political Survival*; Rosato, "Flawed Logic."

18. James and Oneal, "Influence of Domestic and International Politics," 310-311; Richard J. Stoll, "The Guns of November: Presidential Reelections and the Use of Force, 1947–1982," *Journal of Conflict Resolution* 28, no. 2 (1984): 232.

19. James D. Fearon, "Domestic Political Audiences and the Escalation of International Disputes," *American Political Science Review* 88, no. 3 (1994): 577–592.

20. Rosato, "Flawed Logic"; Carles Boix and Milan W. Svolik, "The Foundations of Limited Authoritarian Government: Institutions, Commitment, and Power-Sharing in Dictatorships," *Journal of Politics* 75, no. 2 (2013): 300–316.

21. John W. Kingdon, *Agendas, Alternatives, and Public Policies*, 2nd ed. (New York: Addison Wesley, 2003): 84.

22. Felicity Barringer, "The 1992 Campaign: Campaign Issues; Clinton and Gore Shifted on Abortion," *New York Times*, July 20, 1992. https://www.nytimes.com/1992/07/20/us/the-1992-campaign-campaign-issues-clinton-and-gore-shifted-on-abortion.html.

23. Kingdon, *Agendas*, 85.

24. George, "Two Cultures of Academia and Policy Making," 149.

25. George, "The Case for Multiple Advocacy in Making Foreign Policy," *The American Political Science Review* 66, no. 3 (1972): 752.

26. Matthew A. Baum, "Going Private: Public Opinion, Presidential Rhetoric, and the Domestic Politics of Audience," *Journal of Conflict Resolution* 48, no. 5 (2004): 603–631.

27. Chester A. Crocker, interview with author, Washington, D.C., August 20, 2009.

28. Bud Schultz and Ruth Schultz, *The Price of Dissent: Testimonies to Political Repression in America* (Berkeley: University of California Press, 2001); Baum, "Going Private."

29. Andru E. Wall, "Demystifying the Title 10-Title 50 Debate: Distinguishing Military Operations, Intelligence Activities & Covert Action," *Harvard National Security Journal* 3 (2011): 85–142.

30. Hedley Bull, *The Anarchical Society: A Study of Order in World Politics*, 3rd ed. (New York: Columbia University Press, 2002); Robert Keohane, *After Hegemony: Cooperation and Discord in the World Political Economy* (Princeton, NJ: Princeton University Press, 1984).

31. Robert O. Keohane and Joseph S. Nye Jr., "Power and Interdependence in the Information Age," *Foreign Affairs* 77, no. 5 (September–October 1998): 81–94.

32. Keohane, *After Hegemony*.

33. Robert O. Keohane and Joseph S. Nye, *Power and Interdependence* (Boston: Addison Wesley, 1977).

34. Keohane and Nye, "Power and Interdependence in the Information Age."

35. Thomas A. Pugel, *International Economics*, 12th ed. (New York: McGraw-Hill, 2004): chap. 3; Robert Axelrod, *The Evolution of Cooperation* (New York: Basic Books, 1984).

36. Kenneth Waltz, *Theory of International Politics* (Boston: McGraw-Hill, 1979); Keohane, *After Hegemony*.

37. Robert Keohane, "International Institutions: Two Approaches," *International Studies Quarterly* 32 (1988): 383.

38. Keohane, *After Hegemony*, 89.

39. Axelrod, *Evolution of Cooperation*; Robert Axelrod and Robert Keohane, "Achieving Cooperation Under Anarchy: Strategies and Institutions," *World Politics* 38, no. 1 (1985): 226–254.

40. Keohane, *After Hegemony*, 92–96.

41. Charles Lipson, International Cooperation in Economic and Security Affairs. World Politics 37, no. 1 (1984): 7

42. Lawrence Freedman and Efraim Karsh, *The Gulf Conflict: 1990–1991* (London: Faber and Faber, 1993).

43. Daryl Press, "Power, Reputation, and Assessments of Credibility During the Cuban Missile Crisis," Paper presented at the American Political Science Association, San Francisco, California, August 30–September 2, 2001: 3.

44. Although not all international relations scholars agree that reputations matter, empirical evidence supports this claim. For two contrasting opinions see Press, "Power, Reputation, and Assessments of Credibility During the Cuban Missile Crisis," and Mark Crescenzi, "Reputation and Interstate Conflict," *American Journal of Political Science* 51, no. 2 (2007): 382–396.

45. Joseph Nye, *Soft Power: The Means to Success in World Politics* (New York, NY: Public Affairs, 2004).

46. Article 2(4) of the UN Charter specifically states, "All members shall refrain in their international relations from the threat or use of force against the territorial integrity or political independence of any state, or in any other manner inconsistent with the Purposes of the United Nations." Although scholars as well as policy analysts disagree on the conditions that justify intervening in the domestic affairs of another state (see Anthony C. Arend and Robert Beck, International Law and the Use of Force: Beyond the UN Paradigm (New York: Routledge, 1993): chap. 5), the UN Charter only authorizes the use of force when sanctioned by the UN Security Council (Article 39 and 42) or in response to an armed attack (Article 51).

47. Waltz, *Theory of International Politics*.

48. Michael Walzer, *Just and Unjust Wars: A Moral Argument with Historical Illustrations* (New York: Basic Books, 1977).

49. Stephan Tankel, "Laskhar-e-Taiba: From 9/11 to Mumbai," *Developments in Radicalisation and Political Violence*, (April/May 2009), http://www.ps.au.dk/fileadmin/site _files/filer_statskundskab/subsites/cir/pdf-filer/Tankel_01.pdf.

50. Peter Lavoy, *Learning to Live with the Bomb: India, the United States, and the Myths of Nuclear Security* (Basingstoke, UK: Palgrave Macmillan, 2004).

51. Bernard Brodie, *Strategy in the Missile Age* (Princeton, NJ: Princeton University Press, 1959).

52. Walzer, *Just and Unjust Wars*.

53. Waltz, *Theory of International Politics*; John J. Mearsheimer, *Tragedy of Great Power Politics*.

54. Chaim Kaufmann, "Intervention in Ethnic and Ideological Civil Wars," in *The Use of Force: Military Power and International Politics*, ed. Robert J. Art and Kenneth N. Waltz, 6th ed. (Lanham, MD: Rowman and Littlefield), 394–414.

55. Snyder, *Alliance Politics*, chap. 5.

56. Groh, "War on the Cheap."

57. Seth G. Jones, *In the Graveyard of Empires: America's War in Afghanistan* (New York: Norton, 2010).

58. Eric V. Larson, *Casualties and Consensus: The Historical Role of Casualties in Domestic Support for U.S. Military Operations* (Santa Monica, CA: Rand, 1996).

59. UNSC Report S/2001/357, "Report of the Panel of Experts on the Illegal Exploitation of Natural Resources and Other Forms of Wealth of the Democratic Republic of the Congo," https://www.securitycouncilreport.org/atf/cf/%7b65BFCF9B-6D27-4E9C -8CD3-CF6E4FF96FF9%7d/DRC%20S%202001%20357.pdf.

60. Snyder, *Alliance Politics*, 166–167.

61. Kichiro Fukusaku and Akira Hirata, "The OECD and ASEAN: Changing Economic Linkages and the Challenge of Policy Coherence," *OECD and ASEAN Economies, The Challenge of Policy Coherence. OECD, Paris* (1995): 312.

62. Dominic D. P. Johnson and Dominic Tierney, "The Rubicon Theory of War: How the Path to Conflict Reaches the Point of No Return," *International Security* 36, no. 1 (Summer 2011): 7–40.

63. Kaufmann, "Intervention in Ethnic and Ideological Civil Wars," 405.

64. Ibid.

65. William E. Odom, *On Internal War: American and Soviet Approaches to Third World Clients and Insurgents* (Durham, NC: Duke University Press, 1992).

66. Kaufmann, "Intervention in Ethnic and Ideological Civil Wars," 406.

67. Odom, *On Internal War.*

68. Gregory Bart, "Special Operations Forces and Responsibility for Surrogates' War Crimes," *Harvard National Security Journal* 5, no. 2 (2014): 513–536.

69. Stephen D. Biddle, "Allies, Airpower, and Modern Warfare: The Afghan Model in Afghanistan and Iraq," *International Security* 30, no. 3 (2005): 161–176; Richard Andres, Craig Wills, and Thomas E. Griffiths, "Winning with Allies: The Strategic Value of the Afghan Model," *International Security* 30, no. 3 (2005–2006): 124–160.

70. Kathleen M. Eisenhardt, "Agency Theory: An Assessment and Review," *Academy of Management Review* 14, no. 1 (1989): 57–74.

71. James D. Fearon, "Rationalist Explanations for War," *International Organization* 49, no. 3 (Summer 1995): 379–414.

72. Robert Axelrod, *The Evolution of Cooperation* (New York, NY: Basic Books, 1984).

73. Robert Jervis, "War and Misperception," *Journal of Interdisciplinary History* 18, no. 4 (1988): 677.

74. Alexander George, *Bridging the Gap: Theory and Practice in Foreign Policy* (Washington, DC: United States Institute of Peace Press, 1993): 129.

75. Morris Fiorina, "Group Concentration and the Delegation of Legislative Authority," paper presented at the Conference on Social Science and Regulatory Policy, Reston, Virginia, January 22–23, 1982.

76. Barry M. Mitnick, "Agency Theory," in *The Blackwell Encyclopedic Dictionary of Business Ethics*, eds. R. E. Freeman and P. H. Werhane (Malden, MA: Blackwell, 1998): 12.

77. Susan P. Shapiro, "Agency Theory," *Annual Review of Sociology* 31 (2005): 281.

78. Roderick D. Kiewiet and Mathew McCubbins, *The Logic of Delegation* (Chicago: University of Chicago Press, 1991): 25–28.

79. Clark, "Trading Butter for Guns."

80. Xiaoming Zhang, "China's Involvement in Laos During the Vietnam War, 1963–1975," *Journal of Military History* 66, no. 4 (2002): 1141–1166.

CHAPTER 5

1. "Kennan and Containment, 1947," Office of the Historian, U.S. State Department, https://history.state.gov/milestones/1945-1952/kennan, accessed July 31, 2017.

2. Memorandum of Conference with President Eisenhower, January 3, 1961.

3. John Girling, "Laos: Falling Domino?" *Pacific Affairs* 43, no. 3 (1970): 377.

4. *The Pentagon Papers*, 1971, sec. 2: 146-178.

5. Girling, "Laos"; Walt Haney, "The Pentagon Papers and the United States Involvement in Laos," Vol. V of *The Pentagon Papers*, Senator Gravel Edition (Boston, MA: Beacon Press, 1972): 251.

6. Girling, "Laos"; Timothy N. Castle, *At War in the Shadow of Vietnam: United States Military Aid to the Royal Lao Government, 1955–75* (New York: Columbia University Press, 1995).

7. Paul F. Langer, "Laos: Search for Peace in the Midst of War," *Asian Survey* 8, no. 1 (1968): 82.

8. Joseph J. Zasloff, "Laos 1972: The War, Politics and Peace Negotiations," *Asian Survey* 13, no. 1 (1973): 61; E. H. S. Simmonds, "The Evolution of Foreign Policy in Laos Since Independence," *Modern Asian Studies* 2, no. 1 (1968): 10.

9. William J. Rust, *Before the Quagmire: American Intervention in Laos 1954–1961* (Lexington: University of Kentucky Press, 2012): 20.

10. U.S. Congress, House Committee on Government Operations, *United States Aid Operations in Laos*, Hearings before the Subcommittee on Foreign Operations and Monetary Affairs, 86th Congress, 1st Session, 1959, 46.

11. Philippe Devillers, "The Laotian Conflict in Perspective," *Laos: War and Revolution*, eds. Nina S. Adams and Alfred W. McCoy (New York: Harper and Row, 1970): 42–45.

12. Castle, *At War in the Shadow of Vietnam*, 17.

13. J. T. Folda Jr., Joint Message, Office of Secretary of Defense to Deputy Assistant Secretary of Defense, ISA, Robert H. Knight, August 11, 1959.

14. Chae-Jin Lee, "Communist China and the Geneva Conference on Laos: A Reappraisal," *Asian Survey* 9, no. 7 (July 1969): 522–523.

15. Devillers, "The Laotian Conflict in Perspective," 46–47; Roland A. Paul, "Laos: Anatomy of an American Involvement," *Foreign Affairs* 49, no. 3 (1971): 571.

16. Senate Committee on Foreign Relations, U.S. Agreements and Commitments Abroad, Part 2, Kingdom of Laos 1969, 419; *Foreign Relations of the United States, 1961– 1963, Vol. XXIV: Laos Crisis*, ed. Edward Keefer (Washington, DC: U.S. Government Printing Office, 1994): 14–15, 500–501.

17. Seth Jacobs, *The Universe Unravelling: American Foreign Policy in Cold War Laos* (Ithaca, NY: Cornell University Press, 2012): 1–6.

18. Edward J. Marolda and Oscar P. Fitzgerald, *The United States Navy and the Vietnam Conflict, Volume I: From Military Assistance to Combat* (Washington, DC: U.S. Government Printing Office, 1986): 55.

19. Memorandum of Conversation, Department of State, Washington, January 13, 1958.

20. Castle, *At War in the Shadow of Vietnam*, 130.

21. Jacobs, *Universe Unravelling*, 6–7.

22. Keith Quincy, *Harvesting Pa Chay's Wheat: The Hmong and America's Secret War in Laos* (Spokane: Eastern Washington University Press, 2000): 181; William M. Leary, *CIA Air Operations in Laos, 1955–1974* (Washington, DC: Center for the Study of Intel-

ligence, 1999), https://www.cia.gov/library/center-for-the-study-of-intelligence/kent-csi/vol43no3/pdf/v43i3a07p.pdf.

23. Memorandum from the Chairman of the Joint Chiefs of Staff (Lemnitzer) to President Kennedy, July 7, 1961.

24. Rust, *Before the Quagmire*, 5.

25. Rust, *Before the Quagmire*, chap. 8.

26. Memorandum of Conversation, Secretary of State, January 17, 1961.

27. Marolda and Fitzgerald, *United States Navy and the Vietnam Conflict*, 55.

28. Douglas S. Blaufarb, *Organizing and Managing Unconventional War in Laos, 1962–1970* (Santa Monica, CA: Rand, 1972):, 17–18.

29. Alfred H. Paddock Jr., "Personal Memories of Operation White Star in Laos, 1961," *Small Wars Journal Blog* (April 10, 2013), http://smallwarsjournal.com/blog/personal-memories-of-operation-white-star-in-laos-1961.

30. Zasloff, "Laos 1972," 62.

31. Wilfred Burchett, "Pawns and Patriots: The US Fight for Laos," in *Laos: War and Revolution*, eds. Nina S. Adams and Alfred W. McCoy (New York: Harper and Row, 1970): 303.

32. Blaufarb, *Organizing and Managing Unconventional War in Laos*; Timothy N. Castle, *At War in the Shadow of Vietnam: U.S. Military Aid to the Royal Lao Government 1955–1975* (New York: Columbia University Press, 1993); Timothy N. Castle, *One Day Too Long: Top Secret Site 85 and the Bombing of North Vietnam* (New York: Columbia University Press, 1999).

33. Blaufarb, *Organizing and Managing Unconventional War in Laos*, 78.

34. Ibid.

35. Castle, *At War in the Shadow of Vietnam*, 43.

36. Ibid., 57.

37. Ibid., 57.

38. Ibid., 80.

39. Ibid.; Quincy, *Harvesting Pa Chay's Wheat*.

40. Rust, *Before the Quagmire*, 5.

41. David M. Barrett, *Lyndon B. Johnson's Vietnam Papers: A Documentary Collection* (College Station: Texas A&M University Press, 1997): 52.

42. Department of State Bulletin, April 15, 1969, 567–572; D. Gareth Porter, "After Geneva: Subverting Laotian Neutrality," in *Laos: War and Revolution*, eds. Nina S. Adams and Alfred W. McCoy (New York: Harper and Row, 1970): 193–194; Blaufarb, *Organizing and Managing Unconventional War in Laos*, 18.

43. Blaufarb, *Organizing and Managing Unconventional War in Laos*, 8–9; Paul, "Laos," 537.

44. Barrett, *Lyndon B. Johnson's Vietnam Papers*, 48.

45. Quoted in Blaufarb, *Organizing and Managing Unconventional War in Laos*, 37.

46. Ibid., 37.

47. Timothy N. Castle, *One Day Too Long: Top Secret Site 85 and the Bombing of North Vietnam* (New York: Columbia University Press, 1999): 121.

48. Blaufarb, *Organizing and Managing Unconventional War in Laos*, x.

49. Blaufarb, *Organizing and Managing Unconventional War in Laos*, x; Castle, *At War in the Shadow of Vietnam*.

50. Senate Committee on Foreign Relations, U.S. Agreements and Commitments Abroad, Part 2, Kingdom of Laos 1969, 377, 398, 406.

51. *No. 6564. Declaration 1 On the Neutrality of Laos. Signed at Geneva, On 23 July 1962*, https://treaties.un.org/doc/publication/unts/volume%20456/volume-456-i-6564 -english.pdf, accessed July 25, 2017.

52. Barrett, *Lyndon B. Johnson's Vietnam Papers*, 42.

53. Ibid., 43.

54. Blaufarb, *Organizing and Managing Unconventional War in Laos*, 8–9.

55. Senate Committee on Foreign Relations, U.S. Agreements and Commitments Abroad, Part 2, Kingdom of Laos 1969, 399–402. During this subcommittee hearing, William Sullivan testified that "the North Vietnamese operate with enormous numbers of forces in Laos, totally clandestinely. They deny that their people are there, and this, therefore, in terms of the mechanism of the 1962 agreements, gives them a totally unfair, totally legal protection." Sullivan suggested that if the United States openly admitted that it was breaking the Geneva Accords, Hanoi would score a tremendous political victory and would likely gain the upper hand in Laos (402).

56. Bureau of Economic Analysis, U.S. Department of Commerce, "U.S. International Transactions, 1960–Present," http://www.bea.gov/International/index.htm#bop, accessed October 10, 2009.

57. Senate Committee on Foreign Relations, U.S. Agreements and Commitments Abroad, Part 2, Kingdom of Laos 1969.

58. Quoted from John Ely, *War and Responsibility: Constitutional Lessons of Vietnam and Its Aftermath* (Princeton, NJ: Princeton University Press, 1993): 202n92.

59. Senate Committee on Foreign Relations, U.S. Agreements and Commitments Abroad, Part 2, Kingdom of Laos 1969: 399.

60. Ibid., 402.

61. Ibid., 404.

62. Quoted in Barrett, *Lyndon B. Johnson's Vietnam Papers*, 44.

63. Ibid., 100.

64. U.S. Senate, Subcommittee on United States Security Agreements and Commitments Abroad Hearings (October 20, 21, 22 and 28, 1969): 547.

65. John Ely, *War and Responsibility: Constitutional Lessons of Vietnam and Its Aftermath* (Princeton, NJ: Princeton University Press, 1993): 81–82.

66. Blaufarb, *Organizing and Managing Unconventional War in Laos*, 18.

67. Ely, *War and Responsibility*, 82–83.

68. Ibid., 92.

69. Fred Branfman, "Presidential War in Laos, 1964–1970," in *Laos: War and Revolution*, eds. Nina S. Adams and Alfred W. McCoy, 213–282 (New York: Harper and Row, 1970), 267–268.

70. Christopher Robbins, *The Ravens: The Men Who Flew in America's Secret War in Laos* (New York: Crown, 1987): 240n5; Ely, *War and Responsibility*, 89.

71. Castle, *At War in the Shadow of Vietnam*, 104–105; Robbins, *The Ravens*, 108–109.

72. Ely, *War and Responsibility*, 83. Ely specifically explains that 50 USC § 403j(b) allowed CIA funds to be spent without regard to the usual regulations governing expenditures.

73. Fred Branfman was an International Volunteer Service employee at the time and later became a journalist operating in Laos. See Branfman, "Presidential War in Laos, 1964–1970," 270n18.

74. Two different pieces of evidence lend credence to Christopher Robbins's claim (*The Ravens*, 36n5) that visitors were taken to a smaller base at Sam Thong. First, Senator Symington notes that he did not recall seeing Long Tieng when he was in Laos; see Ted Shackley, *Spymaster: My Life in the CIA* (Washington, DC: Potomac Books, 2005): chap. 17. Second, a *New York Times* article (Henry Kamm, "U.S. Runs a Secret Laotian Army," *New York Times* (October 26, 1969): 24) reported that the real base was Long Tieng and that Sam Thong was "only a show window."

75. Ely makes this comparison to demonstrate the lengths to which some officials would go to keep operations in Laos hidden.

76. A portion of Colonel Tyrell's testimony remains classified, so it is impossible to say whether Tyrell lied to the committee about flying operational missions in Laos or simply did not know that it was happening.

77. Castle, *At War in the Shadow of Vietnam*, 86–87n35

78. Staff Sergeant Kelly Ogden, 16th Special Operations Wing Public Affairs, "Dagger Point: Retired Lt. Col. Jerry Klingaman Discusses Operations in Laos," August 4, 2006, https://www.hurlburt.af.mil/News/Features/Display/Article/206689/dagger-point -retired-lt-col-jerry-klingaman-discusses-operations-in-laos/.

79. *Congressional Record—Senate* (December 15, 1969): 39168–39172.

80. U.S. Senate, Subcommittee on United States Security Agreements and Commitments Abroad Hearings (October 20, 21, 22 and 28, 1969): 521.

81. Robbins, *The Ravens*.

82. Castle, *At War in the Shadow of Vietnam*, 83.

83. Carl von Clausewitz, *On War*, eds. and trans. Michael Howard and Peter Paret (Princeton, NJ: Princeton University Press, 1976): 87.

84. There is some discrepancy about how and why the Hmong moved to these protected areas. Fred Branfman ("Presidential War in Laos") suggests that American personnel came up with the idea and Porter ("After Geneva") suggests it was Vang Pao. Tim Castle (interview with author, Washington, D.C., October 5, 2009) explains that the Hmong had few other choices than to move to defensible areas and try to deflect Pathet Lao advances because the Hmong were not welcomed in the lowland areas based on their ethnicity, and their culture and way of life required the space and freedom gained from living on the mountaintops in northern Laos.

85. Porter, "After Geneva," 183–184.

86. Robbins, *The Ravens*, 134.

87. Barrett, *Lyndon B. Johnson's Vietnam Papers*.

88. Castle, *At War in the Shadow of Vietnam*; Castle, *One Day Too Long*, 84.

89. Blaufarb, *Organizing and Managing Unconventional War in Laos*, 20.

90. *Foreign Relations of the United States, 1961–1963, Vol. XXIV: Laos Crisis*, ed. Edward Keefer (Washington, DC: U.S. Government Printing Office, 1994): 263.

91. Castle, *At War in the Shadow of Vietnam*, 40.

92. Ibid., 57–58.

93. Ibid., 58, 83.

94. Arthur J. Dommen, "Toward Negotiations in Laos," *Asian Survey* 11, no. 1 (1971): 41–50.

95. Blaufarb, *Organizing and Managing Unconventional War in Laos*.

96. Robbins, *The Ravens*; Castle, *At War in the Shadow of Vietnam*, 87.

97. Quincy, *Harvesting Pa Chay's Wheat*, 310–313.

98. Robert Shaplen, "Letter from Laos," *New Yorker* (May 4, 1968).

99. Branfman, "Presidential War in Laos," 254.

100. William Lofgren and Richard Sexton, "Air War in Northern Laos: 1 April–30 November 1971," U.S. Air Force Project CHECO Report, June 22, 1973, U.S. Air Force Historical Research Center, Maxwell AFB, Montgomery, AL: 44, 86.

101. "Thailand, Laos, and Cambodia: January 1972. A Staff Report Prepared for the Use of the Subcommittee on U.S. Security Agreements and Commitments Abroad," *Senate Committee on Foreign Relations* (1972), https://www.vietnam.ttu.edu/star/images/239 /2390718005.pdf.

102. Blaufarb, *Organizing and Managing Unconventional War in Laos*, 83–84.

103. Paul, "Laos," 544.

104. Douglas Blaufarb notes that U.S. accomplishments in Laos "have been achieved at comparatively modest cost. To date, the US has met its minimum goals with resource inputs that make the 1962–1970 unconventional war in Laos perhaps the most cost-effective of all such US ventures in Southeast Asia." Blaufarb, *Organizing and Managing Unconventional War in Laos*, 85–86.

105. This point was made to the author during an interview with officers working for U.S. Special Operations Command, Washington, D.C., April 1, 2009.

106. Nixon, however, does allude to this concern when he tells Alexander Haig (Conversation number 571-8, November 13, 1971) that the American public is growing weary of U.S. involvement in Southeast Asia. "We've gone to the well too many times now with regard to Vietnam. November 3, Cambodia, Laos. Laos is the last. I can't go and make another Nov. 3rd speech. The American people won't respond to that." See https://www .nixonlibrary.gov/forresearchers/find/subjects/silent-majority.php.

107. Quoted from John Ely, *War and Responsibility*, 202.

108. William Sullivan testimony, Senate Committee on Foreign Relations, U.S. Agreements and Commitments Abroad, Part 2, Kingdom of Laos 1969; U. Alexis Johnson testimony, Senate Armed Services Committee, Hearings on Fiscal Year 1972 Authorizations, July 22, 1971.

109. Robert Shaplen, "Our Involvement in Laos," *Foreign Affairs* 48, no. 3: 493.

110. Langer, "Laos," 82.

111. John Lewallen, "The Reluctant Counterinsurgents: International Voluntary Services," in *Laos: War and Revolution*, eds. Nina S. Adams and Alfred W. McCoy (New York: Harper and Row, 1970): 362.

112. Although scholars such as Bernard Fall (*Anatomy of a Crisis* (Garden City, NY: Doubleday, 1967): 189) contend that the United States offered the Hmong an independent Hmong state in return for their assistance in fighting the Pathet Lao and the Vietnamese, Douglas Blaufarb, in a declassified study of U.S. participation in Laos, notes that no such deal took place. The agreement was that the Hmong would fight for a unified Laos and would not seek independence. Blaufarb substantiates this claim by stating that "the language of instruction in the elementary schools which sprang up under the protection of Vang Pao was Lao; the Lao flag flew at his installations; the King's and Souvana's pictures were very much in evidence; his radio called itself the Voice of the Union of Lao Races." Vang Pao accepted the CIA's mandate that he not seek independence, but he did not accept the notion that the Hmong would be subjected to the domination of the RLG in Vientiane. Like so many other facets of the situation in Laos, this duality only undermined the possibility of a unified, coalition government capable of exerting its authority throughout Laos. Blaufarb, *Organizing and Managing Unconventional War in Laos*, 79, 96; Senate Committee on Foreign Relations, U.S. Agreements and Commitments Abroad, Part 2, Kingdom of Laos 1969, 521.

113. Blaufarb, *Organizing and Managing Unconventional War in Laos*, 96.

114. Ibid., 37.

115. FRUS 1961–1963, Vol. XXIV: 282, 911.

116. Blaufarb, *Organizing and Managing Unconventional War in Laos*, 86.

CHAPTER 6

1. John A. Marcum, *The Angolan Revolution* (Cambridge, MA: MIT Press, 1969); Basil Davidson, *In the Eye of the Storm: Angola's People* (Garden City, NJ: Doubleday, 1972).

2. Abiodun Alao, *Brothers at War: Dissidence and Rebellion in Southern Africa* (London: British Academic Press, 1994): 3.

3. Willem S. van der Waals, "Angola 1961–1974: 'N Studie in Rewolusionere Oorlog," PhD diss., Universiteit van die Oranje-Vrystaat, 1990.

4. Chester A. Crocker, interview with author, Washington, D.C., September 2, 2009; William Minter, *Operation Timber: Pages from the Savimbi Dossier* (Trenton, NJ: Africa World Press, 1988): 9.

5. Frederick R. A. Botha, interview with author, Pretoria, South Africa, August 20, 2009.

6. Johannes Geldenhuys, interview with author, Pretoria, South Africa, August 18, 2009; Botha, interview with author, August 20, 2009.

7. Robin Hallett, "The South African Intervention in Angola, 1975–76," *African Affairs* 77, no. 308 (1978): 363–365; Botha, interview with author, August 20, 2009.

8. Piero Gleijeses, *Conflicting Missions: Havana, Washington and Africa, 1959–1976* (Chapel Hill: University of North Carolina Press, 2002): 352; Alao, *Brothers at War*, 3, 17.

9. Hallett, "South African Intervention in Angola."

10. Wayne S. Smith, "A Trap in Angola," *Foreign Policy*, no. 62 (1986): 64. My interview with Crocker confirms Smith's claim (Crocker, interview with author, September 2, 2009).

11. U.S. imports and exports to South Africa were roughly equivalent to those of both Germany and the United Kingdom, roughly $1 billion. Foreign investment, however, was

significantly higher among European countries. The United Kingdom had nearly double the amount of foreign investment (30 percent) compared to 16 percent for the United States. Germany, France, Switzerland, and the Netherlands account for most the remaining foreign investment. See Lawrence G. Franko, "The European Connection: How Durable?," in *South Africa into the 1980s*, eds. Richard Bissell and Chester Crocker (Boulder, CO: Westview Press, 1979): 188–193.

12. Richard E. Bissell, "How Strategic Is South Africa?," in *South Africa into the 1980s*, eds. Richard Bissell and Chester Crocker (Boulder, CO: Westview Press, 1979): 214–215.

13. Keith Sommerville, "The U.S.S.R. and Southern Africa Since 1976," *Journal of Modern African Studies* 22, no. 1 (1984): 76; Arthur J. Klinghoffer, "The Soviet Union and Angola," in *The Soviet Union in the Third World: Successes and Failures*, ed. Robert H. Donaldson (Boulder, CO: Westview Press, 1981): 108.

14. Julius Nyerere, "Crusades in Conflict," *The Guardian* (January 13, 1976).

15. Hallett, "The South African Intervention in Angola," 379.

16. Hallett, "The South African Intervention in Angola," 384n63.

17. Willem van der Waals, interview with author, Pretoria, South Africa, August 30, 2009.

18. Botha, interview with author, August 20, 2009.

19. Fred Bridgland, *Jonas Savimbi: A Key to Africa* (New York: Paragon House, 1987): chap. 4.

20. Stanly Uys, "UNITA Begged Vorster to Send Troops to Angola," *The Guardian* (February 16, 1976).

21. Bridgland, *Jonas Savimbi*, 311.

22. Botha, interview with author, August 20, 2009.

23. Geldenhuys, interview with author, August 18, 2009; Botha, interview with author, August 20, 2009.

24. van der Waals, interview with author, August 30, 2009.

25. Hallett, "The South African Intervention in Angola."

26. Hallett, "The South African Intervention in Angola," 385; Chester A. Crocker, interview with author, Washington, D.C., January 2, 2009.

27. Crocker, interview with author, January 2, 2009.

28. Hallett, "The South African Intervention in Angola," 363.

29. Geldenhuys, interview with author, August 18, 2009.

30. van der Waals, interview with author, August 30, 2009.

31. Smith, "A Trap in Angola," 65.

32. Franko, "European Connection," 79; Crocker, interview with author, January 2, 2009.

33. Chester A. Crocker, *High Noon in Southern Africa: Making Peace in a Rough Neighborhood* (New York: Norton, 1992): 36.

34. Geldenhuys, interview with author, August 18, 2009.

35. van der Waals, interview with author, August 30, 2009.

36. Ibid.

37. Geldenhuys, interview with author, August 18, 2009; Botha, interview with author, August 20, 2009.

38. Peter Batchelor, *Disarmament and Defence Industrial Adjustment in South Africa* (Stockholm: SIPRI, 1998); Botha, interview with author, August 20, 2009.

39. Bridgland, *Jonas Savimbi*, 62.

40. Minter, *Operation Timber*.

41. Geldenhuys, interview with author, August 18, 2009.

42. James Barber and John Barratt, *South Africa's Foreign Policy: The Search for Status and Security 1945–1988* (Cambridge, UK: Cambridge University Press, 1990).

43. Crocker, interview with author, September 2, 2009.

44. Smith, "A Trap in Angola," 64.

45. Crocker, interview with author, September 2, 2009.

46. Johannes Geldenhuys, *At the Front: A General's Account of South Africa's Border War* (Johannesburg, South Africa: Jonathan Ball, 2009); Magnus Malan, *My Life with the SA Defence Force* (Pretoria, South Africa: Protea, 2006); Helmoed-Romer Heitman, *War in Angola: The Final South African Phase* (Gibraltar: Ashanti, 1990).

47. Barber and Barratt, *South Africa's Foreign Policy*, 276–277.

48. Frederick R. A. Botha, interview with author, Pretoria, South Africa, August 20, 2009.

49. Crocker, interview with author, January 2, 2009.

50. Botha, interview with author, August 20, 2009; Crocker, interview with author, January 2, 2009.

51. Crocker, interview with author, January 2, 2009.

52. Botha, interview with author, August 20, 2009.

53. Helmoed R. Heitman, interview with author, Cape Town, South Africa, August 23, 2009.

54. Victoria Brittain, *Death of Dignity: Angola's Civil War* (Chicago: Pluto Books, 1998): 27.

55. van der Waals, interview with author, August 30, 2009.

56. Geldenhuys, interview with author, August 18, 2009.

57. Bridgland, *Jonas Savimbi*, chap. 5.

58. The focus is on how conditions affected South Africa's costs and benefits. Civilians living in within the battlespace reflected a benefit to South Africa and not necessarily to the civilians themselves.

59. van der Waals, interview with author, August 30, 2009.

60. Although Savimbi and eleven other members of UNITA went to China to receive training in Maoist principles of revolutionary war as well as weapons training (Bridgland, *Jonas Savimbi*, 65–67), van der Waals commented that he provided training in the late 1970s to UNITA commanders on the strategy of Mao's revolutionary war (van der Waals, interview with author, August 30, 2009).

61. van der Waals, interview with author, August 30, 2009.

62. Keith Sommerville, "The U.S.S.R. and Southern Africa since 1976," *Journal of Modern African Studies* 22, no. 1 (1984): 76.

63. Botha, interview with author, August 20, 2009.

64. van der Waals, interview with author, August 30, 2009.

65. For example, South Africa purchased weapons from China to give to UNITA instead of providing weapons through normal supply chains.

66. van der Waals, interview with author, August 30, 2009.

67. Crocker, interview with author, January 2, 2009.

68. van der Waals, interview with author, August 30, 2009.

69. Botha, interview with author, August 20, 2009; Crocker, interview with author, September 2, 2009.

70. Gleijeses, *Conflicting Missions*, 352.

71. I refer to Kaufmann's explanation for how ethnicity influences sides in civil wars in general and apply that same logic to the conflict in Angola. See Chaim Kaufmann, "Intervention in Ethnic and Ideological Civil Wars," in *The Use of Force: Military Power and International Politics*, ed. Robert J. Art and Kenneth N. Waltz, 6th ed. (Lanham, MD: Rowman and Littlefield, 2004): 394–414.

72. van der Waals, interview with author, August 30, 2009; Geldenhuys, interview with author, August 18, 2009.

73. W. Martin James, *Historical Dictionary of Angola* (Oxford, UK: Scarecrow Press, 2004): 51.

74. Geldenhuys, interview with author, August 18, 2009; Helmoed R. Heitman, *War in Angola: The Final South African Phase* (Los Angeles: Ashanti, 1990).

75. Geldenhuys, interview with author, August 18, 2009.

76. Heitman, *War in Angola*, 11.

77. Roger Trinquier, *Modern Warfare: A French View of Counterinsurgency* (Westport, CT: Praeger Security International, 2006); David Galula, *Pacification in Algeria 1956–1958* (Santa Monica, CA: Rand, 2006).

78. Crocker, interview with author, September 2, 2009

79. Botha, interview with author, August 20, 2009.

80. Ibid.

81. Geldenhuys, interview with author, August 18, 2009; Botha, interview with author, August 20, 2009.

82. van der Waals, interview with author, August 30, 2009.

83. Geldenhuys, interview with author, August 18, 2009.

84. van der Waals, interview with author, August 30, 2009.

85. Heitman, interview with author, August 23, 2009.

86. van der Waals, interview with author, August 30, 2009.

87. Geldenhuys, interview with author, August 18, 2009.

88. Crocker, interview with author, September 2, 2009.

89. van der Waals, interview with author, August 30, 2009.

90. Crocker, interview with author, September 2, 2009.

91. van der Waals, interview with author, August 30, 2009.

92. Alao, *Brothers at War*, 32.

93. In conversations with Chester Crocker, Savimbi was dismissive of dos Santos, labeling him as a Soviet puppet. Crocker, interview with author, September 2, 2009.

CHAPTER 7

1. Neil DeVotta, "Control Democracy, Institutional Decay, and the Quest for Eelam: Explaining Ethnic Conflict in Sri Lanka," *Pacific Affairs* 73, no. 1 (2000): 58.

2. Robert C. Oberst, "Federalism and Ethnic Conflict in Sri Lanka," *Publius* 18, no. 3 (1988): 181.

3. DeVotta, "Control Democracy, Institutional Decay, and the Quest for Eelam," 58–59.

4. Urmila Phadnis and Nancy Jetly, "Indo–Sri Lankan Relations: The Indira Gandhi Years," in *Indian Foreign Policy: The Indira Gandhi Years*, eds. A. K. Damodaran and U. S. Bajpai (New Delhi: Radiant, 1990): 152.

5. The nonalignment movement was a group of states that remained outside the sphere of influence of the United States or the Soviet Union.

6. Sri Lanka leased over one thousand acres to the United States for a Voice of America antenna farm; India worried that it would be used to monitor naval and land communications as well as communicate with American submarines in the Indian Ocean. S. D. Muni, *Pangs of Proximity: India and Sri Lanka's Ethnic Crisis* (Oslo: PRIO, 1993): 55. Additional Indian concerns revolved around an increase in the number of U.S. Navy vessels docking at the port in Trincomalee and the lease of an oil storage facility to a company with ties to the U.S. government.

7. Venkateshwar P. Rao, "Ethnic Conflict in Sri Lanka: India's Role and Perception," *Asian Survey* 28, no. 4 (1988): 424.

8. Devin T. Hagerty, "India's Regional Security Doctrine," *Asian Survey* 31, no. 4 (April 1991): 351–352.

9. DeVotta, "Control Democracy, Institutional Decay, and the Quest for Eelam," 63.

10. Ibid., 64; Kumar Rupesinghe, "Ethnic Conflicts in South Asia: The Case of Sri Lanka and the Indian Peace-Keeping Force," *Journal of Peace Research* 25, no. 4 (1988): 345.

11. Rohan Gunaratna, *Indian Intervention in Sri Lanka: The Role of India's Intelligence Agencies* (Colombo, Sri Lanka: South Asian Network on Conflict Research, 1993): 53; Rao, "Ethnic Conflict in Sri Lanka," 419.

12. K. M. de Silva, *Regional Powers and Small State Security* (Washington, DC: Woodrow Wilson Center Press, 1995): 102.

13. Phadnis and Jetly, "Indo–Sri Lankan Relations," 152–153.

14. Rao, "Ethnic Conflict in Sri Lanka," 420–421; Devin T. Hagerty, "India's Regional Security Doctrine," 354.

15. Muni, *Pangs of Proximity*, 53–56.

16. Gunaratna, *Indian Intervention in Sri Lanka*, chap. 4.

17. Muni, *Pangs of Proximity*, chap. 3.

18. Rao, "Ethnic Conflict in Sri Lanka," 433.

19. Ibid.; Muni, *Pangs of Proximity*, 90–104.

20. de Silva, *Regional Powers and Small State Security*, 113.

21. Prime Minister Indira Gandhi addressed the Lok Sabha (a house in the Indian Parliament) and explained that Tamil ethnic ties and the flow of refugees into Tamil Nadu directly involved India in Sri Lanka's crisis (*Lok Sabha Debates*, vol. 38, col. 418, 1983).

22. Muni, *Pangs of Proximity*, 52; Rao, "Ethnic Conflict in Sri Lanka," 420.

23. A. J. Wilson, *The Break-Up of Sri Lanka: The Sinhalese-Tamil Conflict* (Honolulu: University of Hawaii Press, 1988): 203.

24. Muni, *Pangs of Proximity*, 37–38.

25. Hagerty, "India's Regional Security Doctrine," 354–355.

26. Muni, *Pangs of Proximity*, 69–73; Hagerty, "India's Regional Security Doctrine," 353–354.

27. *Jain Commission Interim Report*, section 3; Adrian Wijemanne, *War and Peace in Post-Colonial Ceylon: 1948–1991* (Hyderabad, India: Orient Longman, 1996), 32–33; Gunaratna, *Indian intervention in Sri Lanka*, 118, 342–343.

28. Hagerty, "India's Regional Security Doctrine," 355–356.

29. Ibid., 362.

30. Rupesinghe, "Ethnic Conflicts in South Asia," 346.

31. de Silva, *Regional Powers and Small State Security*, 91.

32. Muni, *Pangs of Proximity*, 74.

33. "Growth of Sri Lankan Tamil Militancy in Tamil Nadu: Chapter 1–Phase 1 (1981–1986)," *Jain Commission Interim Report*, Sections 1–2.

34. Rao, "Ethnic Conflict in Sri Lanka," 432–433.

35. Oberst, "Federalism and Ethnic Conflict in Sri Lanka," 186.

36. Robert C. Oberst, "Federalism and Ethnic Conflict in Sri Lanka," *Publius: The Journal of Federalism* 18, no. 3 (January 1988): 175–194.

37. Rupesinghe, "Ethnic Conflicts in South Asia," 347.

38. Wilson, *The Break-Up of Sri Lanka*, 205.

39. Wijemanne, *War and Peace in Post-Colonial Ceylon: 1948–1991*, 39.

40. *Jain Commission Interim Report*, sections 1–2.

41. Rao, "Ethnic Conflict in Sri Lanka," 432.

42. Dagmar Hellmann-Rajanayagam, "The Tamil Militants—Before the Accord and After," *Pacific Affairs* 61, no. 4 (1988–1989): 607–609.

43. Bryan Pfaffenberger, "Sri Lanka in 1987: Indian Intervention and Resurgence of the JVP," *Asian Survey* 28, no. 2 (1988): 138.

44. *Jain Commission Interim Report*, section 27.6.

45. First was the conference in Thiumpu, and then Bangalore at the SAARC Summit in November 1986.

46. Tamil groups had reservations about Colombo's willingness to accept a solution that would grant Tamil autonomy short of secession, but the Tamil groups lowered their sights from secession based on the notion that India would convince Colombo to honor it. See Muni, *Pangs of Proximity*, 82.

47. Hagerty, "India's Regional Security Doctrine," 355.

48. Dagmar Hellmann-Rajanayagam, "The Tamil Militants—Before the Accord and After," *Pacific Affairs* 61, no. 4 (1988–1989): 618.

49. Rao, "Ethnic Conflict in Sri Lanka," 425–427; Hagerty, "India's Regional Security Doctrine," 354–355.

50. Rao, "Ethnic Conflict in Sri Lanka," 429.

51. Ibid., 610.

52. Hagerty, "India's Regional Security Doctrine," 357.

53. All Tamil militant groups engaged in some form of illicit activities; LTTE just happened to be the most effective. See *Jain Commission Interim Report*, sections 5–6.

54. *Jain Commission Interim Report*, Sections 11–15.

55. de Silva, *Regional Powers and Small State Security*, 89; Muni, *Pangs of Proximity*, 94–95.

56. de Silva, *Regional Powers and Small State Security*, 90.

57. Hellmann-Rajanayagam, "The Tamil Militants," 604.

58. Rupesinghe, "Ethnic Conflicts in South Asia," 350.

59. de Silva, *Regional Powers and Small State Security*, 95.

60. Wilson, *The Break-Up of Sri Lanka*, 204.

61. Ibid., 203.

62. Hellmann-Rajanayagam, "The Tamil Militants," 606.

63. Ibid.

64. Muni, *Pangs of Proximity*, 74.

65. Wilson, *The Break-Up of Sri Lanka*, 203.

66. Janatha Vimukthi Peramuna (JVP) was a political party that engaged in terror and antigovernment propaganda to gain control of the capital. JVP relied heavily on pro-Sinhala rhetoric and used India's intervention in 1987 to highlight the weakness of Jayewardene's administration. See Muni, *Pangs of Proximity*, 101.

67. Gunaratna, *Indian intervention in Sri Lanka*, 341.

68. Muni, *Pangs of Proximity*, 71–72.

69. Ambalavanar Sivarajah, "Indo–Sri Lanka Relations and Sri Lanka's Ethnic Crisis: The Tamil Nadu Factor," in *South Asian Strategic Issues: Sri Lankan Perspectives*, ed. Shelton Kodikara (New Delhi: Sage, 1990): 145–148.

70. *Jain Commission Interim Report*, section 27.

71. Gunaratna, *Indian Intervention in Sri Lanka*, 2–3.

72. Muni, *Pangs of Proximity*, 78.

73. Rao, "Ethnic Conflict in Sri Lanka," 435.

CHAPTER 8

1. James G. March, *Primer on Decision Making* (New York: Simon and Schuster, 1994): 36-37.

2. Yuen Foong Khong, *Analogies at War: Korea, Munich, Dien Bien Phu, and the Vietnam Decisions of 1965* (Princeton, NJ: Princeton University Press, 1992): 13.

3. Dominic D. P. Johnson and Dominic Tierney, "The Rubicon Theory of War: How the Path to Conflict Reaches the Point of No Return," *International Security* 36, no. 1 (Summer 2011): 7–40.

INDEX